I0128867

U.S. Freemasons

Libraries of the Supreme Council

Of the 33d degree for the southern jurisdiction of the United States at Washington

U.S. Freemasons

Libraries of the Supreme Council
Of the 33d degree for the southern jurisdiction of the United States at Washington

ISBN/EAN: 9783337302061

Printed in Europe, USA, Canada, Australia, Japan

Cover: Foto ©Suzi / pixelio.de

More available books at **www.hansebooks.com**

LIBRARIES

OF

THE SUPREME COUNCIL

OF

THE 33ᴰ∴ DEGREE

FOR

THE SOUTHERN JURISDICTION OF THE UNITED STATES AT WASHINGTON

FIRST DIVISION

THE PIKE LIBRARY OF THE SUPREME COUNCIL

1ST JANUARY, 1884

NEW YORK

PRESS OF J. J. LITTLE & CO

10 TO 20 ASTOR PLACE

1884

PREFACE.

UPON the shelves, the two Libraries here catalogued constitute one, the books being intermingled. Upon the Catalogues the Pike Library is always to be kept separate.

That neither may be made to seem larger than it is, each book is only once entered in the Catalogue.

The name of the Donor is inscribed in every book presented ; and a list of all Donors, including every giver of even a single book, is printed herewith.

The Libraries are kept insured in the sum of twenty-five thousand dollars.

RULES OF THE LIBRARY.

1. BOOKS are to be loaned from these Libraries (those of special artistic value or great cost excepted), to Masons of any of the Degrees, and to persons not Masons, to whom they can be safely entrusted, with assurance of proper treatment and punctual return.

2. No book can be taken from the Libraries except on the written order of the Grand Commander, nor without the receipt of the Borrower, written on a card.

3. No book borrowed can be retained more than one calendar month.

WILLIAM M. IRELAND, 33°, Secr.·. General,

Ex-officio Librarias.

DONORS

OF

BOOKS TO THE GENERAL LIBRARY.

THE DEPARTMENT OF THE INTERIOR.
THE DEPARTMENT OF WAR.
THE DEPARTMENT OF THE NAVY.
THE TREASURY DEPARTMENT.
THE DEPARTMENT OF AGRICULTURE.
THE SMITHSONIAN INSTITUTION.
ROBERT F. BOWER, Iowa.
CHARLES F. BROWN, California.
THOMAS H. CASWELL, California.
MARTIN COLLINS, Missouri.
WILMOT G. DE SAUSSURE, South Carolina.
ROBERT S. DYRENFORTH, Washington.
J. GRIFFIN ELY, Hamburgh, Conn.
EDMUND FLAGG, Washington.
ABRAHAM E. FRANKLAND, Tennessee.
AUGUSTUS H. GARLAND, Arkansas.
ALBERT S. GATSCHETT, Washington.
JAMES B. GIBBS, Washington.
JOHN HAIGH, Somerville, Massachusetts.
HORACE E. HAYDEN, Wilkes-Barre, Pa.
GEORGE C. HENNING, Washington.
EUGENE ESPRIT HUBERT, Paris, France.
ALPHONSO C. IRELAND, Philadelphia.
WILLIAM M. IRELAND, Washington.
ODELL S. LONG, West Virginia.
NATHANIEL LEVIN, South Carolina.
D. H. McCOMAS, Michigan.
EDWIN B. MACGROTTY, Washington.
GILMOR MEREDITH, Maryland.
JOHN M. MILLER, Baltimore.
ROBERT S. PATTISON, Governor of Pennsylvania
ALBERT PIKE, Washington.
JOSEPH T. K. PLANT, Washington.
BEN: PERLEY POORE, Massachusetts.
GUSTAVE REVILLIOD, Geneva, Switzerland.
WILLIAM S. ROOSE, Washington.

SAMUEL T. SCHOFIELD, Washington.
F. A. DA SILVA, Lishoa, Portugal.
WILLIAM R. SMITH, Washington.
CHARLES SPALDING, Topeka, Kansas.
JACOB TELFAIR, City of New York.
HENRY M. TELLER, Colorado.
JAMES D. WALKER, Arkansas.
FREDERICK WEBBER, Kentucky.
DAVID WEISENFELD, Baltimore.
JOSEPH E. WELLS, Macon, Georgia.
ASHTON S. H. WHITE, Washington.
MARCUS J. WRIGHT, Washington.
S. A. ZOLA, Cairo, Egypt.

LIBRARY A.

THE PIKE LIBRARY

OF THE

SUPREME COUNCIL.

PURCHASED 14TH OF MAY, 1881.

CLASS I.

HISTORICAL.

PIKE LIBRARY

OF

THE SUPREME COUNCIL

CLASS I.

ADAMI MURIMUTHENSIS CHRONICA. Large 8vo. Eng. Hist. Soc. Pub. Londini, 1846.

ALABAMA, History of. By Alfred James Pickett. 2 vols. Charleston, 1851.

ALFRED. The Life of King Alfred. By Dr. Reinhold Pauli. London, 1852.

ALISON, ARCHIBALD. History of Europe, with Atlas. 21 vols. Edinburgh, 1848.

AMERICAN ELOQUENCE. Speeches and Addresses of Eminent American Orators. 2 vols.

AMERICAN MILITARY POCKET ATLAS. Being approved Maps of the British Colonies. London, 1776.

AMERICAN REVOLUTION, The History of the. By David Ramsay, M.D., of South Carolina. Dublin, 1795.

AMERICAN STATESMAN, The. A Political History. By Andrew W. Young. New York, 1856.

ANCIENT HISTORY, Lectures on. By B. G. Niebuhr. Translated by Dr. Schmitz. 3 vols. London, 1852.

ANGLO-SAXONS, History of the; to the Norman Conquest. By Sharon Turner. 2 vols. Philadelphia, 1841.

ANGLO-SAXON CHURCH, History and Antiquities of the. By John Lingard. 2 vols. London, 1845.

ANTIQUITIES OF THE GREEKS, The Historical. By William Wacsmuth. 2 vols.

AQUITAINE ET LANGUEDOC, Histoire de la Gaule Méridionale. Par M. J. Cénac Moncaut. 2 vols. Paris, 1848.

ARKANSAS. Journal of the Sessions of the Convention held in Little Rock. 1861.

ARCHIPELAGO, INDIAN, History of the. By Horace St. John. 2 vols. London, 1853.

ARCHBISHOPS, The Three; Lanfranc, Anselm, A'Becket. By Washington and Mark Wilks. London and Edinburgh. No date.

AUSTRIA, House of. By William Coxe. 3 vols. London, 1847.

BALDASSARI, L'Abbé. Histoire de Pie VI. Bruxelles, 1840.

BARTOLI, DANIEL, Jesuite. Histoire de Saint Ignace Loyola. 2 vols. Paris et Versailles, 1844.

BANCROFT, GEORGE. History of the U. S., from the Discovery of the American Continent. 10 vols.

—— History of the Formation of the Constitution of the U. S. 2 vols.

BATTLES OF THE BRITISH NAVY. By Joseph Allen. 2 vols. London, 1852.

BAYARD, The Chevalier. By the Loyal Servant. 2 vols. London, 1825.

BAYARD, DE. Histoire du Gentil Seigneur. Composée par le Loyal Serviteur. Par Loredan Lárchey. Paris, 1882.

BEAUMARCHAIS AND HIS TIMES. By Louis de Loménie. Translated by Henry S. Edwards. 2 vols. [2 copies.] London, 1856.

BEAUMARCHAIS ET SON TEMPS. Par Louis de Loménie. 2 vols. Paris, 1880.

BEDÆ VENERABILIS. Historia Ecclesiastica. Opera Historica Minora. 2 vols. Large 8vo. Eng. Hist. Soc. Pub. Londini, 1838–1841.

BEDE, The Venerable. Ecclesiastical History, and the Anglo-Saxon Chronicle. By J. A. Giles. London, 1849.

BEDFORD, Duke of; Correspondence of the. By Lord John Russell. 3 vols. London, 1846.

BISHOP BURNET'S HISTORY OF HIS OWN TIME. From the Restoration of Charles II. to Treaty of Utrecht. 2 vols. London, 1840.

BISHOPS, The Seven; Proceedings and Tryal of, in the reign of James II., 1688. London, 1716.

BLAIR'S CHRONOLOGICAL TABLES. By J. Willoughby Rosse. London, 1856.

BLANC, LOUIS. The History of Ten Years, 1830–1840. 2 vols. London, 1845.

BOKHARA, History of. By Arminius Vambéry. London, 1873.

BONAPARTE, ON HOLLAND. By Louis Bonaparte, ex-King of Holland. 3 vols. London, 1820.

BOSTON, History of the Siege of. By Richard Frothingham. 1872.

BOURRIENNE, Memoires de M., Ministre d'État sous Napoléon. 10 vols. Paris, 1829.

BRANDENBURG, Memoirs of the House of. London, 1757.

BRASSEUR DE BOURBOURG. Histoire des Nations Civilisées du Mexique et de L'Amérique Centrale. 4 vols. Paris, 1859.

BRITAIN, The Church History of. By Thomas Fuller. 3 vols. London, 1842.

BRITISH ADMIRALS, Lives of the. By Dr. John Campbell. 8 vols. London, 1817.

BRITISH COLONIAL LIBRARY. Description of the Colonies of the British Empire. By R. M. Martin. 10 vols. London, 1844.

BRITONS, Ancient, History of the. By Rev. J. A. Giles. 2 vols. Oxford, 1854.

BURNET's LIVES. Characters and an Address to Posterity. By Gilbert Burnet. Edited by John Jebb. London, 1833.

BURNHAM FAMILY, Genealogical Records of the. By Roderick H. Burnham. Hartford, 1869.

BURTON, THOMAS, Diary of. From 1656 to 1659. Edited by John Jowill Rutt. 4 vols. London, 1828.

BUCHON, J. A. C. Choix de Chroniques et Mémoires sur L'Histoire de France. Paris, 1836.

CABET, M. Histoire de la Revolution Française. 4 vols. [2 copies.] Paris, 1840.

CAMBRIDGE, History of the University of. By Thos. Fuller. London, 1840.

CAPEFIGUE. Hugues Capet et la Troisième Race. 2 vols. Paris, 1845.

—— Histoire de Philippe-Auguste. 2 vols. Paris, 1842.

—— Philippe d'Orléans. Paris, 1845.

—— Histoire de la Restauration. 4 vols. Paris, 1845.

CARLYLE, THOMAS. The French Revolution: A History. Chapman and Hall. 3 vols. [2 copies.] London.

CAUSES CÉLÈBRES. Répertoire Général des. Anciennes et Modernes, de B. St. Edone. 1st series. 4 vols. Paris, 1834.

—— Same. 2d series. 5 vols. Paris, 1835.

—— Same. 3d series. 4 vols. Paris, 1835.

—— Same. Part 2d. Paris, 1835.

CHANCERY, Court of, History of the. With Practical Remarks. By Jos. Parks. London, 1828.

CHARLES I.; CROMWELL; CHARLES II., Historical Sketches of. Including the King's Trial and Execution. 4to. London, 1828.

CHARLES I., The Fall of the Monarchy of. 1637–1649. By S. R. Gardner. 2 vols. London, 1882.

—— In the Isle of Wight. By George Hillier. London, 1852.

—— Historical Notices of Events in the Reign of. By Nehemiah Wallington. 2 vols. London, 1869.

CHARLES II., Diary of the Times of. By Hon. H. Sidney. 2 vols. London, 1843.

—— In the Channel Islands. By S. Elliott Hoskins, M.D., F.R.S. 2 vols. London, 1854.

CHARTERS AND CONSTITUTIONS, and other Organic Laws of the U. S. Compiled by Ben. Perley Poore. 2 vols.

CHRISTIAN CHURCH, History of the. By William Jones. Philadelphia, 1832.

CHRONIQUE DE LA TRAISON ET MORT DE RICHARD DEUX ROY D'ENGLETERRE. Large 8vo. Eng. Hist. Soc. Pub. Londres, 1846.

CHRONICLES OF ERI. Being the History of Gaal Sciot Iber, or the Irish People. By O'Connor. 2 vols. London, 1822.

CITIZEN CAUSSIDIÈRE, Memoirs of. Secret History of Revolutions of 1848. 2 vols. London, 1848.

CLARENDON GALLERY. Lives of Friends and Contemporaries of Lord Chancellor Clarendon. By Lady Theresa Lewis. 3 vols. London, 1852.

CLARENDON'S HISTORY OF THE REBELLION AND CIVIL WARS IN ENGLAND. By Edward, Earl of Clarendon. 2 vols. Large 8vo. Oxford, 1840.

CLAVIGERO, D. Francisco Saverio. Historia Antigua de Megico. 2 vols. Londres, 1826.

CODEX DIPLOMATICUS, Anglo-Saxonum. 6 vols. Large 8vo. Eng. Hist. Soc. Pub. Londini, 1839–1848.

COMINES, PHILIP DE, Historical Memoirs of. London, 1817.

COMMYNES, PHILIPPE DE. Mémoires. Par R. Chantelauze. Paris, 1881.

CONDÉ, Life of Louis, Prince of. By Lord Mahon. New York, 1845.

—— Same. New Edition. London, John Murray, 1872.

CONFEDERATE GOVERNMENT. Its Rise and Fall. By Jefferson Davis. 2 vols. New York, 1881.

CONSTITUTIONAL CONVENTION. Its History, Powers and Modes of Proceeding. By John Alexander Jameson. Chicago, 1873.

COOPER, J. FENIMORE. History of the Navy of the U. S. A. Abridged. Philadelphia, 1841.

CORTES, HERNANDO, Despatches of, Addressed to Emperor Charles V. By George Folsom. London, 1843.

—— Historia de Mejico. Nueva York, 1828.

COUNCIL FIRE, The. By A. B. Meacham. 2 vols. 1878–82.

CRIMEA, British Expedition to the. By W. H. Russell. London, 1858.

CROMWELL, OLIVER. The Protectorate of, and the State of Europe. Edited by Robt. Vaughan. 2 vols. London, 1839.

CROMWELL, OLIVER, Letters and Speeches of. With Elucidations. By Thomas Carlyle. 4 vols. London, 1850.

CRUSADES, Chronicles of the. By Lord John de Joinville. London, 1848.

CURIOSITÉS DE L'HISTOIRE DES CROYANCES POPULAIRES, AU MOYEN AGE. Paris, 1859.

—— De l'Histoire des Arts. Paris, 1858.

DAVILA, ENRICO CATERINO. Storia delle Guerre Civili di Francia. 8 vols. Londra, 1801.

DEBATES IN THE LORDS. History and Proceedings of the House of Lords, 1741–42. 8 vols. London, 1743.

DEBATES OF CONGRESS, Abridgment of the. From 1789 to 1856. By Thos. H. Benton. 5 vols.

DE BOUILLON, GODEFROID. Par J. Collin de Plancy. Paris, 1848.

DE HEMINGBURGH, WALTERI. Chronicon Domini. 2 vols. Large 8vo. Eng. Hist. Soc. Pub. Londini, 1848.

D'HÉRICAULT, CHARLES. La Revolution, 1789–1882. Paris, 1883.

DEMOCRACY IN AMERICA. By Alexis de Tocqueville.

DE MEDICI, LORENZO, The Life of. By William Roscoe. 3 vols. Philadelphia, 1803.

DE MONTOR, ARTAUD. Histoire du Pape Leon XII. 2 vols. Bruxelles, 1843.

—— Histoire du Pape Pie VIII. Bruxelles, 1844.

DE RETZ, The Cardinal, Memoirs of. 4 vols. Dublin, 1777.

DES LANDES, Histoire Politique, Religieuse et Littéraire. Par P. H. Dorgan. Auch, 1846.

DESTRUCTION AND RECONSTRUCTION. Personal Experiences of the Late War. By Richard Taylor. New York, 1879.

DE TOCQUEVILLE, ALEXIS. The Old Régime. New York, 1856.

—— L'Ancien Régime et la Révolution. [2 copies.] Paris, 1877.

DEVEREUX. The Earls of Essex. By Walter Bourchier Devereux. 2 vols. London, 1853.

DIPLOMACY OF THE REVOLUTION. An Historical Study. By Wm. Henry Trescott. New York, 1857.

DIPLOMATIC HISTORY OF THE ADMINISTRATIONS OF WASHINGTON AND ADAMS, 1789-1801. By Wm. Henry Trescott. Boston, 1857.

ELLIOTT, Lord. His Mission to Spain in 1835. London, 1871.

ENGLAND, The Saxons in. History of the Commonwealth to the Norman Conquest. By John Mitchell Kemble. 2 vols. London, 1849.

2

ENGLAND AND NORMANDY, Ecclesiastical History of. By Ordericus
Vitalis. 4 vols. London, 1856.

—— In the Middle Ages. Essays on Subjects connected with Her
History. Thomas Wright. 2 vols. London, 1846.

—— Letters of the Kings of. By James O. Halliwell. 2 vols. London, 1848.

—— The History of the Worthies of. By Thos. Fuller. 3 vols.
London, 1840.

—— History of. From the Earliest Times to the year 1588. By Sir
James Mackintosh. Philadelphia, 1835.

—— History of the Commonwealth of ; to the Restoration of Charles
II. By Wm. Godwin. 4 vols. London, 1824.

—— History of. From B.C. 55 to A.D. 1572. By Sir James Mackintosh. 10 vols. London. No date.

—— History of. From the Accession of James the II. By Thos.
Babington Macaulay. 4 vols. London, 1855.

—— Constitutional History of. From the Accession of Henry VII.
to the Death of George II. By Henry Hallam. 3 vols. Boston,
1854.

—— History of. During the Reign of George the Third. By Wm.
Massey, M.P. 2 vols. London, 1858.

—— History of. From Peace of Utrecht to Peace of Versailles, 1713
–1783. By Lord Mahon. 7 vols. Boston, 1854.

—— History of. In the XVIIIth Century. By W. E. H. Lecky. 4
vols. New York, 1882.

—— The Historic Lands of. By J. Bernard Burke. London,
1849.

ENGLISH PEOPLE, History of the. By John Richard Green. 4 vols.
Chicago, 1881.

ENGLISH REVOLUTION, History of the. By Guizot. Paris, 1841.

ESSEX, The History of. Its Churches, Monuments, etc. 4to. London, 1814.

ETRURIA, History of. By Mrs. Hamilton Gray. 2 vols. London,
1844.

EUSEBIUS PAMPHILUS. Life of Constantine. London, 1874.

EVERGLADE TO CAÑON with the 2d Dragoons, in Florida, Mexico,
Virginia and Indian Country. By Theodore F. Rodenbough,
U. S. A.

EVELYN, JOHN. Diary and Correspondence of. By Wm. Bray. 4
vols. London, 1857.

EWING, THOMAS, of Ohio ; Memorial of. By His Daughter, Mrs.
Ella B. E. Sherman. 1873.

FEDERAL GOVERNMENT, History of the. From 1789 to 1839. By Alden Bradford. Boston, 1840.

FERDINAND AND ISABELLA, History of the Reign of. By Wm. H. Prescott. 3 vols. Boston, 1838.

FIELD, DUNGEON AND ESCAPE. By Richardson.

FLORENCE OF WORCESTER, The Chronicle of. Translated from the Latin. By Thomas Forester. London, 1854.

FLORENTII, WIGORNIENSIS, MONACHI. Chronicon ex Chronicis. 2 vols. Large 8vo. Eng. Hist. Soc. Pub. Londini, 1848.

FOREIGN RELATIONS OF THE U. S., Papers Relating to ; in President's Message, Dec. 2d, 1872.

FORREST, LIEUT.-GEN'L N. B., Campaigns of, and of Forrest's Cavalry. By Gen'l Jordan and T. P. Pryor. 1868.

FRANCE. Histoire Nationale. Par J. A. C. Buchon. 2 vols. Paris, 1836.

—— History of the Civil Wars of. Imprinted at London by Thos. Orwin for Thomas Woodcock, 1591.

—— Curiosités de l'Histoire de France. Par P. L. Jacob. Paris, 1858.

—— Mémoires Particuliers à l'Histoire de France. 2 vols. Paris, 1756.

—— Mémoires of the Court of. From the Diary of the Marquis de Dangeau. 2 vols. London, 1825.

—— Histoire-Musée de la République. Par Augustin Challamel. 2 vols. Paris, 1842.

—— Histoire de, la Révolution Française. Par A. Thiers. 2 vols. Bruxelles, 1846.

FRANCHE-COMTÉ, Histoire, Ancienne et Moderne. Eugène Rouge-bief. Paris, 1851.

FREDERICK THE SECOND, The Life of. By Lord Dover. 2 vols. London, 1832.

FREDERICK THE GREAT. By Thomas Carlyle. 10 vols. London, 1872.

—— Posthumous Works of. Translated from the French by Thos. Holcroft, 1789. 13 vols. London, 1789.

FRENCH REVOLUTION, Annals of the. By Bertrand de Moleville. Translated by R. C. Dallas. 3 vols. London, 1813.

—— History of the. By A. Thiers. 4 vols. Philadelphia, 1842.

FRENCH REVOLUTIONS. From 1789 to 1849. By T. W. Redhead. 3 vols. Edinburgh, 1849.

FROISSART'S CHRONICLES of England, France, Spain and the Adjoining Countries. By Thomas Johnes. 2 vols. London, 1839.

FROUDE'S HISTORY OF ENGLAND. 7 vols. London, 1870.

GALFRIDI, LE BAKER DE SWINBROKE. Chronicon Angliæ, Temporibus Eduardi II. et Eduardi III. J. A. Giles. London. 1847.

GARIBALDI. I Mille. Torino, 1847.

GEOFFREY OF MONMOUTH. In Twelve Books. By J. A. Giles. London, 1842.

GEORGE II., Memoirs of the Reign of. By Horace Walpole. 3 vols. Edited by Lord Holland. Henry Colburn. London, 1846.

GEORGE III., Memoirs of the Reign of. By Horace Walpole. 4 vols. Edited by Sir Denis le Marchant. Bentley. London, 1845.

—— His Court and Family. 2 vols. London, 1824.

GEORGE IV., Diary Illustrative of the Times of. By Lady Charlotte Bury. 4 vols. London, 1839.

—— Same. By John Galt. 4 vols. London, 1839.

GERMANY, A History of. By Frederick Kohlrauch. London, 1844.

GESTA STEPHANI. Regis Anglorum et Ducis Normanorum. Large 8vo. Eng. Hist. Soc. Pub. Londini, 1846.

GESTE, EDMUND, Life of. By Henry Geast Dugdale. London, 1839.

GIBBON, EDWARD. History of the Decline and Fall of the Roman Empire. 4 vols. New York, 1836.

GILDAS, DE EXCIDIO BRITTANIÆ. Large 8vo. Eng. Hist. Soc. Pub. Londini, 1838.

GIROUETTES, Dictionnaire des, ou nos Contemporains. Paris, 1815.

GRAMMONT, COUNT, Memoirs of. Reign of Charles II. 2 vols. 8vo. London.

—— Same. 2 vols. 8vo. London, 1811.

GRAY'S DEBATES. Of the House of Commons, from 1667 to 1694. 10 vols. London, 1769.

GRECIAN ANTIQUITIES. By John Potter, D.D. 2 vols. Edinburgh, 1832.

GREECE, Manual of the Political Antiquities of. By Charles Fred'k Hermann. Oxford, 1836.

—— Chronology of. To the Death of Augustus. By Henry Fynes Clinton. Oxford, 1851.

—— Mitford's History of. A New Edition. 8 vols. London, 1829.

—— Ancient History of. By John Gillies. Part I. 4 vols. London, 1820.

—— Same. Part II. 4 vols. London, 1820.

—— Same. New York, 1852.

—— History of. By George Grote. 12 vols. Reprint from London Edition. Boston, 1851.

GREEK REVOLUTION, History of the. By Thos. Gordon. 2 vols. London, 1844.

GRENVILLE PAPERS. Correspondence of Rich'd Grenville, Earl Temple and Rt. Hon. Geo. Grenville. 2 vols. London, 1852.

GREVILLE'S JOURNALS OF THE REIGNS OF GEORGE IV. AND KING WILLIAM IV. Chas. C. F. Greville. 2 vols. New York, 1875.

GUERRE, DE L'INDÉPENDANCE ITALIENNE, 1848–1849. Par le Général Ulloa. 2 vols. Paris, 1859.

GUERRES DES FRANÇAIS EN ITALIE, 1794–1814. 26 Cartes et Plans. 2 vols. Paris, 1859.

GUESCLIN, BERTRAND DU, The Life and Times of. By D. F. Jamison. 2 vols. Charleston, 1864.

GUJARAT, Political and Statistical History of. Translated from the Persian of Ali Mohammed Khan. By Jas. Bird. London, 1835.

GUY, JOLI, Private Secretary to Cardinal De Retz; Memoirs of. 2 vols. Dublin, 1777.

HALLAM, HENRY. Europe during the Middle Ages. 2 vols. London, 1846.
—— Same. Supplemented Notes to. London, 1848.

HARDWICKE, LORD CHANCELLOR, Life of, with Selections from Correspondence, etc. By George Harris. 3 vols. London, 1847.

HATTON, SIR CHRISTOPHER. Memoirs of His Life and Times. By Sir Harris Nicolas. London, 1847.

HEEREN'S HISTORICAL RESEARCHES. By A. H. L. Heeren. 6 vols. London, 1846.

HENRICI QUINTI, Regis Angliæ, Gesta. Large 8vo. Eng. Hist. Soc. Pub. London, 1850.

HENRY'S HISTORY OF ENGLAND. With Andrew's Continuation [2 vols.]. The Duke of Buckingham's Copy, from the Stowe Library. 14 vols. 1800.

HENRY V., Memoirs of. By J. Endell Tyler. 2 vols. London, 1838.

HERODOTUS. From the Text of Schweighauser, with English Notes. Edited by C. S. Wheeler, A.M. 2 vols. Boston, 1843.
—— A New and Literal Version, from the Text of Baer. By Henry Carey. London, 1852.

HISTOIRE DES GUERRES CIVILES des Espagnols dans les Indes. Par J. Baudoin. 2 vols. Amsterdam, 1706.

HISTOIRE DE LA GUERRE CIVILE EN AMÉRIQUE. Par M. Le Comte de Paris. 6 vols. Paris, 1883.

HISTORICAL COLLECTIONS. From 1618 to 1648. 6 vols. London, 1703–1708.

HISTORIETTES. De Tallement des Reaux. Par MM. De Monmerque et Paulin. 7 vols. Paris, 1854.

HISTORY OF THE CIVIL WAR IN AMERICA. By Comte de Paris. 3 vols. Philadelphia.

HUC, M. Le Christianisme en Chine, en Tartarie et au Thibet. 4 vols. Paris, 1855.

HUTCHINSON, COL. JOHN, Memoirs of; and the Siege of Latham House. H. G. Bohn. London, 1848.

IMPEACHMENT OF ANDREW JOHNSON, President of the U. S. Published by Order of the Senate. 3 vols. 1868.

INDEPENDENCE OF THE U. S., History of the War of. By Charles Botta. 2 vols. New Haven, 1839.

INDIANS. Laws of Colonial and State Governments, Relating to Indian Affairs, 1683 to 1831 inclusive. Washington, 1832.

—— Speeches in Congress on Bill for Removal of the Indians, April and May, 1830. Boston, 1830.

INGULPH'S CHRONICLE of the Abbey of Croyland. By Henry T. Riley. London, 1854.

INQUISITION, History of the. By Philip à Limborch. Translated by Samuel Chandler. 2 vols. 4to. London, 1731.

JACQUES CŒUR. The French Argonaut and his Times. By Louisa Stuart Costello. 2 copies. London, 1847.

JAMES II. A History of the Early Part of his Reign. By Rt. Hon. Chas. James Fox. 4to. London, 1808.

JAY, JOHN, The Life of. By his Son, William Jay. 2 vols. New York, 1833.

JOMINI. Opérations Militaires. Par le Général Baron de Jomini. With Atlas. 5 vols. Paris, 1816.

KEARSAGE AND ALABAMA, The Story of the. By Surgeon John M. Browne, U. S. N. San Francisco, 1868.

KING'S MOUNTAIN AND ITS HEROES. By Lyman C. Draper. Cincinnati, 1881.

LAMARTINE. Histoire des Girondins. 8 vols. Paris, 1847.

—— History of the French Revolution of 1848. London, 1849.

—— Trois Mois au Pouvoir. Paris, 1848.

LANMAN, CHARLES. Dictionary of the U. S. Congress. Philadelphia, 1859.

LE LOYAL SERVITEUR, Du Bellay. Chroniques et Mémoires sur l'Histoire de France. Buchon. 1836.

LEE, GENERAL ROBERT E, Reminiscences of.   By Rev. J. Wm. Jones, 1874.

LEO X., Life and Pontificate of.   By Wm. Roscoe.   2 vols.   London, 1846.

LIVES OF CELEBRATED SPANIARDS.   By T. R. Pearson.   London, 1833.

LIVES OF SIMON, Lord Lovat and Duncan Forbes, of Culloden.   By John Hill Burton.   London, 1847.

LIVERY COMPANIES.   History of the Twelve Great Livery Companies of London.   By Wm. Herbert.   2 vols.   London, 1836.

LONDONDERRY, MARQUIS OF.   Story of the Peninsular War.   London, 1856.

LORENZO DE' MEDICI, The Life of.   By Wm. Roscoe.   London, 1851.

LOUIS THE XIV., Life and Times of.   By G. P. R. James.   2 vols.   London, 1851.

LOUISIANA, History of.   The American Domination.   By Charles Gayarré.   New York, 1866.

—— Historical and Descriptive Sketches of.   By Major Amos Stoddard.   Philadelphia, 1812.

LOUISIANE, Histoire de la.   Par le Page du Pratz.   3 vols.   Paris, 1757.

LUDLOW, EDMUND, Lieut.-Gen'l, Memoirs of.   3 vols.   Vevay, Switzerland, 1699.

MACHIAVELLI, NICOLAS.   The History of Florence.   2 vols.   Glasgow, 1761.

—— Same [New Translation].   London, 1851.

—— Works of.   8 vols.   Italia, 1813.

MADISON, JAMES.   Selections from his Private Correspondence.   Privately printed by James C. McGuire.   Washington, 1853.

MAGNA CHARTA, Historical Essay on.   By Richard Thompson.   London, 1829.

MALAY ANNALS.   Translated by Dr. John Leyden.   London, 1821.

MALLET DU PAN.   Memoirs and Correspondence.   By A. Sayous.   2 vols.   London, 1852.

MALTA, Knights of; History of the.   By Major Whitworth Porter.   2 vols.   London, 1858.

MANYPENNY, GEORGE W.   Our Indian Wards.   1880.

MARCHMONT, Earls of.   Selections from their Papers, 1685 to 1750.   3 vols.   London, 1831.

MARLBOROUGH, JOHN CHURCHILL, First Duke of; Letters and Dispatches of.   By Sir George Murray.   3 vols.   London, 1845.

MARLBOROUGH, JOHN CHURCHILL, Memoirs of the Duke of. With Original Correspondence. By William Coxe. 3 vols. London, 1848.

—— Same. 3 vols. London, 1876.

MARTYRS, Letters of the. Published in 1564. By Rev. Edward Bickersteth. London, 1837.

MATTHEW OF WESTMINSTER. The Flowers of History, Relating to Great Britain. By C. D. Yonge. 2 vols. London, 1853.

MAZARIN, Madame la Duchesse de, Mémoires de. 24mo. Cologne. Pierre du Marteau. Old, no date.

McCARTHY, JUSTIN. A History of Our Own Times. 4 vols. London, 1880.

MEACHAM, ALFRED B., Life of. By Dr. T. A. Bland. 1883.

MELVIN, JAMES. A Journal of the Expedition to Quebec in 1775, under Col. Benedict Arnold.

MEXICAN WAR. Messages of the President of the U. S. on the Subject. 1848.

MEXICO. The Twelve Months Volunteer. Journal of a Private in 1846–1847.

—— War with. Official Reports, and Appendix. 2 vols. Washington, 1848.

MICHELET, J. Histoire de France. A. Lacroix & Co., Editeurs. 19 vols. Paris, 1879.

—— Histoire de France. Vol. 1. Royal 8vo. Bruxelles, 1840.

MODERN EUROPE, History of. By William Russell. 4 vols. London, 1833.

MODERN HISTORY, Manual of. By W. C. Taylor. New York, 1854.

MOHAMMED, Khan of Kabul. Life of the Amir. By Mohun Lal. 2 vols. London, 1846.

MONARCHIE FRANÇAISE, Décadence de la. Par Eugène Pelletan. Paris.

MONSTRELET'S CHRONICLES of England, France, Spain, and the Adjoining Countries. By Thomas Johnes. 2 vols. London, 1840.

MONTEIL, A. A. Histoire des Françaises des divers états. 5 vols. Paris, 1853.

MOSBY, JNO. S., Partisan Life with. By Major John Scott. New York, 1867.

MOTLEY, JNO. LATHROP. The Life and Death of John of Barneveld. 2 vols. New York, 1880.

NAPIER, Sir W. F. P. History of the War in the Peninsula. 6 vols. London, 1853, with Vol. of Maps and Plans Enlarged by hand, at a cost of $320

NAPOLÉON. Confidential Correspondence with his Brother Joseph, sometime King of Spain. 2 vols. London, 1855.

NAPOLÉON EN 1815. Les Cent Jours. Par Fleury de Chaboulon. 2 vols. London, 1820.

NAPOLÉON, Histoire de l'Empereur. Par Laurent de l'Ardèche. Illustrée par Horace Vernet. Paris, 1840.

—— Histoire de. Par M. de Norvins. 4 vols. Paris, 1828.

—— His Captivity at St. Helena, from Letters and Journals of Sir Hudson Lowe. By Wm. Forsyth. 3 vols. London, 1853.

—— Same. By Gen'l Count Montholon. 2 vols. London, 1846.

—— Mémoires pour servir à l'Histoire de France, sous Napoléon : écrits à Saint-Hélène. Montholon. 6 vols. 1823.

—— Same. Gourgaud. 2 vols. 1823.

—— The Fall of. By Lt.-Col. J. Mitchell. 3 vols. London, 1826.

—— The Life of. By William Hazlitt. 3 vols. Philadelphia, 1880.

NAPOLEON'S OWN MEMOIRS. Dictated to the Count de Montholon. 4 vols. London, 1824.

NENNII, Historia Britonum. Large 8vo. Eng. Hist. Soc. Pub. Londini, 1838.

NEWBERRY, The Annals of. By John Belton O'Neill. Charleston, 1859.

NICOLAY, REV. C. G. A Manual of Geographical Science, Mathematical, Physical, Historical and Descriptive. London, 1852.

NORTH CAROLINA, The Chronology of. By D. K. Bennett. New York, 1858.

NORWAY, The Heimskringla, or Chronicles of the Kings of. By Samuel Laing. 3 vols. London, 1844.

OBITUARY ADDRESSES on Clay and Webster. 1852 and 1853.

OLD ENGLISH CHRONICLES. Edited by J. A. Giles. London, 1848.

OLIVE BRANCH. By Matthew Cary. Philadelphia, 1815.

ORDERLY BOOK OF ARMY Stationed at Williamsburg, Va., from March 18 to August 28, 1776. 4to.

OREGON AND CALIFORNIA, History of. By Rob't Greenhow. Boston, 1845.

PAINE, THOMAS. Common Sense. 1776.

PASTON LETTERS. Original Letters, during the Reigns of Henry VI., Edward IV. and Richard III. By John Fern. 2 vols. London, 1840.

PELOPONNESIAN WAR. From the Greek of Thucydides. By Wm. Smith, A.M. Philadelphia, 1836.

PENN, SIR WILLIAM, Kn't. Memorials of His Professional Life and Times. By Grenville Penn. 2 vols. London, 1833.

PEPYS, SAMUEL, Diary and Correspondence of. By Richard Lord Braybrooke. 4 vols. London, 1854.

PERU AND MEXICO, Historical Researches on the Conquest of. By John Ranking. London, 1828.

PERU, Conquest of, History of the. By Wm. H. Prescott. 2 vols. Boston. 1857.

PHILIP THE II., History of the Reign of. By Wm. H. Prescott. 2 vols. Boston, 1857.

—— Same. By Chas. Gayarré; and Letter of George Bancroft, New York, 1866.

PONTIAC, History of the Conspiracy of, and the War of the North American Tribes. By Francis Parkman, jr. Boston, 1837.

POPES, History of the, from the Foundation of the See of Rome to the Death of Benedict XIV., 1758. By Archibald Bower. 7 vols. 4to. London, 1766.

—— History of. By Leopold Ranke. Translated by E. Foster. 3 vols. London, Bohn, 1847.

PROTESTANT REFORMATION, Cobbett's History of the, and Monastic Institutions. London and Dublin, 1825.

QUEENS, The, Before the Conquest. By Mrs. Matthew Hall. 2 vols. London, 1854.

RAPPORTS, Opinions et Discours, Choix de : Prononcés à la Tribune Nationale. 20 vols. 1789 à 1815.

RECUEIL des Manifestes, Discours, Décrets, etc., etc., de Napoléon Buonaparte. Par Lewis Goldsmith. 1810.

REFORMATION OF THE CHURCH OF ENGLAND, The History of. By Gilbert Burnet. 2 vols. London, 1841.

REMINISCENCES OF A NONAGENARIAN. By Sarah Anna Emery. Newburyport, 1879.

RÉVOLUTION D'ANGLETERRE. Charles I., 1630–1660. Par Philarète Chasles. Paris. 1844.

RICARDI DIVISIENSIS. De Rebus Gestis Ricardi Primi Regis Angliæ. Large 8vo. Eng. Hist. Soc. Pub. London, 1838.

RICHARDSON'S TABLE BOOK of Remarkable Occurrences. By M. A. Richardson. 8 vols. Newcastle-upon-Tyne, 1841 to 1846.

RICHARD OF DEVIZES, Chronicle of. Translated and Edited by J. A. Giles. London, 1841.

RICRAFT'S SURVEY of England's Champions and Patriots. By Josiah Ricraft. London, 1647.

ROBESPIERRE. Œuvres de Maximilian Robespierre. Par Armand Carrel. 3 vols. Paris. 1840.

ROBINSON, WM., D.D., The Works of. By Dugald Stewart. 10 vols. London, 1821.

ROGER OF WENDOVER. Flowers of History. Translated from the Latin. By J. A. Giles. 2 vols. London, 1849.

ROGERI DE WENDOVER. Chronica sive Fiores Historiarum. With Appendix. 5 vols. Large 8vo. Eng. Hist. Soc. Pub. Londini, 1842.

ROLAND, MADAME, Mémoires Particuliers de. Par Fs. Barrière. Paris, 1847.

ROLLIN'S ANCIENT HISTORY. With a Life of the Author. By James Bell. 2 vols. New York, 1836.

ROMAN EMPERORS, History of the. By Rev. Robt. Lynam. Edited by Rev. Jno. T. White. 2 vols. London, 1850.

ROMAN HISTORY, Credibility of the Early. By Sir George Cornewall Lewis. 2 vols. London, 1855.

ROME, History of, to the Age of Augustus. By Henry Bankes. 2 vols. London. 1818.

—— Lectures on the History of. By B. G. Niebuhr. Translated by r. Schmitz. 3d Edition. 3 vols. 8vo. London, 1853.

—— History of the. By B. G. Niebuhr. Translated by Hare and Thirlwall. 3 vols. 8vo. New Edition. London, 1855.

ROVIGO, Duke of, Memoirs of the. Written by Himself [M. Savary]. 3 vols. London, 1828.

ROYAL NAVY, History of. From the Earliest Times to the Wars of the French Revolution. By N. H. Nicolas. 2 vols. London. 1847.

RUPERT, Prince, and the Cavaliers, Memoirs of. Eliot Warburton. 3 vols. London, 1849.

RUSSIA, History of. From the Foundation of the Empire to the Close of the Hungarian War. By Rabbe and Duncan. 2 vols. London, 1854.

RUSSIE EN 1839. Par le Marquis de Custine. Bruxelles, 1843.

SAINT-JUST, Œuvres de. Représentant du Peuple à la Convention Nationale. Paris, 1834.

SARACENS, History of the. By Simon Ockley. London, 1848.

SEBASTOPOL, Siege of, Engineer and Artillery Operations at the. 3 vols. London, 1859. With Vol. of Maps.

SCHILLER, FREDERICK. History of the Thirty Years' War. Revolt of the Netherlands. London, 1851.

SCHLOSSER, F. C.   History of the XVIIIth Century.   Translated by
D. Davison.   8 vols.   London, 1852.

SCHOULER, JAMES.   History of the U. S. Under the Constitution.   2
vols.   Washington, 1882.

SCOTLAND, Annals of.   From the Accession of Malcolm III., A.D. 1507
to Accession of House of Stuart, A.D. 1371.   By Sir David Dal-
rymple.   3 vols.

—— History of the Church of.   From A.D. 203 to the End of the
Reign of James VI.   By Rev. John Spottiswoode.   3 vols.
Edinburgh, 1851.

—— History of.   From the Earliest Period.   By Aikman.   6 vols.
Glasgow, Blackie & Sons, 1855.

·—— Same.   By Malcolm Laing.   4 vols.   London, 1819.

—— The History of.   By John Struthers.   2 vols.   Edinburgh and
Glasgow, 1828.

—— Buchanan's History of.   2 vols.   Edinburgh, 1762.

SCOTT'S NAVAL LIFE.   Recollections of a Naval Life.   By Capt.
James Scott.   3 vols.   London, 1834.

SICILIAN VESPERS, History of the War of the.   By Michel Amari.   3
vols.   London, 1850.

SIOUX WAR AND MASSACRES of 1862 and 1864.   By L. V. D.
Heard.

SISMONDI.   Republicas de Italia.   By J. C. L. de Sismondi.   2 vols in
one.   Paris, 1837.

SOPHIA DOROTHEA.   Consort of George I.   2 vols.   London, 1845.

SOUTH CAROLINA.   Biographical Sketches of the Bench and Bar.
By Jno. Belton O'Neall.   Charleston, 1859.

—— History of Upper Country of.   By Jno. H. Logan.   Charleston,
1856.

SOUTHERN GENERALS.   Their Lives and Campaigns.   By Wm. Parker
Snow.

SOUTHERN HISTORICAL PAPERS.   By Southern Historical Society.
January, 1876, to December, 1882 ; and Index.   10 vols.

SOUTHERN REFUGEE, Diary of a.   By a Lady.   New York, 1868.

SPAIN, Sieges in ; Journals of.   By Sir John T. Jones.   3 vols.   London, 1846.

STATESMAN'S MANUAL.   By Edwin Williams.   4 vols.

ST. JOHN OF JERUSALEM, History of the Order of.   By John Taafe.
4 vols.   London, 1852.

STORIA D'ITALIA.   1789–1814.   Scritte da Carlo Botta.   4 vols.   Italia,
1826.

ST. PAUL'S, Chapters in the History of Old.   By W. Sparrow Simpson.
London, 1881.

STUART, MARIE, Lettres, Instructions et Mémoires de. Par Prince Alexandre Labonoff. 7 vols. London, 1844.

STUART, PRINCE CHARLES, The Young Pretender, Memoirs of. By Chas. Louis Klose. 2 vols. London, 1846.

SUCHET. Mémoires du Maréchal Suchet, Duc d'Albufera. 2 vols. Paris, 1828. Copy presented by the Author to Belliard, Min. of War.

SULLY, The Duke of, Memoirs of. 6 vols. London, 1778.

SUNDON, VISCOUNTESS. Memoirs and Correspondence of Lady Sundon. By Mrs. Thompson. 2 vols. London, 1850.

TENNESSEE, Annals of. By J. G. M. Ramsay. Charleston, 1853.

THIERRY, AUGUSTIN. Histoire de la Conquête de l'Angleterre. 4 vols. Paris, 1846.

THORNTON'S GAZETTEER of the Countries Adjacent to India. 2 vols. London, 1844.

THUCYDIDIS. De Bello Peloponnesiaco Libri Octo. London, 1824.
—— The History of. By Rev. S. T. Bloomfield. Vols. I. and II. London, 1829.

TITUS LIVIUS, The History of Rome, by. By Spillam, Edmonds, & McDevitte. 4 vols. London, 1850–'53.

TRIVETI, F. NICHOLAI. Annales. Large 8vo. Eng. Hist. Soc. Pub. Londini, 1845.

UNITED STATES, National History of. By Lossing and Williams. 2 vols. New York.

VESPUCCI, AMERIGO, Vita de. Bandini. Firenze, 1745.

VICTOIRES ET CONQUÊTES des Français, de 1792 à 1815. 27 vols. Paris, 1817.
—— Same. Maps and Plans.

WALLENSTEIN, The Life of. By Lt.-Col. J. Mitchell. London, 1840.

WALPOLE, HORACE, Private Correspondence of. 3 vols. London, 1837.

WAR IN FRANCE AND BELGIUM IN 1815, History of the. Captain W. Siborne. 2 vols. 8vo. London, 1844.
—— Same. American Edition. Philadelphia, 1845.

WAR OF THE REVOLUTION, Memoirs of the, in the Southern Department of the U. S. By Henry Lee, of the Partisan Legion.

WAR OF THE REBELLION, Report on the Conduct of the. 1863, 1865, 1866, and Supplement. 8 vols.
—— Of the Rebellion, Southern History of the. By Edward A. Pollard. 4 vols. Richmond.

WAR OF THE REBELLION.   Official Records of the Union and Confederate Armies.   Series I., Vol. I. to VIII.

WAR PICTURES.   From the South.   By B. Estvàn.   New York, 1864.

WARS, Tales of the ; or, Naval and Military Chronicle.   2 vols.   London, 1838.

WASHINGTON CITY, Siege of.   By Capt. F. Colborne Adams.

WASHINGTON, The Writings of.   With Life of the Author.   By Jared Sparks.   12 vols.   Boston, 1838.

WASHINGTON, GEORGE, The Diary of.   From 1789 to 1791.   Richmond, 1861.

WEARING OF THE GRAY.   Personal Portraits, Scenes and Adventures of the War.   By John Esten Cooke.

WELLESLEY, RICHARD, MARQUESS, Memoirs and Correspondence of.   By Robt. R. Pearce.   3 vols.   London, 1846.

WESTMINSTER.   History of Ancient Palace and Late Houses of Parliament.   By Brayley and Britton.   London, 1836.

WILLELMI PARVI DE NEWBURGH.   Historia Rerum Anglicarum.   2 vols.   Large 8vo.   Eng. Hist. Soc. Pub.   Londini, 1856.

WILLELMI MALMESBIRIENSIS, MONACHI.   Gesta Regum Anglorum.   2 vols.   Large 8vo.   Eng. Hist. Soc. Pub.   Londini, 1840.

WILLIAM OF MALMESBURY.   Chronicle of the Kings of England.   Translated by J. A. Giles.   London, 1847.

WOMAN IN BATTLE.   A Narrative of Madame Loreta Janeta Velasquez.   Richmond, 1876.

CLASS II.

PHILOSOPHICAL AND RELIGIOUS.

CLASS II.

ÆLOIM, ou les Dieux de Moise. Par P. Lacour, 2 vols. Bordeaux, 1839.

ALCORAN OF MOHAMMED. By George Sale. London.

ALLIES, THOS. WM. The Church of England Cleared from the Charge of Schism. Oxford, 1848.

ANDERSON, CHRISTOPHER. Annals of the English Bible. 2 vols. London, 1845.

ANDREWS, LANCELOTI. Preces Privatæ Quotidianæ. Græcè et Latinè. Londini, 1848.

ANNALES DU MAGNÉTISME ANIMAL. 4 vols. Paris, 1814.

APOCALYPSES APOCRYPHÆ. Constantinus Tischendorf. Lipsiæ, 1866.

ARABIA, The Historical Geography of. By Rev. Chas. Foster. 2 vols. London, 1844.

ARCHIVES DE MAGNÉTISME ANIMAL. Par le Baron d'Henin de Cuvillers. 8 vols. in 4. Paris, 1820.

—— Same. Vols. 3 to 8 inclusive, in 3. Paris, 1820.

ARISTOTLE. Nicomachean Ethics. Translated by Browne. London, 1850.

—— Organon, or Logical Treatises. Translated by Owen. 2 vols. London, 1853.

—— Rhetoric and Poetic. Translated by Buckley. London, 1851.

ART MAGIC SPIRITISM. Edited by Emma Hardinge Britten. New York, 1876.

BARNI, JULES. Philosophie de Kant. 2 copies. Paris, 1851.

BARON, RICHARD. The Pillars of Priestcraft and Orthodoxy Shaken. 4 vols. London, 1768.

BARROW, ISAAC. His Works and Life. By Rev. Jas. Hamilton. 3 vols. Edinburgh, 1841.

BEDÆ, VENERABILIS. Opera. Edidit J. A. Giles, LL.D. 12 vols. Londini, 1843, 1844.

       Vol. I. Vita, Poemata, Epistolæ.

        II. Historiæ Ecclesiasticæ. Libra I., II., III.

       III.   "   "   " IV., V.

       IV. Opuscula Historica.

3

BEDÆ, VENERABILIS.—*Continued.*

Vol. V. Homilæ.
 VI. Opuscula Scientifica, et Appendix.
 VII. Comment. in Script. Sacra.
 VIII. " " "
  IX. " " "
  X. " " "
  XI. " " "
  XII. " " "

BELLOWS, HENRY W. Re-statements of Christian Doctrine. New York, 1860.

BIBLE. The Holy Bible. Philadelphia.

—— A Key to the. A Summary of Biblical Knowledge. Rev. Thos. Timpson. London, 1840.

BIBLIA HEBRAICA. Londini, Jacobi Duncan, 1844.

BIBLIOTHÈQUE DU MAGNÉTISME ANIMAL. 4 vols. Paris, 1817.

BIET, F. JOSEPH. L'École Juive d'Alexandrie. Paris, 1854.

BOSSUET, Sermons Choisis de. Paris, 1845.

—— Œuvres Philosophiques. Paris, 1844.

—— Oraisons Funèbres. Paris, 1847.

BOURDALOUE, Œuvres de. 3 vols. Paris, 1840.

Tome Premier. Avent, Carême, Dominicales.

 " Deuxième. Suite de Dominicales. Mystères, Panégyriques.

 " Troisième. Sermons pour les Vêtures ; Orations Funèbres ; Exhortations, Pensées, Essai d'Avent.

BUCHANAN, REV. JAS. Faith in God, and Modern Atheism Compared. 2 vols. Edinburgh, 1855.

BUNSEN. Ancient Christianity and Mankind. Philological Section. London, 1854.

—— Reliquiæ Literariæ. Vol. I.

—— Reliquiæ Canonicæ. Vol. II.

—— Historical Section. Hippolytus and His Age. Vol. I. 2 copies. London, 1854.

-- - Philosophical Section. Outlines of Philosophy of Universal History. 2 vols. London, 1854.

CANNE, JOHN. Necessity of Separation from the Church of England. London, 1349.

CHILLINGWORTH, WM., The Works of. 3 vols. Oxford, 1838.

CHRISTIAN EXAMINER. 3 vols. Boston.

Vol. LXIII., Fifth Series, Vol. I., July, Sept., Nov., 1857.

Vol. LXIV., Fifth Series, Vol. II., Jan'y, March, May, 1858.

Vol. LXV., Fifth Series, Vol. III., July, Sept., Nov., 1858.

CHRISTIANITY, Ancient; and Doctrines of the Oxford Tracts for the Times.. Supplement. 2 vols. London, 1840.

CHURTON, EDWARD. The Early English Church. London.

CICERO, Offices, Three Books of. Translated by Edwards.

CLAVEL, F. T. B. Histoire Pittoresque des Religions. 2 vols. Paris, 1844.

CLAVIS CALENDARIA. John Brady. 2 vols. London, 1812.

COMTE, AUGUSTE. Discours sur l'Ensemble du Positivisme. Paris, 1848.

—— Cours de Philosophie Positive. 6 vols. Paris, 1852.

COQUEREL, ATHANASE. Christologie. 2 vols. Paris, 1858.

COUSIN, VICTOR, Œuvres de. Paris, 1846 to 1851.

—— Première Série. 7 vols. Philosophie Moderne.

—— Troisième Série. Fragments Philosophiques. 4 vols.

—— Quatrième Série. Littérature. 3 vols.

—— Cinquième Série. Instruction Publique. 3 vols.

—— Sixième Série. Discours Politiques.

CRANMER, THOMAS, Miscellaneous Writings and Letters of. Parker Society Pub., Cambridge, 1846.

CREATION [THE] AND THE SCRIPTURE. The Revelation of God. By Gilbert Chichester Monell, M.D. New York, 1882.

DELEUZE, J. P. F. Lettre et Réponse, sur le Magnétisme Animal. Paris, 1818.

—— Défense du Magnétisme Animal. Paris, 1819.

DE MAISTRE, Le Comte J. Du Pape. Lyon, 1845.

—— De l'Église Gallicane. Lyon, 1845.

DE PLANCY, COLLIN. Dictionnaire Critique des Reliques et des Images. 3 vols. Paris, 1821.

DESCARTES, Œuvres de. Par M. Jules Simon. Paris, 1850.

DEVOTIONS for the Family and the Closet. From the Manual of a Country Clergyman. New York, 1854.

DE WETTE. Introduction to the Canonical Scriptures of the Old Testament. Translated and Enlarged by Theo. Parker. 2 vols. Boston, 1850.

DIDEROT, Œuvres Choisies de. 2 vols. Paris, 1847.

DIOGENES, LAERTIUS. Lives and Opinions of Eminent Philosophers. London, 1853.

DIO L'Universo. Per S. P. Zecchini. Torino, 1875.

DISDIER, HENRI. Conciliation Rationnelle, du Droit et du Devoir. 2 vols. Genève, 1859.

DOWLING, JOHN, D.D. Romanism, The History of.

EUSEBIUS PAMPHILUS, Ecclesiastical History of. Translated by Rev. C. F. Crusé. London, 1851.
EVANSON, EDWARD. The Four Evangelists. Dissonance and Evidence of their Authenticity. Ipswich, 1794.

FAITH, The Eclipse of ; or a Visit to a Religious Sceptic. London, 1857.
—— Same. A Defense of. By the Author. London, 1854.
FEUERBACH, LUDWIG. The Essence of Christianity. Translated by Marian Evans.
FLEMING, WILLIAM. The Vocabulary of Philosophy. London, 1857.
FOISSAC, M. P. Sur le Magnétisme Animal. Paris, 1833.
FOSTER, REV. CHARLES. Mahometanism Unveiled. 2 vols. London, 1829.
FRIDERICUS, FRANCKE. Libri Symbolici Ecclesiæ Lutheranæ. Lipsiæ, 1847.

GENESIS, The Book of, in Hebrew. With Translation by De Sola, Lindenthal and Raphall. London, 1844.
GILLY, W. S. Vigilantius and his Times. London, 1844.
GIOBERTI, VINCENZO. Il Gesuita Moderno. 5 vols. Losanna, 1846.
GRÉGOIRE. Histoire des Sectes Religeuses. 6 vols. Paris, 1828.

HALES, WILLIAM, D.D. Analysis of Chronology and Geography, History and Prophecy. 4 vols. London, 1830.
HAMILTON, SIR WM., Philosophy of. Edited by O. W. Wight.
HEBREW SCRIPTURES, His'l and Critical Enquiry into the Interpretation of. By John W. Whittaker. Cambridge, England, 1819.
HECKER, J. F. C. The Epidemics of the Middle Ages. London.
HELVETIUS. De l'Esprit. Paris, 1843.
HENGSTENBERG, E. W. On the Genuineness of the Pentateuch. 2 vols. Translated by J. E. Ryland. Edinburgh, 1847.
—— Dissertations on the Genuineness of the Pentateuch. 2 vols. Translated by J. E. Ryland. Edinburgh, 1847.
—— On the Genuineness of Daniel, etc. Edinburgh, 1848.
—— On the Psalms. A Commentary. 3 vols. Translated by Fairbairn and Thomson. Edinburgh, 1851.
—— St. John, the Revelation of, Expounded. Vol. II. Translated by Fairbairn. Edinburgh, 1852.
HOFFMAN, MURRAY. The Episcopal Church, The Law of.
HOBBES' LATIN WORKS. By Sir William Molesworth, Bart. 5 vols. Londini, 1839.
—— English Works. By Sir William Molesworth, Bart. 11 vols. London, 1839.

HOOKER, RICHARD, The Works of. With Life of the Author. By
   Izaak Walton. 2 vols. Oxford, 1839.
HOPE, THOMAS. An Essay on the Origin of Man. 3 vols. London,
   1831.
HUME, DAVID, The Philosophical Works of. 4 vols. Edinburgh,
   1854.

JEWISH LITERATURE. By Steinschneider. London, 1857.
JEWS, Rites and Ceremonies of the. By David Levi. London, 1782.
—— Ceremonies, Customs, Rites and Traditions of the. By Hyam
   Isaacs. London, 1836.
JONES, JOHN. Ecclesiastical Researches. London, 1812.
JOSEPHUS, FLAVIUS, The Works of. By William Whiston. 4 vols.
   London, 1848.
JULIAN, Emperor of Rome, Orations of. Translated by Taylor. Lon-
   don, 1793.
—— Œuvres Complètes de. 3 vols. Paris, 1821.

KABALA, Extracts from the. By Albert Pike. Manuscript.
KABBALA DENUDATA. Vol. I. Sulzbach, 1677.
—— Vol. II. Frankfort, 1684.
KANT. Leçons de Metaphysique. Paris, 1843.
—— Critique de la Raison Pratique. Paris, 1848.
—— Logique. Par Jh. Tissot. Paris, 1840.
—— Critique du Jugement. 2 vols. Paris, 1846.
—— Critique de la Raison Pure. 2 vols. Paris, 1845.
KINGSLEY, REV. CHAS. Alexandria and Her Schools. Cambridge,
   1854.
KNEELAND, ABNER. A Review of the Evidences of Christianity.

LAW OF GOD. The Book of Genesis. By Isaac Leeser.
LEIBNIZ. Lettres et Opuscules Inédits. Paris, 1854.
—— Œuvres de. Par M. A. Jacques. Première Série. [2 copies.]
   2 vols. Paris, 1846.
—— Same. Deuxième Série. [2 copies.] 2 vols. Paris, 1846.
LIBERAL TRACTS, A Collection of.
LOCKE, JOHN, The Philosophical Works of. London, 1843.
LORDAT, Réponses. Dualité du Dynamisme Humain. Montpellier,
   1854.

MACKAY, ROBERT WM. The Progress of the Intellect. 2 vols. London, 1850.

MAGNÉTISME, Le, et le Somnambulisme. Paris, 1844.

MAGNÉTISME ANIMAL, Sur le. Rapport Confidentiel. Paris, 1839.

MAILLE, M. S. Exposé des Cures Opérées par le Magnétisme. 2 vols. Paris, 1826.

MAITLAND, S. R. The Dark Ages. London, 1844.

MALEBRANCHE, Œuvres de. Par M. Jules Simon. Première Séric. Paris, 1846.

—— Same. Deuxième Série. Paris, 1846.

MANSEL, HENRY LONGUEVILLE. Limits of Religious Thought. Boston, 1859.

MANUAL OF PLAIN SONG. By Rev. Thomas Helmore. London, 1850.

MASSILLON. Sermons et Morceaux Choisis. Paris, 1848.

MATTER, JACQUES. Histoire Critique du Gnosticisme. 3 vols. Paris, 1843.

—— Histoire de l'École d'Alexandrie. 3 vols. Paris, 1840.

—— Same. Vols. I. and II. in 1. Paris, 1840.

MATTEUCCI, C. Phénomènes Électro-Physiologiques des Animaux. Paris, 1844.

MICHÆLIS, JOHN DAVID. Laws of Moses, Commentaries on the. 4 vols. Translated by Alex. Smith. London, 1814.

MILL, JOHN STUART. On Liberty. London, 1864.

MISHNA, Eighteen Treatises from the. By D. A. De Sola and M. J. Raphall. London, 1843.

MONTESQUIEU. Esprit des Lois. Paris, 1858.   .

MORMON. Le Livre de Mormon. Par Jos. Smith, jr. Paris, 1852.

NEANDER, DR. AUGUSTUS. History of the Christian Church. 2 vols. London, 1851.

—— History of the Christian Religion and Church. New York.

—— Life of Jesus Christ, in its Historical Connection and Development. New York.

—— The Christian Religion and Church, General History of. 8 vols. London, 1850.

NEWMAN, FRANCIS WM. A History of the Hebrew Monarchy. London, 1853. 2 copies.

—— Theism, Doctrinal and Practical. 4to. London, 1858.

—— Reply to the "Eclipse of Faith," and Defense of. By the Author. London, 1854.

—— Phases of Faith. London, 1854.

NEWMAN, JOHN HENRY. The Arians of the Fourth Century. London, 1854.

NEW TESTAMENT. Greek. London, 1859.
—— The Apocryphal. Not Included in the New Testament. London, 1820.
NOBLE, DANIEL. The Human Mind in its Relations with the Brain and Nervous System. London, 1858.
NOURRISSON, M. Progrès de la Pensée Humaine. Paris, 1858.

OERSTED, HANS CHRISTIAN. The Soul in Nature. London, 1852.

PARKER, THEODORE. Ten Sermons of Religion.
—— Sermons of Theism, Atheism and the Popular Theology.
PASCAL, BLAISE, Lettres à un Provincial, par. Paris, 1849.
PASCAL ET NICOLE, Pensées de. Paris, 1854.
PATRUM ECCLESIASTICORUM, Bibliotheca. Curante E. G. Gersdorf. Tauchnitz. Lipsiæ.
—— Vol. I. Clementis Romani Sanct. 1838.
Vols. II. and III. Cypriani. 1838.
Vols. IV. to VII. Tertulliani. 1839.
Vol. VIII. Ambrosii Episcope. Mediol. De Off. Clericorum. 1839.
Vol. IX. Idem, Hexæmeri. 1840.
Vol. X. Lactantii, Firmiani, op. 1842.
Vol. XII. Annobii, Orations, adv. Nationes. 1846.
PAUL, THÉODORE. Jérome Savonarole. Précurseur de la Réforme. Genève, 1857.
PELLETAN, EUGÈNE. Les droits de l'Homme. Paris, 1858.
—— Profession de Foi du dix-neuv^me Siècle. Pagnerre, Edit. Paris.
PENTATEUCH AND HAFTAROTH. The Five Books of Moses. By Dr. A. Benisch. 2 vols. Rödenheim, 1864.
PHILO JUDÆUS, Works of. Translated by Yonge. 4 vols. London, 1854.
PHILOSOPHER'S BANQUET, The. Printed for Nicolas Vavasour. London, 1633.
PLATO, Works of. Translated. 5 vols. London, 1852.
—— The Gorgias of. By Woolsey.
POWELL, REV. BADEN. Christianity Without Judaism. London, 1857.
PRIAULX, OSMOND DE BEAUVOIR. Quæstiones Mosaicæ, or the Book of Genesis. London, 1842.
PRIESTLY, JOSEPH. History of Early Opinions Concerning Jesus Christ. 4 vols. Birmingham, 1786.
PSALTER. Oxford and Cambridge Psalter. London.

QUINET, EDGAR. Œuvres Complètes. Le Génie des Religions : De l'Origine des Dieux. Paris, 1857.

RABBI JESHUA.   An Eastern Story.   New York, 1881.

REGHELLINI DE SCHIO.   Examen du Mosaïsme et du Christianisme.
3 vols.   Paris, 1834.

RELIGIONS DE L'ANTIQUITE.   Par Frédéric Creuzer.   Traduit, refondu
et complété par Guigniaut.   Planches et Explication.   10 vols.
Paris, 1838.

RENAN, ERNEST.   Religious History and Criticism, Studies of.

—— Le Livre de Job.   Paris, 1860.

RENVERSEMENT de la Morale Chrétienne.   [Caricature of Monkery.]
Enriché de 50 Figures.   Small 4to.   Se vend en Holland.

RICARD, J. J. A.   Magnétisme Animal.   Traité Théorique et Pratique.
Paris, 1841.

—— Journal de Magnétisme Animal.   3 vols in 2.   Toulouse, 1859.

RITTER, HEINRICH.   The History of Ancient Philosophy.   4 vols.
Oxford, 1838.

RITTER, DR. HEINRICH.   Histoire de la Philosophie Chrétienne.   2
vols.   Paris, 1843.

ROSSETTI, GABRIELE.   The Anti-papal Spirit, Disquisitions on.   London, 1834.

SAINTS, Lives of the.   By Rev. Alban Butler.   12 vols.   Dublin and
London, 1866.

ST. AUGUSTINE, The Works of.   Edited by Rev. Marcus Dods, D.D.
5 vols.   Edinburgh, 1872.

SALVADOR.   Jésus Christ et sa Doctrine.   2 vols.   Paris, 1838.

SALVERTE, EUSEBE.   De la Civilisation depuis les Premiers Temps
Historiques.   Paris, 1813.

SALZADE, Ch. de la.   Lettres sur le Magnétisme Animal.   Paris, 1847.

SCHWEGLER, ALBERT.   History of Philosophy.   In Epitome.

SEPTUAGINT, An Apology for the.   By E. W. Grinfield.   London,
1850.

SHOBERL, FREDERIC.   Persecutions of Popery.   2 vols in 1.   London,
1844.

SIMON, JULES.   Le Devoir.   Paris, 1857.

—— Histoire de l'École d'Alexandrie.   3 vols.   Paris, 1845.

SKELTON, REV. PHILIP, Complete Works of.   6 vols.   London, 1824.

SMITH, GEORGE.   Sacred Annals.   London, 1850.

—— The Patriarchal Age.

—— The Gentile Nations.   2 vols.

—— The Hebrew People.   [2 copies.]   2 vols.

SMITH, GAMALIEL.   [Jeremy Bentham.]   Not Paul, but Jesus.   London, 1823.

SOCRATES, The Ecclesiastical History of, Comprising a History of the Church. London, 1853.

SOZOMON AND PHILOSTORGIUS.   Comprising a History of the Church. London, 1855.

SPARROW, ANTHONY.   Articles, Injunctions, Canons, etc., of the Church of England. London, 1675.

SPICILEGIUM SYRIACUM.   By Rev. Wm. Cureton.   London, 1855.

SPINOZA, Œuvres de.   Par Emile Saisset.   Première Série.   Paris, 1842.

—— Same.   Seconde Série.   Paris, 1842.

STILLINGFLEET, EDWARD, D.D.   Origines Britannicæ ; or Antiquities of British Churches. London, 1837.

STRACHEY, EDWARD.   Hebrew Politics in the Times of Sargon and Sennacherib. London, 1853.

STRAUSS, DAVID FRIEDRICH.   The Life of Jesus, Critically Examined. 3 vols. London, 1846.

SUPERSTITION UNVEILED.   Series of Lectures, Unveiling the Christian Mythology. London.   Privately printed.

TALMUD, De Babylone.   Par L. Chiarini.   Leipsic, 1831.

—— Selections from the.   Translated from the Original by H. Polano. 1876.

TAYLOR, JEREMY, The Whole Works of. 3 vols. 8vo. London, 1836.

TAYLOR, REV. ROBERT.   The Diegesis ; A Discovery of the Early History of Christianity. London, 1841.

TAYLOR, THOMAS.   Two Treatises of Proclus, the Platonic Successor.

—— Lucanus ; Taurus ; Firmicus.   Select Theorems on the Perpetuity of Time, of Proclus. London, 1831.

THEODORET AND EVAGRIUS.   A History of the Church.   London, 1854.

THOLUCK, AUGUSTUS.   Commentary on the Gospel of John.

TRENCH, RICHARD CHENEVIX.   The Fitness of the Holy Scripture.

UNITARIAN.   How I Became a Unitarian.   By a Clergyman of the P. E. Church.

VACHEROT, E.   Histoire Critique de l'École d'Alexandrie. 3 vols. Paris, 1846.

VANINI, Œuvres Philosophiques de.   Paris, 1842.

VESPERALE ROMANUM cum Psalterio ex Antiphonali Romano.   Mechliniæ, 1870.

VETUS Testamentum Græcum, juxta Septuagintum.

VON BOHLEN, PETER.   Introduction to the Book of Genesis.   London, 1855.

WARD, REV. W. G.   The Ideal of a Christian Church.   London, 1854.

WARBURTON, WILLIAM, D.D.   The Divine Legation of Moses demonstrated.   3 vols.   2 copies.   London, 1846.

WATERWORTH, REV. J.   The Canons and Decrees of the Council of Trent.   London, 1848.

WHITE, REV. JOSEPH BLANCO.   Practical and Internal Evidence against Catholicism.   London, 1826.

WISE, ISAAC M.   The Origin of Christianity.

WRIGHT, THOMAS.   Early Christianity in Arabia.   London, 1855.

CLASS III.

ANTIQUITIES.

.

CLASS III.

ANCIENT FRAGMENTS. Cory. Translated by E. Richmond Hodges. London, 1876.

APULEIUS, Works of, translated; With Metrical Version of Cupid and Psyche, and Mrs. Tighe's Psyche. London, 1853.

—— LUCIUS, The Golden Ass of, Of Medaura. 2 vols. London, 1822.

ARCHÆOLOGIA AMERICANA. Transactions and Collections of the American Antiquarian Society. 6 vols.

ARNOLD, EDWIN. The Light of Asia; or the Great Renunciation.

ARTHUR, WILLIAM. A Mission to the Mysore.

BELLONII PETRI CENOMANI. Opera. Translated from French into Latin by Atrebas. Antverpiæ, 1539.

BETHAM, SIR WM. Etruria Celtica; Etruscan Literature and Antiquities Investigated. 2 vols. Dublin, 1842.

—— The Gael and Cymbri. Dublin, 1834.

BIBLICAL LEGENDS OF THE MUSSULMANS. By Weil. London, 1846.

BONOMI, JOSEPH. Nineveh and its Palaces. London, 1857.

BOTTA, M. On the Discoveries at Nineveh. 1st Series. London, 1850.

BOULLAND, J. F. A. AUGUSTE. Histoire des Transformations Religeuses et Morales des Peuples. Paris, 1839.

BUNSEN, CHRISTIAN, C. J. Egypt's Place in Universal History. 5 vols. London, 1848.

—— Same. Vol. I.

BURNOUF, E. Introduction à l'Histoire du Buddhisme Indien. 4to. Paris, Imprimerie Royale, 1844.

BUSBEQUIUS, D. Legationis Turcicæ. Hanoviæ, 1605.

BRYANT, JACOB. A New System; or An Analysis of Antient Mythology. 6 vols. London, 1807.

CALMET, AUGUSTINE. The Phantom World. Edited by Rev. Henry Christmas. 2 vols. London, 1850.

CARUANA, A. A. Phœnician and Roman Antiquities. Recent Discoveries at Notabile, 1881, 1882. Malta, Gov. Printing Off., 1882.

CHAMPOLLION, Le Jeune. Précis du Système Hiéroglyphique. Planches et Explication. 2 vols. Paris, 1828.
—— Egypte Ancienne. Paris, Firmin Didot Frères, 1847.
—— Grammaire Egyptienne. Folio. Paris, Firmin Didot Frères. 1836.
—— Dictionnaire Egyptienne. Folio. Paris, Firmin Didot Frères, 1841.
COLEMAN, CHARLES. The Mythology of the Hindus. 4to. London, 1832.
CONWAY, MONCURE DANIEL. Demonology and Devil Lore. 2 vols.
CRAUFURD, Q. Ancient and Modern India. Its Laws, Theology, etc. London, 1817.

DAVIES, EDWARD. Mythology and Rites of the British Druids. London, 1809.
—— Celtic Researches, on Origin and Traditions of Ancient Britons. London, 1804.
DEANE, REV. JOHN BATHURST. Worship of the Serpent. London, 1830.
DE GEBELIN, COURT. Monde Primitif, Analysé et Comparé avec le Moderne. 9 vols. Paris, 1773-1782.
DE ISIDE ET OSIRIDE. Plutarchi. Cambridge, 1744.
DI CESNOLA, LOUIS PALMA. Cyprus. Its Ancient Cities, Tombs and Temples. New York, 1878.
DIDRON, M. Christian Iconography. E. J. Millington. Vol. I. London, 1851.
DRUMMOND, SIR W. Origines. Remarks on the Origin of Several Empires, States and Cities. 4 vols. London, 1825.
DULAURE. Histoire Abrégé des différens Cultes. 2 vols. Paris, 1825.
DUNLAP, S. F. Vestiges of the Spirit-History of Man.
DUPUIS. Origine de tous les Cultes, Abrégé. Paris, 1847.
—— Same. Ou Religion Universelle, with Atlas. 11 vols. Paris, 1835.

EDIE, JOHN. Early Oriental History. London, 1852.
EICHHOFF, F. G. Parallèle des Langues de l'Europe et de l'Inde. 4to. Paris, Imprimerie Royale, 1836.

FELLOWS, SIR CHARLES. Coins of Ancient Lycia. London, 1855.
—— Discoveries in Lycia. London, 1841.
FORNANDER, ABRAHAM. The Polynesian Race. Its Origin, etc. Vol. I. London, 1878.

FORSTER, REV. CHARLES. The Monuments of Egypt. London, 1853.

FOSBROKE, THOS. DUDLEY. Encyclopædia of Antiquities and Archæology and British Monachism. 3 vols. London, 1843.

GELL, SIR WILLIAM. Pompeiana. Topography, Edifices and Ornaments of Pompeii. Large 8vo. 2 vols. London, 1832.

GELL, SIR WILLIAM, AND JOHN P. GANDY. Pompeiana. London, 1852.

GLIDDON, GEO. R. Ancient Egypt. 4to.

GOLDZIHER, IGNAZ. Mythology Among the Hebrews. Translated by Russell Martineau. London, 1877.

GOULIANOF, J. A. DE. Archéologie Egyptienne. 3 vols. Leipsic, 1839.

GRAY, MRS. HAMILTON. Tour to the Sepulchres of Etruria, in 1839. London, 1843.

GREEN, WM. B. The Blazing Star. The Jewish Kabbala, etc.

GUHL AND KONER. The Life of the Greeks and Romans. Chatto & Windus. London, 1881.

HAMAKER, HENRICI ARENTII. Miscellanea Phœnicia. 4to. Lugduni Batavorum, 1828.

HAMILTON, WM. J. Researches in Asia Minor, Pontus and Armenia. 2 vols. London, 1842.

HARCOURT, REV. L. VERNON. Doctrine of the Deluge. 2 vols. London, 1838.

HARDY, R. SPENCE. Eastern Monachism. London, 1860.

HAUG, DR. PHIL MARTIN. The Parsees : Essays on the Sacred Writings, Language and Religion of Bombay. Bombay, 1862.

HERBERT, A. Cyclops Christianus. London, 1849.

HIGGINS, GODFREY. The Celtic Druids. 4to. London, R. Hunter, 1827. Cost $20.

—— Anacalypsis. 2 vols. 4to. London, Longmans, 1836. Cost $65.

JABLONSKI, PAUL ERNEST. Opuscula. Edited by Iona Gulielmus Te Water. 4 vols. Lugduni Batavorum, 1804.

JENNINGS, HARGRAVE. The Rosicrucians : their Rites and Mysteries. London, 1870.

JOHNES, ARTHUR JAMES. Origin of the Human Race. London, 1846.

JOHNSON, SAMUEL. Oriental Religions : India. Boston, 1873.

JONES, GEORGE. History of Ancient America. London, 1843.

KENRICK, JOHN. Ancient Egypt under the Pharaohs. 2 vols. New York.

—— Primæval History, An Essay on. London, B. Fellowes.

KESSON, JOHN.   The Cross and the Dragon.   London, 1854.

KING, C. W.   The Gnostics and their Remains.   London, Bell & Daldy, 1864.

KNIGHT, R. P.   The Worship of Priapus, An Account of.   London, ; T. Spilsburg, 1786.

—— RICHARD PAYNE.   Symbolical Language of Ancient Art and Mythology.   New York.

LACOUR, P.   Essai sur les Hiéroglyphes Égyptiens.   Bordeaux, 1821.

LA FINLANDE.   Léouzon le Duc.   2 vols.   8vo.   Paris, 1845.

LANDSEER, JOHN.   Sabæan Researches.   4to.   London, 1823.

LAYARD, AUSTEN HENRY.   Nineveh and Its Remains.   1st Expedition.   2 vols.   London, 1849.

—— Nineveh and Babylon.   2d Expedition.   New York, 1853.

LEPSIUS, RICHARD.   Egypt, Ethiopia, and the Peninsula of Sinai.   London, 1853.

LETRONNE, M.   Zodiaques de Dendera et d'Esne.   4to.   Paris, 1845.

LEVI, ÉLIPHAS.   Dogma et Rituel de la Haute Magie.   2 vols.   Paris, 1856.

—— La Clef des Grands Mystères.   Paris, 1861.

—— La Science des Esprits.   Paris, 1865.

—— Histoire de la Magie.   Paris, 1860.

LOFTUS, WM. KENNETT.   Travels and Researches in Chaldæa and Susiana.   New York, 1857.

MACROBII, Opera.   Londini, 1694.

MALAN, REV. S. C.   Who is God in China ?   London.

MALLET, M.   Northern Antiquities.   Translated by Bishop Percy.   London, 1847.

MANKIND : Their Origin and Destiny.   By an M.A. of Balliol College, Oxford.   London, 1872.

MANUEL D'ICONOGRAPHIE CHRÉTIENNE.   Didron and Durand.   Paris, 1845.

MAURICE, THOMAS.   Indian Antiquities of Hindostan.   7 vols.   London, 1806–1812.

MELEKARTHA, The Temple of.   3 vols.   London, Holdsworth & Ball, 1831.

MILNE, REV. WILLIAM.   The Sacred Edict.   Translation.   London, 1817.

MOOR, EDWARD.   Oriental Fragments.   London, Smith, Elder & Co., 1834.

MULLER, C. O.   Ancient Art and its Remains.   Translated by John Leitch.   London, 1852.

MULLER, C. O. Introduction to a Scientific System of Mythology. Translated by John Leitch. London, 1844.

MULLER, MAX. Rig-Veda Sanhita. Translation. Hymns to the Maruts. Vol. I. London, 1869.

—— Science of Religion, and Paper on Buddhist Nihilism.

—— Chips from a German Workshop. 3 vols. London, 1867, 1870.

NOSTRADAMUS, MICHAEL, The True Prophecies of. Folio. London, John Salusbury, 1685.

O'BRIEN, HENRY. The Round Towers of Ireland. London, 1834.

OSBURN, WILLIAM. The Monumental History of Egypt. 2 vols. London, 1854.

PAULUS, DR. Magicon : Prophecies Concerning Popery, etc.

PAUTHIER, M. G. Les Livres Sacrés de l'Orient. Paris, 1852

—— Confucius et Mencius. Paris, 1841.

PERUVIAN ANTIQUITIES. Rivero and Von Tschudi. Translated by Hawks.

PHENIX, The. Collection of Old and Rare Fragments.

PIERIUS-VALERIANUS, IOANNES. Hieroglyphica. 4to. Erasmus Kempffer, Francofvrti ad Mœnvm, 1614.

PIGOTT, GRENVILLE. A Manual of Scandinavian Mythology. London, 1839.

PIKE, ALBERT. Indo-Aryan Deities and Worship. Rig-Veda. Manuscript. 3 vols. 4to. Bound. 7 unbound.

—— Irano-Aryan. Theosophy and Creed. Zend Avesta. Manuscript. 3 vols. 4to.

—— Lectures of the Arya. Manuscript. 8 vols. Viz. :

　Vol. I. Emigrations ; Country ; Manners. Indo- and Irano-Aryan.

　　II. The Veda ; Aryan Languages. Indo-Aryan I.

　　III. Deities of the Veda ; Agni Indra. Indo-Aryan II.

　　IV. 　" 　" 　Vishnu, etc. Indo-Aryan III.

　　V. 　" 　" 　Rudra, etc. Indo-Aryan IV.

　　VI. The Gâthâs. The Doctrine of Zarathrustra. Irano-Aryan I.

　　VII. Ahura Mazda, and the Amĕsha Çpĕntas. Irano-Aryan II.

　　VIII. The Gâthâs, and Legendary. Irano-Aryan III.

—— Lectures on the Veda. 1, 2, 3. Manuscript.

PORTAL, FRÉDÉRIC. Les Symboles des Égyptiens. Paris, 1840.

POSTON, C. D. The Parsees : A Lecture for Private Circulation.

PRINSEP, JAMES. Indian Antiquities, Essays on. Edited by Edward Thomas. 2 vols. London, 1858.

RAWLINSON, GEORGE.   The History of Herodotus.   2 vols.   London, 1858.

RIG-VEDA SANHITA.   Translation.   By Prof. Wilson.   4 vols.   London, 1850 to 1866.

—— Hymns of, Original.   Prof. Aufrecht.   2 vols.   Roman letter. Bonn, 1877.

—— Translation.   French.   Langlois.   Paris, 1870.

SAINT-HILAIRE, J. BARTHÉLEMY.   Le Bouddha et sa Religion.   8vo. Paris, 1860.

SALVERTE, EUSÈBE.   Des Sciences Occultes.   Paris, 1856.

SANSKRIT TEXTS, Original.   J. Muir.   5 vols.   London, 1868 to 1873.

—— Same.   1st edition.   Vol. I.   London, 1858.

SCHLEGEL, GUSTAVE.   Thiam Ti Hwui.   The Hung League.   4to. Batavia, 1866.

SEELY, JOHN B.   The Wonders of Elora, in the East Indies.   London, 1825.

SHARPE, SAMUEL.   The Decree of Canopus.   London, 1870.

SMALL, GEORGE.   A Handbook of Sanskrit Literature.   London, 1866.

SMITH, GEORGE.   Assyrian Discoveries.   New York, 1875.

SPINETO, The Marquis.   Elements of Hieroglyphics and Egyptian Antiquities.   London, 1845.

STEPHENS, THOMAS.   Literature of the Kymry.   Llandovery, 1849.

STEVENSON, REV. J.   Sanhita of the Sâma-Veda ; Translation of.

STODDARD, SIR JOHN.   Introduction to the Study of Universal History.   London.

THE TEMPLE.   Especially as it stood in the dayes of Our Saviovr. Described by John Lightfoot.   London, 1650.

THOMSON, J. COCKBURN.   The Bhagava-Gîtâ ; or the Sacred Lay. Hertford, 1855.

THORPE, BENJAMIN.   Northern Mythology.   3 vols.   London, 1851.

VILLANUEVA, JOACHIMO LAURENTIO.   Ibernia Phœnicea.   Dublin, 1831.   2 copies.

VILLANUEVA AND O'BRIEN.   Phœnician Ireland.   London and Dublin, 1833.

VOLNEY, C. F.   New Researches on Ancient History.   New York, 1856.

WATHEN, GEO. H.   Arts, Antiquities and Chronology of Ancient Egypt. London, 1843.

WILKINSON, SIR GARDNER.   Manners and Customs of the Ancient
   Egyptians.   4 vols.   London, 1847.
WILLIAMS, MONIER.   Non-Christian Religious Systems.   Hinduism.
   London, 1877.   .

ZEND-AVESTA, The.   English Translation by Bleeck, from German of
   Spiegel.   Hertford, 1864.

CLASS IV.

TRAVELS.

CLASS IV.

ADALBERT, PRINCE OF PRUSSIA, Travels of. 2 vols. London, David Bogue, 1849.

ALEXANDER, JAS. EDWARD. Voyage Among the Colonies of Western Africa. 2 vols. London, Henry Colburn, 1838.

ATKINSON, THOS. WITLAM. Oriental and Western Siberia. London, Hurst & Blackett, 1858.

BAKER, SIR SAMUEL W. The Nile Tributaries of Abyssinia. London, Macmillan & Co., 1867.

BARTH, HENRY. Travels and Discoveries in North and Central Africa. 5 vols. New York, Appleton & Co., 1857.

BARTRAM, WILLIAM. Travels through North and South Carolina, Georgia, etc. Dublin, 1793.

BELCHER, SIR EDWARD. Narrative of a Voyage Round the World. 2 vols. London, Henry Colburn, 1843.

BELL, JAMES STANISLAUS. Journal of a Residence in Circassia, during 1837–'38 and '39. 2 vols. London, 1840.

BELTRAMI, J. C. A Pilgrimage in Europe and America. 2 vols. London, Hunt & Clarke, 1828.

BORROW, GEORGE. The Bible in Spain. Philadelphia, Campbell & Co., 1843.

CAILLIÉ, RÉNÉ. Travels through Central Africa to Timbuctoo. 2 vols. London, Henry Colburn & Richard Bentley, 1830.

CHEEVER, GEORGE B., D.D. Wanderings of a Pilgrim. New York, Wiley & Putnam, 1845–'46.

CLARKE, E. D. Travels in Scandinavia. 3 vols. London, T. Cadell & W. Davies, 1838.

DUNCAN, JOHN. Travels in Western Africa. 2 vols. London, Richard Bentley, 1847.

ERMAN, ADOLPH. Travels in Siberia. 2 vols. London, Longmans, 1848.

FORBES.   Eleven Years in Ceylon.   2 vols.   London, Richard Bentley, 1841.

HAMEL, J.   Early English Voyages to Northern Russia.   London, Richard Bentley, 1857.

HARRIS, W. CORNWALLIS.   Adventures in Africa.   Philadelphia, T. B. Peterson.

HERNDON AND GIBBON.   Valley of the Amazon.   2 vols.   Washington, Robert Armstrong, 1853.

HOOKER, WM. JACKSON.   Tour in Iceland in 1809.   2 vols.   London, John Murray, 1813.

HOWITT, WILLIAM.   Remarkable Places.   2 vols.   Philadelphia, Carey & Hart, 1842.

HUNTER, JOHN D.   Manners and Customs of Indian Tribes.   Philadelphia, J. Maxwell, 1823.

JANCIGNY, DE, M. DUBOIS.   Japon, Indo-Chine.   Paris, Firmin Didot Frères, 1850.

KING, HORATIO, Ex-Postmaster-General U. S.   Sketches of Travel, or Twelve Months in Europe.

LAIRD AND OLDFIELD.   Expedition to the Interior of Africa.   2 vols.   London, Richard Bentley, 1837.

LAL MOHAN.   Travels in the Pânjâb, etc.   London, William H. Allen & Co., 1846.

LANMAN, CHARLES.   Adventures in the Wilds of the U. S. and British Provinces.   2 vols.

LE VERT, MADAME OCTAVIA WALTON.   Souvenirs of Travel.   2 vols.   New York, 1857.

LIVINGSTONE, DAVID.   Researches in South Africa.   London, John Murray, 1857.

MACGILLIVRAY, JOHN.   Voyage of the Rattlesnake.   London, T. & W. Boone, 1852.

MARCEL, J. J.   Modern Egypt.   Paris, Firmin Didot Frères, 1848.

MARGOLIUTH, REV. MOSES.   A Pilgrimage to the Land of My Fathers.   2 vols.   London, Richard Bentley, 1850.

MARTIN, R. MONTGOMERY.   China ; Political, Commercial and Social.   2 vols.   London, James Madden, 1847.

MAUNDEVILLE, SIR JOHN, Kt.   Voyage and Travel.   London, Edward Lumley, 1839.

MEDWIN, THOMAS. The Angler in Wales. 2 vols. London, Richard Bentley, 1834.

MUDIE, JAMES. The Felonry of New South Wales. London, Whaley & Co., 1837.

MUNK, S. Palestine ; Description Géographique, Historique et Archéologique. Paris, Firmin Didot Frères, 1845.

NORMAN, B. M. Rambles in Yucatan. New York, J. & H. G. Langley, 1843.

PIKE'S EXPEDITIONS to the Sources of the Mississippi. By Major Z. M. Pike. Philadelphia, 1810.

PINKERTON, ROBERT, D.D. Observations on the State of Russia and its Inhabitants. London, Seeley & Sons, 1833.

RIPA, FATHER, Memoirs of, During 13 Years' Residence at the Court of Peking ; and Cheever's Wanderings.

Ross, W. A. Yacht Voyage to Norway, Denmark and Sweden. 2 vols. London, Henry Colburn, 1848.

SPENCER, CAPT. Travels in Turkey, Russia, the Black Sea and Circassia. London, Routledge & Co., 1855.

STEEDMAN, ANDREW. Wanderings and Adventures in Southern Africa. 2 vols. London, Longmans & Co.. 1835.

STEPHENS, JOHN L. Incidents of Travel. 2 vols. New York, Harper & Bros., 1848.

SWINBURNE, HENRY. The Courts of Europe. 2 vols. London, Henry Colburn, 1841.

WELLSTED, J. R. Travels in Arabia. 2 vols. London, John Murray, 1838.

CLASS V.

LITERATURE.

CLASS V.

AGE, A New Spirit of the. Edited by R. H. Horne.

ALLSTON, WASHINGTON. Lectures on Art and Poems. Rich'd Henry Dana, Editor. 1850.

AMOURS ET GALANTERIES DES ROYS DE FRANCE. Par Saint Edmé. 2 vols. Paris, 1830.

AN AUTHOR'S MIND. The Book of Title Pages. By M. F. Tupper.

ANGLER, The Complete. By Izaak Walton and Charles Cotton. London, 1842.

—— Same. Fac-Simile Reprint of 1st Edition of 1653.

ANGLER'S MANUAL, The British. By T. C. Hofland. London, 1839.

ANGLER'S COMPANION. To Rivers and Lochs of Scotland. By Thos. Tod Stoddart. Edinburgh, 1847.

ANGLER, The, in Wales. Thomas Medwin. 2 vols. London, 1834.

ARMS, The Pursuivant of, or Heraldry founded upon Facts. By J. R. Planché. London. No Year.

ARMS AND ARMOUR, An Illustrated History of. By Auguste Demmin. London, 1877.

ASTROLOGY, An 'Introduction to. By Wm. Lilly (Zadkiel). London. 1852.

BACON, FRANCIS, LORD, Works of. 2 vols. Large 8vo. London, 1837.

BALZAC'S CONTES DROLATIQUES. Collected from the Abbeys of Touraine. Illustrated by Gustave Doré. London, 1874.

BEAUTIFUL THOUGHTS. From Greek Authors.

—— From German and Spanish Authors.

—— From French and Italian Authors.

—— From Latin Authors.

BENCH AND BAR, Complete Digest of the Wit, etc., of. By L. J Bigelow.

BENTHAMIANA. Extracts from Works of Jeremy Bentham. By John Hill Burton.

BOLINGBROKE, LORD, The Works of. 4 vols.

BOOK OF THE COURT. By William J. Thomas. London, 1844.

BROAD STONE OF HONOR. By Kenelm Henry Digby. 5 vols.
    Tancredus. London, 1846.
    Godefridus. London.
    Morus. London.
    Orlandus. 2 vols. London, 1876.

BROWNE, SIR THOMAS, Works, Life and Correspondence of. By Simon
    Wilken. 4 vols. London, 1836.

BUBBLES FROM THE BRUNNEN OF NASSAU. By an Old Man.

BUNCLE, JOHN, Life of. 4 vols. in 2. London, T. Beckett, 1770.

BUNYAN, JOHN. The Holy War. Large 8vo. London, 1844.

—— The Pilgrim's Progress. Fac-Simile of London Edition. Printed
    by Nath. Ponder, 1678. London, Elliot Stock.

BURKE, EDMUND. First Principles, Selected from his Writings. By
    Robert Montgomery. London, 1853.

—— Life of. By James Prior. 2 vols.

—— The Works of. 8 vols.

BURROUGHS, JOHN, The Writings of. Houghton, Mifflin & Co. 5
    vols. Boston, 1881.

BURTON'S ANATOMY OF MELANCHOLY. 3 vols.

BYRON, Life of. By Thomas Moore. 6 vols. London, 1854.

CAKES AND ALE. By Barry Gray.

CALIFORNIA SKETCHES. New Series. By O. P. Fitzgerald. 1883.

CALIFORNIA. For Health, Pleasure and Residence. Nordhoff.
    1882.

CAQUETS DE L'ACCOUCHÉE, Les. Par M. Edouard Fournier. Paris,
    1855.

CARLYLE, THOMAS:
    Translations: Musæus, Tieck, Richter. London.
    Sartor Resartus, and Lectures on Heroes. London.
    Latter-Day Pamphlets. London, 1855.
    Past and Present. London, 1845.
    Critical and Miscellaneous Essays. 4 vols. 2 copies. New
    York.

CARTAPHILUS. The Wandering Jew. By David Hoffman, Göttegen.
    3 vols. in 2. London, 1852.

CASTLES IN THE AIR. By Barry Gray.

CAXTON'S BOOK. Essays, Poems, Tales and Sketches. By W. H.
    Rhodes. Edited by Daniel O'Connell. San Francisco, 1876.

CELLINI, BENVENUTO, Memoirs of. Translated by Thomas Roscoe.
    2 vols. in 1. 2 copies. London, 1850.

CEYLON, The Natural History of. By Emerson Tennent. London,
    1868.

CHAMBERS' PAPERS FOR THE PEOPLE. 12 vols. Edinburgh, 1850.

CHANNING, REV. WM. E., The Works of. 6 vols. in 3.

CHARICLES. Illustration of the Private Life of the Ancient Greeks. By Prof. W. A. Becker. London, 1854.

CHASSE, Royale, La. Composée par le Roy Charles IX. Paris, 1857.

CHESS-PLAYERS' HANDBOOK. By Howard Staunton. London, 1847.

CHESS, Works of Damiano, Ruy Lopez and Salvio on. By J. H. Sarratt. London, 1813.

CHRONIQUES DE L'ŒIL DE BŒUF. Par le Comptesse Douairière de B***. 4 vols. Paris, 1845.

CLASSICAL SELECTIONS. From British Prose Writers. London, 1852.

CLAY, HENRY, Life and Speeches of. Edited by Daniel Mallory. 2 vols.

COBBETT, WILLIAM. Legacy to Parsons.

—— Advice to Young Men.

COLERIDGE, SAMUEL TAYLOR. Biographia Literaria. 3 vols. London, 1847.

—— Aids to Reflection. 2 vols. London, 1843.

—— The Friend. A Series of Essays. 3 vols. London, 1850.

—— Essays on his Own Times. [2d Series of The Friend.] 3 vols. London, 1850.

—— Notes on English Divines. 2 vols. London, 1853.

—— Lay Sermons. London, 1852.

—— Confessions of an Inquiring Spirit. London, 1853.

—— Notes : Theological, Political and Miscellaneous. London, 1853.

—— Church and State, Constitution of the. London, 1852.

—— Notes and Lectures upon Shakespeare and Others. 2 vols. London, 1849.

COLERIDGE, HARTLEY. Essays and Marginalia. 2 vols. London, 1851.

—— Lives of Northern Worthies. 3 vols. London, 1852.

COMMON-PLACE BOOK. By Mrs. Jameson.

COMMONS, House of ; Random Recollections of. Grant. 4 vols. London, 1837.

CRADLE OF THE TWIN GIANTS, Science and History. By Henry Christmas. 2 vols. London, 1849.

CRESCENT, THE, AND THE CROSS. By Eliot Warburton.

CROSS AND CRESCENT AS STANDARDS IN WAR. By Jas. J. Macintyre. London, 1854.

CYCLOPÆDIA, New American. Edited by George Ripley and Charles A. Dana. 16 vols. New York, D. Appleton & Co.

CYCLOPÆDIA, The American Annual, and Register of Important Events. 5 vols. New York, D. Appleton & Co.

D'ARBLAY, MADAME, Diary and Letters of. 7 vols. London, 1854.

DAY AFTER TO-MORROW, The. William De Tyne. London, 1858.

DEAN SWIFT'S CHOICE WORKS; In Prose and Verse. With Memoir, etc. New York.

DEATH, Dance of. By William Herman.

DECAMERON, of Giovanni Boccaccio. Illustrated by Stothard. London, 1872.

—— 2 vols. London, 1841.

DE FOE, DANIEL, The Works of, viz.:

The Complete English Tradesman. 2 vols. Oxford, 1841.

A System of Magic. Oxford, 1840.

Political History of the Devil. Oxford, 1840.

New Voyage round the World. Oxford, 1840.

The Plague in London, 1665. 1 vol. 2 copies. 2 vols. Oxford, 1840.

Life of Colonel Jack. 2 copies. 2 vols. Oxford, 1840.

Religious Courtship. 2 copies. 2 vols. Oxford, 1840.

Life and Adventures of Duncan Campbell. Oxford, 1841.

Life of Capt Singleton. 2 copies. Oxford, 1840.

Memoirs of Capt. Carleton. 2 copies. Oxford, 1840.

Roxana. 2 copies. Oxford, 1840.

Robinson Crusoe. New York, 1859.

DEMOSTHENES ON THE CROWN, The Oration of. By J. T. Champlin.

DE QUINCY QUATREMÈRE. On Imitation in the Fine Arts. By J. C. Kant. London, 1837.

DE QUINCEY, THOMAS, The Works of, 21 vols. Boston, 1856., viz.:

Letters to a Young Man, and Other Papers.

Note Book of an English Opium Eater.

Miscellaneous Essays.

Life and Manners.

Autobiographic Sketches.

Confessions of an English Opium Eater.

Essays on the Poets.

The Cæsars.

Narrative and Miscellaneous Papers. 2 vols.

Essays on Philosophical Writers. 2 vols

Biographical Essays.

Memorials. 2 vols.

Theological Essays. 2 vols.

Literary Reminiscences. 2 vols.

Historical and Critical Essays. 2 vols.

DEWEY, ORVILLE, D.D., Works of. 3 vols.
DICTIONARY OF LATIN QUOTATIONS. By H. T. Riley.
DISRAELI, ISAAC. Curiosities of Literature. 3 vols. London, 1859.
—— Amenities of Literature. 2 vols. London, 1859.
—— Calamities and Quarrels of Authors. London, 1859.
—— Literary Character, or History of Men of Genius. London, 1859.
DON QUIJOTE DE LA MANCHA. Cervantes. In Spanish.
DRUNKEN BARNABY'S FOUR JOURNEYS. Printed from the Edition of 1778. London, 1822.

ELLIS, MRS., Prose Works of. 2 vols.
EMERSON, RALPH WALDO. English Traits.
ENGLAND AND ITS PEOPLE, First Impressions of. By Hugh Miller.
ENGLAND UNDER SEVEN ADMINISTRATIONS. By Albany Fonblanque. 3 vols. London, 1837.
ENGLISH COUNTRY LIFE. By Thomas Miller. London, 1859.
ENGLISH REPRINTS; Embracing the following. 5 vols. London, 1869.
    Roger Ascham, 1545.
    James Howell, 1642.
    John Earle, 1628.
    Edward Webbe, 1590.
    Revelation of the Monk of Evesham, 1196.
    Euphues. John Lyly. 1579 and 1580.
    Addison on Paradise Lost, 1712.
    Stephen Gosson, Schoole of Abuse, 1579.
    More, Utopia, 1516.
    George Puttingham, The Art of English Poesie, 1589.
    Master Hugh Latimer, the Ploughers, 1549. Seven Sermons, 1549.
    Nich. Udall, Roister Doister, 1553.
    Milton, Areopagitica, 1644.
ERASMUS. The Praise of Folly. Made English by the Lord Bishop of Peterborough. London, 1740.
ERNE, The. Its Legends and its Fly-Fishing. With Engravings from Designs by Hans Holbein. By Rev. Henry Newland. London, 1851.
ESSAYS AND REVIEWS. By Edwin P. Whipple.
EVANGILES DES QUENOUILLES, Les. Paris, P. Jannet, 1855.
EXCERPTS. Manuscript. Albert Pike.

FABLE OF THE BEES. London, 1795.
  5

FABLES, One Hundred. By James Northcote. London, 1828.

FAMILIAR QUOTATIONS, An Index to. By J. C. Grocott.

FELTHAM, OWEN. Century of Resolves. London, Oxford and Leicester, 1840.

—— Resolves. A Duple Century. The 7th Edition. London, Printed for Henry Seile, 1647.

FLETCHER, ANDREW, of Saltoun, Political Works of. Glasgow, Robert Urie, 1749.

GALLUS, or Roman Scenes of the Time of Augustus. By Prof. W. A. Becker. London, 1849.

GAUTIER, THÉOPHILE. One of Cleopatra's Nights. Translated by Lafcadio Hearn. New York, 1882.

GESTA ROMANORUM, Select Tales from the.

GIBBON'S WORKS. Edward Gibbon's Miscellaneous Works. By John, Lord Sheffield. London, 1837.

GODOLPHIN, MRS., Life of. By John Evelyn. London, 1848.

GOOD THOUGHTS. By Thomas Fuller. London, 1841.

GOVERNMENTS, Confusions and Revolutions of. By Ant. Ascham. London, 1649.

GUESSES AT THE TRUTH. By Two Brothers. 2 vols. London, 1851.

GUIZOT, M. General History of Civilization in Europe.

GYPSIES, The. By Charles G. Leland. Houghton, Mifflin & Co., 1883.

HADDON HALL, Evenings at. Illustrations by George Cattermole. London. No date.

HALLAM, HENRY. Introduction to the Literature of Europe. 4 vols. Paris, Baudry, 1837.

—— Same. 3 vols. London, Murray, 1847.

HAWKER'S INSTRUCTIONS TO YOUNG SPORTSMEN. By Wm. T. Porter, Editor *Spirit of the Times.*

HAWTHORNE, NATHANIEL, The Works of. 12 vols. Boston, Houghton, Mifflin & Co.

—— Dr. Grimshawe's Secret. Edited by Julian Hawthorne. Boston, Osgood & Co.

HAZLITT, WILLIAM. Conversations of James Northcote. London, 1830.

—— Criticisms and Dramatic Essays. London, 1854.

—— Criticisms on Art. London, 1843.

—— Lectures on Dramatic Literature. London, 1840.

—— Lectures on the English Comic Writers. London, 1841.

—— Literary Remains of. 2 vols. London, 1836.

HAZLITT, WILLIAM. Plain Speaker, The. 2 vols. London, 1826.
—— Sketches and Essays. London, 1839.
—— Table-Talk. 2 vols. in 1. New York.
HEADS OF THE PEOPLE, or Portraits of the English. By Kenny Meadows.
HERALDRY in History, Poetry and Romance. By Ellen J. Millington. London, 1858.
—— An Introduction to. By Hugh Clark. London, 1840.
—— Familiar Introduction to. By Archibald Barrington. London, 1848.
HERBERT, GEORGE, The Remains of. By Izaak Walton. London, 1841.
—— The Temple. Sacred Poems. Reprint Facsimile of Original Edition. Cambridge, Thos. Buck, 1633. London, Elliott Stock.
HESPERUS, or Forty-Five Dog-Post Days. Jean Paul Friedrich Richter. Translated by Charles T. Brooks. 2 vols.
HOLMES, OLIVER WENDELL. Professor at the Breakfast Table.
—— Autocrat of the Breakfast Table.
HOLY LIVING AND DYING, with Prayers. By Jeremy Taylor. London, 1839.
HOLY WAR, History of the. By Thomas Fuller. London, 1840.
HOURS WITH THE MYSTICS. By Robert Alfred Vaughan. 2 vols. London, 1856.
HUNT, LEIGH. Imagination and Fancy; or Selections from English Poets. London, 1855.
—— Men, Women and Books. [2 vols. in 1.]
—— His Autobiography and Reminiscences of Friends.
—— A Book for a Corner.
—— Stories from the Italian Poets.
—— The Indicator; a Miscellany for Fields and Fireside.

INDUCTIVE SCIENCES, History of the. By Wm. Whewell. 3 vols.
INEDITED TRACTS, Illustrating the Manners, etc., of Englishmen, in the 16th and 17th Centuries. Printed for the Roxburghe Library. London, 1868.
INVENTIONS, DISCOVERIES AND ORIGINS, History of. Wm. Beckmann. Translated by Wm. Johnston. 2 vols. London, 1846.

JAPAN, Tales of Old. By A. B. Mitford. 2 copies. London, 1876.
JERROLD, DOUGLAS. The Barber's Chair, and the Hedgehog Letters. London, 1874.
JOHNSON, SAMUEL, Life of. By James Boswell. 4 vols. London.
—— Works of, and Essays on his Life and Genius. By Arthur Murphy. 2 vols.

KEATS, JOHN, Life, Letters and Literary Remains of.   By Richard
Monckton Milnes.   2 vols.   London, 1848.
KNIGHTHOOD, Concise History of.   By Hugh Clark, Heraldic En-
graver.   London, 1784.

LAMARTINE.   Voyage en Orient.   2 vols.   1843.
LAMB, CHARLES, Works of.   Prose.   5 vols.   London, 1838.
—— Final Memorials of.   By Sir Thomas Noon Talfourd.   London,
1850.
LANDOR, WALTER SAVAGE.   The Hellenics.   London, 1847.
—— Imaginary Conversations of Greeks and Romans.   London, 1853.
—— The Works of.   2 vols.   London, 1853.
LAW AND LAWYERS.   Edinburgh, Wm. P. Nimmo.
LECTURES ON LITERATURE AND LIFE.   By Edwin P. Whipple.
LIBERAL, The.   Verse and Prose from the South.   2 vols.   Printed
for John Hunt.   London, 1822.
LITTÉRATURE CONTEMPORAINE EN ANGLETERRE, 1830–1874.   Par
Odysse-Barot.   Paris, 1874.
LONGFELLOW, HENRY W.   Outre-Mer ; A Pilgrimage Beyond the Sea.
—— Hyperion.
LOVE.   From the French of M. J. Michelet.   Translated by J. W.
Palmer.
LOWELL, J. RUSSELL.   Conversations on Some of the Old Poets.

MACAULAY'S ESSAYS.   T. Babington Macaulay.   4 vols.
MACHIAVEL.   Œuvres Politiques.   Paris, 1851.
MAGNUSSON, E., AND W. MORRIS.   The Story of Grettir the Strong.
Grettis Saga.   London, 1869.
—— Three Northern Love Stories, and Other Tales.   London,
1875.
MARCO POLO, The Travels of.   By Thos. Wright.   London, 1854.
MARGARET, QUEEN OF NAVARRE, Heptameron of.   Translated from
the French.   Philadelphia, Geo. Barrie.
MARIAGE, Les Quinze Joyes de.   Paris, P. Jannet, 1853.
MARVELL, ANDREW, The Works of.   By Capt. Edward Thompson.
3 vols.   4to.   London, 1776.
MATRIMONIAL INFELICITIES.   By Barry Gray.
MELVILLE'S OMOO.   Narrative of Adventures in the South Seas.   In
2 parts.
MEMORIALS OF HIS TIME.   By Henry Cockburn.
MILL, JOHN STUART.   Principles of Political Economy.   2 vols.
MILTON, JOHN, Prose and Poetical Works of.   By Robert Fletcher.
Large 8vo.   London, 1838.

MILTON, JOHN. Treasures from the Prose Writings of. Boston, 1866.

MITCHELL, DONALD G. [Ik Marvel.] Reveries of a Bachelor.

MITCHELL, DONALD G. [Ik Marvel.] Dream Life.

—— Fresh Gleanings.

—— [Jno. Timon]. The Lorgnette. 2 vols.

MODERN LITERATURE, Sketches of. By George Gilfillan.

MODERN SHOOTER, The. By Capt. Lacy. London, 1846.

MONTAIGNE, The Works of. Edited by William Hazlitt. London, 1842.

—— Same. 4 vols. New York.

MOORE, THOMAS. Memoirs, Journals, etc. By Lord John Russell. 5 vols. London, 1853.

MORT D'ARTHURE. By Sir Thomas Malory. 3 vols. London, 1858.

MOUNTAINEERING IN THE SIERRA NEVADA. By Clarence King. Boston, 1874.

MUSICAL DRAMA, Memoirs of. Hogarth. 2 vols. London, 1838.

MY MARRIED LIFE AT HILLSIDE. By Barry Gray.

NATURE, NIGHT SIDE OF. By Catherine Crowe. London, 1854.

NEW MISCELLANIES. By Charles Kingsley.

NIDDERDALE, Studies in. By Joseph Lucas, F.G.S., F.M.S. London, Elliot Stock.

NOCTES AMBROSIANÆ OF BLACKWOOD. 4 vols.

NORTH STAR AND SOUTHERN CROSS. By Margaretha Weppner. 2 vols.

NOTES AND QUERIES. Vols. I. to XII., and Index. 13 vols. London, 1850 to 1855.

OLD ROME AND NEW ITALY. By Emilio Castelar. Translated by Mrs. Arthur Arnold.

OLD THULE, Tales of. J. Moyr Smith. London, 1879.

ONE OF THE THIRTY; A Strange History. By Hargrave Jennings. London.

OUT OF TOWN. By Barry Gray.

OVERBURY, SIR THOMAS. His Miscellaneous Works in Prose and Verse, by Edward F. Rimbault. London, 1856.

PALACE OF PLEASURE. By William Painter. Edited by Jos. Haslewood. 3 vols. London, 1813. Only 165 copies printed. Little & Brown ask for this and " The Mirror for Magistrates," in 1882, $135.

PALESTINE, or the Holy Land. By Rt. Rev. M. Russell. London, 1854.

PARIS AND ITS ENVIRONS. An Illustrated Hand-Book. Edited by Thomas Forester. London, 1859.

PARIS AND VIENNE. A Prose Tale of Knight-Errantry. W. Caxton, 1485. Reprinted for Roxburghe Library, 1868.

PASCAL, BLAISE, The Provincial Letters of. Edinburgh, 1848.

PELLETAN, EUGENE. Jarousseau, le Pasteur du Désert. Paris, 1877.

PELLICO, SILVIO. Mes Prisons, suivi des Devoirs des Hommes. H. L. Delloye, Éditeur. Paris, 1846.

PHILOSOPHY OF DISCOVERY. By William Whewell.

PHILOSOPHY OF HISTORY. By Frederick von Schlegel. Translated by James Burton Robinson. London, 1848.

PHŒNIX, JOHN. [Lieut. Derby.] The Squibob Papers.

PICTORIAL CALENDAR OF THE SEASONS. By Mary Howitt. London, 1854.

PIKE, ALBERT. Addresses, etc. 3 vols.
—— Some Writings of. 1860–1875. 2d Series.
—— Argument before the Supreme Court of the U. S.
—— Thoughts on Political Questions.
—— Arguments in Jurisprudence.
—— Sabinus, the Evil and the Remedy   Little Rock, 1840.

PLAYING CARDS, Origin and History of. By Wm. Andrew Chatto. London, 1848.

POE, EDGAR A. The Literati, Some Opinions about.
—— The Works of. 4 vols. New York, 1866.

POLYNESIAN RESEARCHES. By William Ellis. 4 vols. London, 1853.

PRESS AND THE PUBLIC SERVICE, The   By a Distinguished Writer. London, 1852.

PROMETHEUS IN ATLANTIS. New York, G. W. Carleton.

PROVERBIAL PHILOSOPHY. By M. Farquhar Tupper.

PROVERBS, Hand-Book of. Collected by Henry G. Bohn. London, 1855.

PSEUDONYMS OF AUTHORS. By John Edward Haynes. New York, 1882.

QUARLES, FRANCIS. Enchiridion. London, 1856.

RABELAIS, The Works of. Illustrated by Gustave Doré. London.
—— Œuvres de Maître François Rabelais. 6 vols. Delarue, Paris.

RABELAIS, The Works of. Explanatory Notes by Duchat, Ozell and Others. 4 vols. London, 1844.

RECREATIONS IN SHOOTING. By Craven. London, 1859.

RELICS OF LITERATURE. By Stephen Collet. London, Thos. Boys, 1823.

RELIQUARY, A Pilgrim's. London, Wm. Pickering, 1845.

REPUBLIC OF LETTERS. By A. Whitelaw. 4 vols. Glasgow, 1835.

RHINE, The. By Victor Hugo.

RITSON, JOSEPH. His Works, viz.:
    Life of King Arthur. London, 1825.
    Annals. 2 vols. Edinburgh, 1828.
    Letters. 2 vols. London, 1833.
    Fairy Tales. London, 1831.
    Memoirs of the Celts, or Gauls. London, 1827.

ROCHESTER, JOHN, EARL OF. Some Passages of his Life and Death. By Gilbert Burnet. Reprint in fac-simile of edition of 1630. Elliott Stock. London, 1875.

ROME IN THE NINETEENTH CENTURY. By Charlotte A. Eaton. 2 vols. London, 1852.

RUTILIUS AND LUCIUS. By Robert Isaac Wilberforce. London, 1842.

SCIENTIFIC IDEAS, History of. By William Whewell. 2 vols.

SCOTLAND, Scenes and Legends of the North of. By Hugh Miller.

SCOTT, SIR WALTER, Life of. By J. C. Lockhart. 7 vols.

—— Same. By George Allen.

SCRIPTURA, or History and Art of Chalcography. By John Evelyn. London, 1755.

SELBORNE, Natural History and Antiquities of. By Rev. Gilbert White. London, 1850.

SHAFTESBURY. Characteristics. 3 vols. No imprint.

SHELLEY'S ESSAYS, ETC. Edited by Mrs. Shelley. 2 vols. London, 1852.

SHOOTING IN THE HIMALAYAS. By Col. Markham. London, 1854.

SIDNEY, SIR PHILIP, Miscellaneous Works of. By Wm. Gray.

—— Life and Times of.

SISMONDI, J. C. L. Simonde de. Translated by Roscoe. 2 vols. London, 1846.

SKETCHES FROM LIFE. By Laman Blanchard. Edited by Sir Edward Bulwer Lytton.

SMITH, SYDNEY, Works of. 3 vols. Philadelphia, Carey & Hart.

SMITH, ADAM. Wealth of Nations.

SMITH, MARGARET. Leaves from Her Journal, 1678–1679.

SOLITUDE, The Genius of. By William R Alger.

SOUVESTRE, ÉMILE. Le Monde,tel qu'il sera. Paris, W. Coquebort.

SPECTATOR, The. 4 vols. London, Thomas Bosworth, 1853.

STORY, WILLIAM W., Life and Letters of. Edited by his son, William
  W. Story. 2 vols.

STRUTT'S QUEEN-HOO HALL. A Romance. By the late Joseph Strutt.
  4 vols. Edinburgh, 1808.

STUDIES IN LITERATURE. By G. W. Griffin.

SWINBURNE, ALGERNON CHARLES. William Blake. A Critical Essay.
  London, 1868.

—— Essays and Studies. London, 1876.

—— A Study of Shakespeare. London, 1880.

—— A Note on Charlotte Brontë. London, 1877.

—— George Chapman. A Critical Essay. London, 1875.

SYDNEY, ALGERNON, The Works of. Printed by W. Strahan, jr. 4to.
  London, 1772.

TAINE, H. A. History of English Literature. Translated from the
  French. By H. Van Laun. 4 vols. London, 1880.

TASSO, TORQUATO, The Life of. By Rev. R. Milman. 2 vols. London, 1850.

THE DREAM-GOD. By John Cuningham.

THIODOLF, THE ICELANDER, and BOOK OF CHRISTMAS. From the
  German of Baron de la Motte Fouqué.

THOREAU, HENRY D., The Works of. 8 vols. Boston, 1833.

TIMON. Livre des Orateurs. 2 vols. Paris, Pagnerre, Éditeur,
  1847.

—— Same. 1844.

TITCOMB, TIMOTHY. Letters to Young People ; Single and Married.

UNDINE ; and Sintram and his Companions. German Romance.
  Friedrich de la Motte Fouqué.

UTOPIA, or the Happy Republic. By Sir Thomas More ; and The
  New Atlantis. By Lord Bacon. London, 1838.

WALTON, IZAAK. Lives of Donne, Wotton, Hooker, Herbert and
  Sanderson. London, 1847.

WEBSTER, DANIEL, Works of. 6 vols.

WHEWELL, WILLIAM. History of the Inductive Sciences. 3 vols.
  London, 1857.

—— History of Scientific Ideas. 2 vols. London, 1858.

—— Novum Organon Renovatum. London, 1858.

—— Philosophy of Discovery. London, 1860.

WHITTIER, JOHN G.   Old Portraits and Modern Sketches.
—— Literary Recreations and Miscellanies.
WILKES, JOHN, Letters of.   4 vols.   London, 1848.
WINES, History of Ancient and Modern.   4to.   London, Baldwin,
   Cradock & Joy, 1824.
WIRT, WILLIAM, Life of.   By John P. Kennedy.   2 vols.

YACHT VOYAGE, A.   W. A. Ross.   2 vols.   London, 1848

ZSCHOKKE, HEINRICH, Tales from the German of.   By Parke Godwin.

CLASS VI.

MAGAZINES.

CLASS VI.

ALL THE YEAR ROUND. October, 1859, to April, 1860. [Vol II.]
AMERICAN MAGAZINE. [Vol. II.]
AMERICAN MONTHLY. N. P. Willis. [Vol. I.]
AMERICAN REVIEW. Vols. I. to VIII. [except vol. VI.] 7 vols.

BLACKWOOD. Vols. I. to LX. [except XI., XXI., XXIV., XXXI., XXXIII., XXXIX.] 5 vols.

DE BOW'S REVIEW. Vols. I. to XXIII. [except V., VI., VII.] 20 vols.

HOUSEHOLD WORDS, Dickens'. Vols. I. to XIX. 19 vols.

KNICKERBOCKER. Vols. XXV. to LI. [except XXIX., XXXII., XLIX.] 24 vols.

ONCE A WEEK. July to December, 1859. [Vol. I.]

PUTNAM'S. 9 vols.

SOUTHERN REVIEW. January, 1867, to July, 1870. 7 vols.

TURF REGISTER. [Vol. XV.]

WHIG REVIEW. July, 1849, to December, 1852 [except July to December, 1850]. 6 vols.

CLASS VII.

JURISPRUDENCE AND LAW.

CLASS VII.

ANALYSE DES PANDECTES DE POTHIER. 2 vols. Paris, 1827.
AUSTIN'S JURISPRUDENCE. London, 1861.

CAUSES CÉLÈBRES ANCIENNES ET MODERNES. Saint Edmé. Série
I., 4 vols.; Série II., 5 vols.; Série III., 4 vols.; Compl., Vol. I.
CHARDON. Traité du Dol et de la Fraude. 3 vols. Paris, 1838.
CIVIL CODE OF LOUISIANA. Morgan. New Orleans, 1861.
CODE NAPOLÉON, Le, expliqué. J. J. Delsol. 3 vols. Paris, 1854.
CODIGO DE COMERCIO DE 1829, de Fernando Septimo. Puebla, 1833.

DEMOLOMBE. Cours de la Code Civile. Vols. I. to X. Paris, 1845.
DIGESTORUM SEU PANDECTORUM JUSTINIÆ LIBRI. Originaux et tra-
duits par Hulot et Berthelot. Paris, 1803.
DOMAT. Loi Civile. By Strahan. Cushing's Edition. 2 vols.
DURANTON. Cours de Droit Français. 22 vols. Paris, 1834.

ÉLÉMENTS DU DROIT CIVIL ROMAIN. Heineccius. 4 vols. Paris,
1805.

FENET, P. A. Travaux Préparatoires du Code Civile. 15 vols.
Paris, 1836.

GAII. Institutionum Commentarii IV. Boulet, ed. Paris, 1827.
GRAILHE, ALEX. Mémoire à plaider, pour la Nouvelle Orleans et
Baltimore. Testament de McDonough.

HORÆ JURIDICÆ SUBSECIVÆ. The Geography, Chronology and Literary History of Grecian, Roman and Feudal Law. Butler.
London, 1804.

JOURNAL DU PALAIS. 1791 à 1858. 106 vols.
——— Lois, Ordonnances, etc. 1845 à 1858. 5 vols.
——— Bulletin des Droits d'Enregistrement, etc. 1851 à 1858.
——— Belge. 1837 à 1856. 19 vols.
JUSTINIAN, Institutes of. Cooper.
——— Sandars. London, 1849.

MACKELDEY.   Manuel de Droit Romain, traduit de l'Allemand par
J. Beving. Bruxelles, 1846.

MAGNIN.   Traité des Minorités, etc.   2 vols.

MALEPEYRE ET JOURDAIN.   Traité des Sociétés Commerciales.

· MARCADÉ, VICTOR.   Explication du Code Napoléon.   6 vols.   Paris,
1852.

MAXIMS OF THE ROMAN LAW ; with Commentaries and Illustrations.
Albert Pike.   MSS.   13 vols.

MOURLON.   Examen du Commentaire du Troplong, sur les Priviléges.
2 vols.

NOTES ON CIVIL CODE OF LOUISIANA.   Albert Pike.   MSS.

PARTIDAS, Las Siete, The Laws of, in force in the State of Louisiana.
By Moreau & Carleton.   2 vols.   1820.

PERSIL, Régime Hypothécaire.   Questions sur les Priviléges et Hy-
pothéques.

POTHIER, Œuvres de.   Ed. de Sifferin.   18 vols.   Paris, 1821.

RÉPERTOIRE DES OUVRAGES DE LÉGISLATION, DE DROIT ET DE JURIS-
PRUDENCE.   1789–1855.   Paris, 1855.

REVUE CRITIQUE DE LÉGISLATION ET DE JURISPRUDENCE.   Tomes
1–13.   Paris, 1851 to 1858.

SALA.   Hispano-Mejicano.   2 vols.   Paris, 1844.

SELDENI, JOANNIS.   Mare Clausum.   London, 1636.

TEULET.   Les Codes de la République Française.   Paris, 1850.

VAZEILLE.   Traité des Prescriptions.
—— Resumé sur les Successions.   3 vols.

WHITE, JOSEPH M.   New Recopilacion of the Laws of Spain and the
Indies, etc.   2 vols.   1839.

ZACHARIÆ.   Cours de Droit Civil Français.   5 vols.   Strasbourg, 1843.

CLASS VIII.

PHILOLOGICAL.

CLASS VIII.

ANALECTA HEBRAICA. Pauli, C. W. H. Oxford, 1839.

BUNSEN, CHRISTIAN CHAS. JOSIAS. Outlines of the Philosophy of Universal History. 2 vols. London, 1854.

DICTIONNAIRE DE L'ACADÉMIE FRANÇOISE, and Supplement. 3 vols. 4to. Paris, 1825 and 1829.

—— François-Anglois et Anglois-François, par Louis Chambaud. London, 1816.

—— Synoptique de tous les Verbes de la Langue Française.

—— De la Langue Bretonne. Par Dom Louis le Pelletier. Folio. 1752.

—— De Langage Choisé. Par Goyer Linguet. Paris, 1846.

—— Synonymique de la Langue Française. Paris, 1826.

DIZIONARIO FRANCESE-ITALIANO ED ITALIANO-FRANCESE. 2 vols. 1813.

DICTIONARY. Sanskrit-English. Theodor Benfey. London, 1866.

—— Latin-English. Andrews, formed on larger Latin-German Lexicon of Freund. New York, 1854.

—— English-Latin and Latin-English. Ainsworth.

—— German and English. G. P. Adler. New York, 1849.

—— French and English. Fleming and Tibbins.

—— French Pronouncing. By Gabriel Surenne. New York, 1848.

—— Anglo-Saxon. From Manuscripts of Jos. Bosworth. Oxford, 1882.

—— Icelandic-English. By R. Cleasby. Enlarged and Completed by Gudbrand Vigfusson. 4to. Oxford, 1874.

—— Classical. J. Lemprière.

—— Spanish and English Pronouncing. Sloane's Newman and Baretti, by Velasquez de la Cadena. New York, 1854.

—— Spanish and English. By Joseph Baretti. 4to. London, 1786.

—— Portuguese-English and English-Portuguese. By Anthony Vieyra. 2 vols. London, 1840.

—— Italian Pocket. By C. Graglia.

—— Italiano-Inglese and English-Italian. John Millhouse. 2 vols. New York, 1866.

DICTIONARY, English. Hyde Clarke. London, 1855.
—— Of English Etymology. By Hensleigh Wedgwood. Vol. 1. London, 1858.
—— Same. Complete. 3d Edition, revised. London, 1878.
—— Of the Scottish Language, as illustrating Civilization in Scotland. By Francisque Michel. Edinburgh, 1882.
DONALDSON, JOHN WM. Varronianus. A Critical and Historical Introduction to the Ethnography of Ancient Italy, and Philological Study of the Latin Language. London, 1852.
—— The New Cratylus ; or Contributions towards a More Accurate Knowledge of the Greek Language. London, 1859.
DE VERE, SCHELE. Outlines of Comparative Philology. New York, 1853.

ENGLISH LANGUAGE, Lectures on the. By George P. Marsh. 4to edition. 2 vols. London, 1843.
ETHNOLOGICAL SOCIETY, American, Transactions of the. New York, 1845.
ETHNOLOGY, Bureau of, Annual Report of. 1879–1880. 4to. J. W. Powell, Director.
ETHNOLOGY AND LINGUISTICS OF THE RED MEN. Matthews, Valentine, Powell, Gatschet.

FERGUSON, ROBERT. English Surnames and their Place in the Teutonic Family. London, 1858.
FOSTER, REV. CHARLES. The One Primeval Language. London, 1852.
—— A Harmony of Primeval Alphabets, on cloth. 1 copy.

GRAMMAIRE COMPARÉE DE LANGUES DE L'EUROPE LATINE. Raynouard. Paris, 1821.
GRAMMAR, Elementary, of the Sanskrit Language. Monier Williams. London, 1846.
—— Practical, of the Sanskrit Language. By Theodor Benfey. 2d Edition. London, 1868.
—— A Sanskrit, for Beginners. By F. Max Müller. 2d Edition. London, 1870.
—— A Sanskrit, of the Classical Language and other Dialects, of Veda and Brahmaṇa. By Prof. Wm. D. Whitney. Leipzig, 1879.
—— Of the Hebrew Language. Rev. Samuel Lee. London, 1844.
—— Hebrew, of Gesenius. 14th Edition, as revised by Rödiger. Translated by Conant. New York, 1846.
—— Comparative, of the Teutonic Languages. Helfenstein. London, 1870.

GRAMMAR, Comparative, of the Sanskrit, Zend, etc.   By Franz Bopp.
Translated by Eastwick. 2d Edition. 3 vols. London, 1856.
—— Of the Anglo-Saxon Language. By Louis F. Klipstein. New
York, 1849.
—— Latin. Andrews and Stoddard. Boston, 1867.

HEBREW CHARTS, containing the Elements of the Language. Rev.
Norman Irish.

INDIA, A Handbook for, with Travelling Map and Plans of Towns.
Part II., Bombay. London, 1859.
INTRODUCTION TO WRITING HEBREW. Gräfenhan. Oxford, 1836.

JONAH AND HOSEA, Notes on the Prophecies of.   Rev. Wm. Drake.
Cambridge, 1853.

KOPP, ULRICO FREDERICO. Palæographica Critica. 4 vols. Mann-
hemii. 1817.

LAFFON DE LADEBAT, CHARLES. Méthode d'apprendre la Langue
Française. Paris, 1876.
—— Méthode d'apprendre la Langue Allemande. Paris, 1877.
—— Anglo-American Method of learning the French Language.
Paris, 1876.
LATHAM, ROBERT GORDON. The English Language. London, 1850.
—— The Germania of Tacitus. Ethnological Dissertation and Notes.
London, 1851.
LEXICONS.
—— Manuale Hebraicum et Chaldaicum. Gesenius. Lipsiæ, 1833.
—— Hebrew, Chaldee and English. Rev. Samuel Lee. London, 1844.
—— Hebrew-English and English-Hebrew. By Selig Newman. 2
vols. London, 1834.
—— Greek. Cornelii Schrevelii. New York, 1828.
—— Greek-English. Liddell and Scott. 4to. Oxford, 1855.
LOWER, MARK ANTHONY. English Surnames. Essay on Family
Nomenclature. 2 vols. London, 1849.

MÜLLER, MAX. Lectures on the Science of Language. New York,
1869.
—— Same. 2d Series. New York, 1871.
—— The Languages of the Seat of War in the East. London, 1855.
MUSEUM, PHILOLOGICAL. Printed by J. Smith, 1832–'33. 2 vols.
Cambridge, England.

PHILOLOGICAL SOCIETY OF LONDON, Proceedings of the. With Appendix, 1842–1843. 6 vols.

RENAN, ERNEST. De l'Origine du Langage. Paris, 1859.
ROGET, PETER MARK. Thesaurus. Revised Edition. 1881.

SACY, SILVESTRE DE. Calila et Dimni, ou Fables de Bidpai en Arabe. Paris, 1816.
SALVERTE, EUSEBE. Les Noms d'Hommes, de Peuples et de Lieux. 2 vols. Paris, 1824.
SURNAMES, English. Their Source and Signification. Charles Wareing Bardsley. London, 1875.
SWINTON, WILLIAM. Rambles among Words. Their Poetry, History and Wisdom. New York, 1859.

TAFEL, LEONARD AND RUDOLPH. Latin Pronunciation and the Latin Alphabet. Philadelphia, 1860.
TOOKE, JOHN HORNE. The Diversions of Purley. London, 1857.
TRENCH, RICHARD CHENEVIX. The Study of Words. New York, 1853.
TYPOGRAPHIA, or the Printer's Instructor. By J. Johnson, Printer. 2 vols. London, 1824.

WELSFORD, HENRY. Mithridates Minor; or an Essay on Language. London, 1848.
WHITING, WM. DWIGHT. Studies, Oriental and Linguistic. New York, 1873.

YATES, Rev. W. Introduction to the Hindustáni Language. Calcutta, 1855.

CLASS IX.

SCIENTIFIC.

CLASS IX.

ALMANAC, Nautical, and American Ephemeris for 1874.
ANCIENT FAUNA OF NEBRASKA, The. By Joseph Leidy, M.D. 1852.
AQUARIUM, The. By Philip Henry Gosse. London, 1856.
ARCANA ENTOMOLOGICA. By J. O. Westwood. 2 vols. London, 1845.
ARCHITECTURE OF THE. HEAVENS. By J. P. Nichol. London, 1851.
ASTRONOMICAL CATECHISM. By Catherine Vale Whitwell. 1818.
ASTRONOMY, Olmstead's, and Mason's Supplement.

BOHÉMIENS, Des, et de leur Musique en Hongrie. Par F. Liszt. Leipzig, 1881.
BOOK OF THE GREAT SEA DRAGONS, ICHTHYOSAURI AND PLESIOSAURI. By Thomas Hawkins. Imperial Folio. London, Wm. Pickering, 1840.
BOULDER, The Story of a. By Archibald Geikie. Edinburgh, 1851.

CEYLON, An Account of, Physical, Historical and Topographical. By Sir James Emerson Tennent. 2 vols. London, 1860.
—— Sketches of the Natural History of. By Sir James Emerson Tennent. London, 1858.
—— History of. By Rev. James Cordiner. 2 vols. 4to. London, 1807.
CHEMISTRY, METEOROLOGY, AND THE FUNCTION OF DIGESTION. Considered with reference to National Theology. By Wm. Prout. London, 1845.
CLASSICAL ATLAS. To illustrate Ancient Geography. By Alex. G. Findlay. London, 1853.
CONCHOLOGY, Popular British. By George Brettingham Sowerby. London, 1854.
CONCHOLOGY OF THE UNITED STATES, Writings of Thomas Say on the. W. J. Binney.
CREATION, Sketches of. Winchell. Illustrated.
CRETACEOUS REPTILES OF THE UNITED STATES. By Joseph Leidy, M.D. 4to. 1865.
CRUISE OF THE BETSEY. Rambles of a Geologist. Hugh Miller.

CRYPTOGAMEN. H. Wagner. Bielefeld, 1853.
CUVIER, M. LE BARON G. Animal Kingdom. By Edward Griffith
and others. 16 vols. Full calf. Published at £26 8s. London,
1827–1835.
—— Discours sur les Revolutions de la Surface du Globe. 4to.
Paris, 1826.
—— Ossemens Fossiles. 6 vols. 4to. Paris, 1821–1823.

DYNAMICS, Physico-Physiological Researches on. By Baron Charles
von Reichenbach.

EARTH AND ITS INHABITANTS, The. By Élisée Reclus. Edited by
E. G. Ravenstein. 5 vols. Large 8vo. New York, Appleton,
1882.
ENCYCLOPÆDIA, Iconographic, of Science, Literature and Art. By J.
G. Heck. Translated and edited by Spencer F. Baird. 6 vols.
ENTERTAINING KNOWLEDGE, Library of. Vegetable Substances.
ENTOMOLOGY, American. By Thomas Say. [3 vols. in 1.]
—— Introduction to. By Kirby & Spence. 2 vols. London, 1843.
—— Same. 1856.
—— Popular British. By Maria E. Catlow. London, 1852.
EXPLORATIONS AND SURVEYS IN NEVADA AND ARIZONA. George M.
Wheeler, Corps of Engineers. 4to. 1871.

FUR-BEARING ANIMALS OF NORTH AMERICA. By Elliott Coues.
1877.

GEOGRAPHICAL SCIENCE, Manual of. 2 vols. London, 1852.
Vol. I. Mathematical, by O'Brien ; Physical, by Ansted ; Char-
tography, by Jackson ; and Terminology, by Rev. C. G. Nicolay.
Vol. II. Descriptive Geography ; Ancient Geography. Rev.
W. L. Bevan. Maritime Discovery and Modern Geography.
Rev. C. G. Nicolay.
GEOGRAPHOS MINORES, Tabulæ in. À Carolo Mullero. Pars Prima.
Paris, Didot, 1855.
GEOLOGICAL, and other Tracts.
—— Manual. By Henry T. de la Beche. Philadelphia, 1832.
—— Map of Europe. By Sir R. I. Murchison, Prof. Nicol, and A.
Keith Johnston. In covers. 4to. London.
—— Observer, The. By Sir Henry T. de la Beche. London,
1851.
—— Reconnoissance of Arkansas, in 1859 and 1860. By David Dale
Owen. 2 copies. 2 vols.

GEOLOGICAL, and other Tracts—*Continued.*

—— Reconnoissance. By G. W. Featherstonhaugh. Made in 1835, from Washington *via* Green Bay and Wisconsin Territory to the Coteau de Prairie.

—— Report. G. W. Featherstonhaugh, U. S. Geologist.

—— Report, South-West Branch Pacific Railroad of Missouri. G. C. Swallow, State Geologist.

—— Science, Relation between Scripture and some parts of. By Jno. Pye Smith. 2 copies. London, 1852.

—— Survey in Kentucky. By David Dale Owen. 4 vols. 1856 and 1857.

—— Same. Maps and Illustrations.

—— Same. Reports of Progress. N. S. Shaler, Director. Vol. V. Frankfort, 1880.

—— Same. The Mounds of the Mississippi Valley, Historically considered. By Lucien Carr. 4to. Pamphlet.

—— Survey of Indiana. By E. T. Cox, State Geologist. Vol. II. 1870.

—— Survey of the State of Iowa. By James Hall, State Geologist ; J. D. Whitney, Chemist and Mineralogist. Parts I. and II. 2 vols.

—— Survey of Missouri, 1st and 2d Annual Reports of the. By G. C. Swallow, State Geologist.

—— Survey, State of New York. Reports of 1837, 1838, 1839.

—— Survey of Ohio. Vol. II. And Maps. 2 vols. 1874.

—— Survey. J. W. Powell, Director. Mineral Resources of the U. S. Williams. 1883.

—— Survey for Fiscal Year ending June 30, 1881. J. W. Powell, Director. Report.

—— Survey of the Territories. Hayden. Vol. IX., Palæontology ; Vol. XI., Rodentia ; Vol. XII., Rhizopods. 3 vols. 4to. 1876–1879.

—— Survey of the Territories. Hayden. North American Pinnipeds, Monograph of. [Allen.]

—— Survey of Nebraska and adjacent Territories. F. V. Hayden. 10 vols. 1867 to 1882.

—— Survey of Wyoming and Idaho. F. V. Hayden. Parts I. and II. Maps. 2 vols. 1878.

—— Survey of the Rocky Mountain Region. Powell. Vol. I., Vol. III., Vol. IV. 3 vols.

—— Survey, U. S. J. W. Powell, Director. 2d Annual Report, 1880–1881. 4to.

—— U. S. Geological and Geographical Surveys of the Territories, Bulletin of. Vols. IV., V. and VI. 3 vols. 1878 to 1881.

GEOLOGICAL, and other Tracts—*Continued.*
—— Survey of Wisconsin, Iowa and Minnesota. By David D. Owen.
4to.
—— Same. Illustrations. 4to. 2 copies
—— Terms, and Handbook of Geology. David Page. Edinburgh,
1859.
—— Travels. By J. A. De Luc. 3 vols. London, 1810.
GÉOLOGIQUE, Description. Des Environs de Paris, and Atlas. By
Cuvier and Brongniart. Folio. Paris, 1835.
GEOLOGISTS AND NATURALISTS, Reports of the Association of Ameri-
can, 1840, 1841, 1842.
GEOLOGY AND AGRICULTURE OF THE STATE OF MISSISSIPPI. By Eug.
W. Hilgard, State Geologist. 1860.
GEOLOGY, OF CANADA. Report of Survey, from commencement to
1863. With Atlas.
—— Certainties of. Wm. Sidney Gibson. London, 1840.
—— Elementary Treatise on. J. A. De Luc. London, 1809.
—— and Extinct Volcanoes of Central France. By G. Poulet Scrope.
London, 1858.
—— of the Black Hills of Dakota. Powell. 1880.
—— of the Henry Mountains. Powell. [2 copies.] 2 vols. 1877.
—— Introduction to. By G. F. Richardson. 2 copies. London,
1851.
—— Introductory, Descriptive and Practical. David Thos. Ansted.
2 vols. London, 1844.
—— Of Lake Superior. Foster and Whitney. 2 vols.
—— Same. Map of Survey.
—— Manual of. By John Phillips. 2 copies. London, 1855.
—— and Mineralogy. Rev. Wm. Buckland. 2 vols. 2 copies.
London, 1858.
—— Mineralogy and Crystallography. By Ansted, Tennant and
Mitchell. London, 1855.
—— Mineralogy and Physical Geography, Elementary Course of.
By David T. Ansted. London, 1850.
—— Popular Sketch - Book of. By Hugh Miller. Edinburgh,
1859.
—— and Revelation, or the Ancient History of the Earth. Rev.
Gerald Molloy.
—— Report on, of South Carolina. Tuomey. 1848.
—— of Tennessee. By James M. Safford, State Geologist. Maps.
1869.
—— Connection of, with Terrestrial Magnetism. By Evan Hopkins.
London, 1851.

GLACIERS ACTUELS, Nouvelles Études et Expériences sur les. By L. Agassiz. Paris, 1847.
—— Atlas, de 3 Cartes et 9 Planches. Folio. Paris.
GOSSE, PHILIP HENRY. A Year at the Shore. London, 1865.
GREAT BRITAIN, Royal Institution of, Journal of the. 2 vols. London, 1831.

HORSE OF AMERICA, The. By Frank Forester. [Henry W. Herbert.] 2 vols. 1857.
HUMBOLDT, ALEXANDER VON. Cosmos. 5 vols. London, 1849.
—— Travels to the Equinoctial Regions of America. 3 vols. London, 1852.
—— Same. Vol. I.
—— Views of Nature. Translated by E. C. Otte and H. G. Bohn. 2 copies. London, 1850.
HUMMING BIRDS, A General History of, or the Trochilidæ. By W. C. L. Martin. London, 1852.

INFUSORIA, History of, Living and Fossil. By Andrew Pritchard. London, 1849.
INSECT LIFE, Episodes of. By Acheta Domestica. 3 vols.
INSECTS, Introduction to the Modern Classification of. By J. O. Westwood. 2 vols. London, 1839.

LACÉPEDE, Œuvres du Comte de. L'Histoire Naturelle, avec Planches. 5 vols. Bruxelles, 1839.
LE MONDE PHYSIQUE. Par Amédée Guillemin. 3 vols. Paris, Hachette et Cie, 1883.
LEPIDOPTERES D'EUROPE. Catalogue Méthodique. By P. A. J. Duponchel. Paris, 1844.
LICHENS, British, Popular History of. By W. Lauder Lindsay. London, 1856.
LIFE HISTORY OF OUR PLANET. By Wm. D. Gunning. 1881.
LINNEAN SOCIETY, Transactions of the, 1788 to 1801. 4to. 6 vols. in 3. London, 1781 to 1802.

MACGILLIVRAY'S BRITISH BIRDS. By Wm. Macgillivray. Vols. I., II. and III. London, 1837 to 1840.
—— Same. Vols. IV. and V. London, 1852.
MACKIE, S. J. First Traces of Life on the Earth, or Fossils of the Bottom Rocks. London, 1860.
MAGNÉTISME TERRESTRE, Atlas du. Par Pierre Beron. 4to.
MAMMALIA, Natural History of. By G. R. Waterhouse. Vol. I., Marsupiata ; Vol. II., Rodentia. London, 1846.

MAMMIFÈRES, Histoire Naturelle des.   By M. Paul Gervais.   Paris, 1855.

MAN, Descent of.   By Charles Darwin.   2 vols.

MANKIND, Types of.   By J. C. Nott and Geo. R. Gliddon.

MANTELL, GIDEON ALGERNON.   Isle of Wight and Dorsetshire.   1st and 3d Editions.   London, 1847 and 1854.

—— Medals of Creation.   2 vols.   London, 1854.

—— Petrifactions.   London, 1851.

—— Wonders of Geology.   2 vols.   London, 1848.

MICROSCOPE, Practical Treatise on the Use of.   By John Quekett.   London, 1848.

—— Its History, Construction and Applications.   By Jabez Hogg.   London, 1854.

—— Same.   4th Edition.   London, 1859.

—— Evenings at the.   By Philip Henry Gosse.   London, 1859.

—— Popular Description of Objects for.   By L. Lane Clarke.   London, 1858.

—— and its Revelations.   By Wm. B. Carpenter.   London, 1856.

—— Same.   6th Edition, 1881.

MINERALOGY, Popular.   By Henry Sowerby.   London, 1850.

—— Manual of.   By James Nichol.   Edinburgh, 1849.

MOLLUSCA, Manual of the.   By S. P. Woodward.   London, 1851–1856.

MOLLUSKS, Terrestrial, and Shells of the United States.   By Amos Binney.   3 vols.

MOLLUSQUES, Histoire Naturelle des.   D. Dupuy.   2 vols.   4to.   Paris, 1847–1852.

MOSSES, British, Popular History of.   By Robert M. Stark.   London, 1860.

MUSIC OF NATURE.   By Wm. Gardiner.

NATURAL HISTORY OF THE INSECTS OF INDIA.   By E. Donovan.   Illustrated.   4to.   London, 1842.

NATURAL HISTORY OF IRELAND.   Birds.   By Wm. Thompson.   3 vols.   London, 1849.

   Vol. I. Raptores and Insessores ; Vol. II. Rasores and Grallatores ; Vol. III. Natatores.

NATURAL HISTORY OF THE EUROPEAN SEAS.   By Prof. Edward Forbes.   London, 1859.

NATURAL HISTORY OF THE UNITED STATES, Contributions to the.   By Louis Agassiz.   Vols. I. and II.

NATURE AND LIFE.   By Fernand Papillon.

NATURE, Harmonies of.   By G. Hartwig.

NEBRASKA, The Ancient Fauna of. Leidy. 4to.
NEWFOUNDLAND, Geological Survey of. By Alex. Murray, and Jas.
P. Howley, Asst.
NUMISMATIQUE ET LA SIGILLOGRAPHIE. Recherches sur la, des Nor-
mands, de Sicile et d'Italie. Par Arthur Engel. Paris, 1882.

ORNITHOLOGY, Northwestern, Handbook of. By Elliott Coues. 1877.

PALÆONTOLOGY AND THE GEOLOGICAL RELATIONS. Summary of
Extinct Animals. By Richard Owen. Edinburgh, 1840.
PARIS EXPOSITION, 1867. Reports of the U. S. Commissioners. 6
vols.
POISSONS FOSSILES, Recherches sur les. Par L. Agassiz. Letter-press.
5 vols. in 2.
—— Atlas, accompanying. Folio. 5 vols in 3. Neufchatel, 1833 to
1843. [Cost, imported in 1855, $360 ; binding, $40.]

RACES, Indigenous, of the Earth. By J. C. Nott and George R. Glid-
don.
ROCKS, Testimony of the. By Hugh Miller. Boston, 1858.
—— Same. Edinburgh, 1860.

SAINTHILL, RICHARD. Numismatic, Antiquarian and Literary Scraps.
[Privately printed.] 2 vols. London, 1844 and 1853.
SANDSTONE, The Old Red. By Hugh Miller. Edinburgh, 1859.
SCIENCE AND THE ARTS, Quarterly Journal of, 1817 to 1830. Edited
at Royal Institution of Great Britain. 30 vols. London.
SCIENCES, Natural, Cyclopædia of. By William Baird. London, 1853.
—— Physical, Cyclopædia of. By J. P. Nichol. London, 1860.
SILLIMAN'S JOURNAL OF SCIENCE AND ART. October, 1844.
SILURIA. By Roderick Impey Murchison. London, 1854.
SMITHSONIAN INSTITUTION. Reports of Boards of Regents of : 1854–
1857. 3 vols.
SPECIES, Origin of. By Charles Darwin. London, Jno. Murray, 1860.
—— Same. New York, Appleton & Co., 1871.
—— Genesis of. By St. George Mivart.
SPECTRUM ANALYSIS, Studies in. By J. Norman Lockyer.
STORMS, Philosophy of. James P. Espy. 1841.

TENERIFFE, An Astronomer's Experiment. By C. Piazzi Smyth. Lon-
don, 1858.
TERRAINS, Tableau des, qui composent l'Ecorce du Globe. By Alex.
Brongniart. Paris, 1829.

7

VEGETABLE PHYSIOLOGY AND SYSTEMATIC BOTANY.   By Wm. B. Carpenter.   London, 1858.

WORLD, The, Before the Deluge.   Louis Figuier.   London, 1865.
—— Relating to the System of.   By J. P. Nichol.   Edinburgh, 1848.
—— The Pre-Historic.   By Élie Berthet.   Translated from the French by Mary J. Safford.
—— Thoughts on Some Important Points.
—— The Ancient.   By David Thomas Ansted.   London, 1848.

ZIMMERMAN, DR. W. F. A.   Le Monde Avant la Création de l'Homme.   Paris and Bruxelles, 1857.
ZOOLOGICAL ILLUSTRATIONS.   By Wm. Swainson.   1820–1823.
   1st Series.   3 vols.   London, Baldwin, Cradock & Joy, 1820.
   2d Series.   3 vols.   London, Baldwin & Cradock, 1829.
ZOOLOGICAL JOURNAL.   Quarterly.   March, 1824, to February, 1830.   5 vols.   London.

CLASS X.

CLASSICAL.

CLASS X.

GREEK CLASSICS.

16mo.   Tauchnitz Edition.   Leipzig.

ÆSCHINES.
ÆSCHYLUS.
ÆSOPUS.
ANACREON.
ANTHOLOGIA.   3 vols.
ANTONINUS, MARCUS.
APPIANUS.   4 vols.
APOLLODORUS.
APOLLONIUS.
ARISTOPHANES.   3 vols.
ARISTOTELES.   16 vols.
ARRIANUS.
ATHENÆUS.   4 vols.

BABRIUS.

CASSIUS, DIO.   4 vols.

DEMOSTHENES.   5 vols.
DIODORUS.   6 vols.
DIOGENES.   2 vols.
DIONYSIUS.   6 vols.

EURIPIDES.   4 vols.

FLAVIUS JOSEPHUS.   6 vols.

HERODIUS.
HERODOTUS.   3 vols.
HESIODUS.
HOMERUS, ILIAS.   2 vols.
HOMERUS, ODYSSEA.   2 vols.

ISÆUS.   [2 copies].
ISOCRATES.   2 vols.

LUCANUS.
LUCIANUS.   4 vols.
LYSIAS.

ORPHICA.

PAUSANIAS.   3 vols.
PHILO.   8 vols.
PINDARUS.
PLATO.   8 vols.
PLUTARCHUS.   Vitæ Parallelæ.   9 vols.
—— Varia Scripta.   6 vols.
POETÆ GRÆCI, GNOMICI.
POLYDIUS.   4 vols.
PTOLEMÆUS.   3 vols.

SMYRNÆUS.
SOPHOCLES.   2 vols.
STOBÆUS.   3 vols.
STRABO.   3 vols.

THEOCRITUS, BION AND MOSCHUS.
THEOPHRASTUS.
THUCYDIDES.   2 vols.

XENOPHON.   6 vols.

LATIN CLASSICS.

16mo.   Tauchnitz Edition.   Leipzig.

ÆLIANUS.

AMMONIUS.

AULUS GELLIUS.

AURELIUS.

CÆSAR, JULIUS.

CATULLUS, TIBULLUS, PROPERTIUS.

CICERO.   11 vols.

CURTIUS.

ERASMUS.   2 vols.

EUTROPIUS.

FLORUS.

HORATIUS.

JUSTINUS.

LIVIUS, TITUS.   6 vols.

LUCRETIUS.

MARCELLUS.

MARTIAL, VALERIUS.

MELAS, POMPONIUS.

MURETUS.   Orationes.   2 vols.

MURETUS.   Epistolæ.

NEPOS, CORNELIUS.

OVIDIUS.   3 vols.

PERSIUS ET JUVENAL.

PHÆDRUS, GUDIUS, VIANUS and FÆRNUS.

PLINIUS II.   5 vols.

—— Epistolæ.

PLAUTUS.   4 vols.

QUINTILIANUS, M. FABIUS.   2 vols.

SILIUS.

SENECA.   6 vols.

SALLUSTIUS.

SUETONIUS.

TACITUS.   2 vols.

TERENTIUS.

VALERIUS MAXIMUS.   Memorabilium.

VELLEIUS.

VIRGILIUS.

VITRUVIUS.

ARISTOPHANEM, Note in.   3 vols.   London, 1829.

CALLIMACHUS, Hymns of.   Translated by Dr. Wm. Dodd.   4to. London, 1755.

DEMOSTHENES.   Oration on the Crown.   By J. T. Champlin.   Boston.

JUVENAL, The Satires of.   With the original text.   By John Stirling. London, 1760.

PLOTINUS.   Opera Omnia.   Porphyrii Liber de Vitâ.   Plotini cum Marsillii Ficini Commentariis.   Wyttenbach, Moser, Creuzer.   3 vols.   Oxonii, 1835.

CLASS XI.

POETRY AND DRAMA.

CLASS XI.

AGNOSTIC, The. Poems. By Henry Niles Pierce, D.D., LL.D., Bishop of Arkansas.

AINSLIE, HEW. Scottish Songs, Ballads and Poems. New York.

ALDRICH, THOMAS BAILEY, Poems of. 2 copies. 2 vols.

ALE. By Barry Gray and John Savage. New York.

ALEXANDER, W. D. S. Hermit of the Pyrenees. London, 1859.

ALMANAC DES MUSES. Nouvel. An. V., An. VIII., An., XI. 3 vols. Paris.

AMERICAN PATRIOTISM, Poems of. Chosen by J. Brander Matthews.

ANGEL IN THE HOUSE. Coventry Patmore. Boston, 1856.

ANONYMOUS POEMS. [See Poetæ Minores, Vol. I.]

ANTIENT ENGLISH POESIE. By John Marston. London, 1794.

ANTI-JACOBIN, Poetry of the. Canning and others. Charles Edmonds. London, 1854.

ARIOSTO, LUDOVICO. L'Orlando Furioso. 2 vols. Paris, 1846.

ARKANSAS GENTLEMAN, The Fine, Life-Wake of. Washington, 1855.

ARNOLD, EDWIN, Poems by. Boston, 1880.

—— Indian Idylls. Boston, 1833.

—— Light of Asia. Boston, 1879.

—— Indian Poetry. London, 1881.

ARNOLD, MATTHEW, Poems of. Boston, 1856.

—— Same. New York, 1880.

ARUNDINES CAMI. Collegit atque edidit Henricus Drury, A.M. Cantabrigiæ, 1843.

AYTOUN, WM. E. Lays of the Scottish Cavaliers, etc. New York, 1852.

BAILEY, PHILIP JAMES. Festus. London, Chapman & Hall, 1854.

—— The Age. Boston, 1858.

—— The Mystic. London, Chapman & Hall, 1855.

BAKER, GEORGE A., Jr. Point Lace and Diamonds. Poems. [See Poetæ Minores, Vol. VIII.]

BALDER. By Sydney Yendys. London, 1854.

BALLADS, Early. By Robert Bell. London, 1856.

BALLADS AND SONGS (Irish).   By the Writers of the Nation, with Original and Ancient Music.   Dublin, 1845.

BALLADS, Old, A Collection of.   3 vols.   London, 1849.

—— Pictorial Book of.   By J. S. Morse.   3 vols.   London, 1723. (Reprint fac-simile.)

BARHAM, REV. RICHARD HARRIS.   Ingoldsby Legends.   New York, 1852.

BAUDELAIRE, CHARLES.   Les Fleurs du Mal.   Paris, Calmann Levy, 1882

BEACH, ELIZABETH T. PORTER.   Pelayo : An Epic of the olden Moorish Time.   [See Poetæ Minores, Vol. VI.]

BEATTIE, JAMES, Poetical Works of.   London, Pickering, 1831.

BEDDOES, THOMAS LOVELL, Poems of.   London, Pickering, 1851.

BÉRANGER, DE, Songs of.   Philadelphia, 1844.

—— Complete Works of.   Exquisitely illustrated.   2 vols.   8vo. Paris, 1847.

BLOOMFIELD, ROBERT, Poetical Works of.   London, 1857.

BOILEAU, DESPRÉAUX, Œuvres de.   (Copy which belonged to Mme. Pompadour, with her coat of arms on covers, and signature on title-page.)   2 vols.   Paris, 1745.

BOURNE, VINCENT, Poems of.   Notes by Jno. Mitford.   London. Pickering.   No year.

BOWLES, W. LISLE.   Scenes and Shadows.   London, Pickering, 1837.

BOWRING.   Batavian Anthology.

—— Poetry of the Magyars.

BRITISH POETS.   Croly.

—— Chaucer to Jonson.   By Southey.   London, 1831.

BROAD GRINS.   My Nightgown and Slippers, etc.   By George Coleman, the younger.   London.   No year.

BROWNE, WILLIAM, The Whole Works of.   By W. Carew Hazlitt. 2 vols.   Roxburghe Library, 1868.

BROWNELL, HENRY HOWARD, Poems by.   [See Poetæ Minores, Vol. IV.]

BROWNING, MRS. E. B.   Aurora Leigh.   New York, 1857.

—— Poems of.   (Prometheus Bound, etc.)   New York, 1551.

—— Poems of.   2 vols.   New York, 1850.

BROWNING, ROBERT.   Poems.   2 vols.   London, 1849.

—— Same.   2 vols.   Boston, 1850.

—— Men and Women.   London, 1855.

—— Same.   Boston, 1850.

—— Christmas Eve and Easter Day.   London, 1850.

—— Agamemnon, La Saisiaz and Dramatic Idyls.   Boston, 1882.

BUCHANAN, ROBERT, Selected Poems of.   London, 1882.

Burns, Robert, Works of. (Hogg-and-Motherwell Edition.) 5 vols. 12mo. Edinburgh, 1852.

Butler, Samuel, Poetical Works of. 2 vols. London, Pickering, 1835.

Butler, Wm. Allen. Two Millions. [See Poetæ Minores, Vol. II.]

Byron, Lord, Works of. 10 vols. London, John Murray, 1854.

Camoens, Poems of. Strangford.

Campbell, Thomas, Poetical Works of. London, Moxon, 1854.

Carew, Thomas, Poems of. Printed for Roxburghe Library, 1870.

Carmina Yalensia. A Collection of Yale College Songs. Arranged by Heald and Dutton.

Cary, Alice and Phœbe, The Poetical Works of.

Cary, Phœbe. Poems of Faith, Hope and Love.

Casseday, Ben. Life in Death. Louisville.

Catullus, Tibullus, etc., Poems of. Bohn's Classical Library. (Translations.)

Chapman, George, Works of. Batrachomyomachia, of Homer. Hesiod's Works ; Juvenal's 5th Satire ; Musæus' Hero and Leander. London, 1858.

—— Iliads of Homer. 2 vols. in 1. London, 1843.

—— Odysseys of Homer. 2 vols. London, 1857.

Charles the Great and Orlando. Translated by Thomas Rodd. 2 vols. London, 1812.

Chatterton, Thomas, Poetical Works of. 2 vols. Cambridge, England, 1842.

Chaucer, Geoffrey, Poetical Works of. 6 vols. London, Pickering, 1845.

—— Same. Large 8vo. London, Moxon, 1843.

Chiquita [Eppie Bowdre Castlen]. Autumn Dreams. [See Poetæ Minores, Vol. VI.]

Christmas Carols. Ancient and Modern. Wm. Sandys. London, 1833.

Churchill, Charles, Poetical Works of. 3 vols. London, Pickering, 1844.

Cist, Lewis J. Trifle in Verse. Cincinnati.

Clark, Willis Gaylord, Literary Remains of. New York.

Cleveland, John. Poems. London, 1669.

Coleridge, Hartley, Poems of. 2 vols. London, Moxon, 1851.

Coleridge, Samuel Taylor. Poems. London, Moxon, 1852.

Collins, William, Poetical Works of. (2 copies.) 2 vols. London, Pickering, 1830 and 1853.

Comic Poets of the Nineteenth Century. Edited by W. Davenport Adams. London. No year.

CONFEDERATE POETRY. Miscellaneous.

CONQUEST OF ENGLAND, The. From Wase's Poem of the Roman de
　　Rou. Translated by Sir Alex. Malet. Large 4to. London, 1860.

COOK, ELIZA, The Poetical Works of. Philadelphia.

—— Same. London. No year.

CORBETT, RICHARD, Poems of. London, 1807.

CORNWALL, BARRY. English Songs and Small Poems. Boston, 1851.

—— Flood of Thessaly and other Poems. London, 1823.

COWPER, WILLIAM, Works of. By Southey. 15 vols. London,
　　1835.

COX, CHRISTOPHER C. Poem read at reunion of Yale Alumni Associ-
　　ation, February, 1875. [See Poetæ Minores, Vol. V.]

CRASHAW, RICHARD, Works of. London, 1858.

CROLY, REV. GEORGE, Poetical Works of. (2 copies.) 2 vols. Lon-
　　don, 1830.

—— Modern Orlando. London, 1855.

CROMEK. Scottish Songs. With Observations and Notices by Robert
　　Burns. 2 vols. London, 1810.

CUTTER, G. W. Poems : National and Patriotic. Philadelphia, 1857.
　　[See Poetæ Minores, Vol. VII.]

DALY, JOHN. Irish Songs ; Original Irish, with translations. Kil-
　　kenny, 1843.

DANA, RICHARD H. Poems and Prose Writings. 2 vols. Boston.

DANIEL, GEORGE, of Beswick, Yorkshire [1616–1657], Poems of.
　　Printed for private circulation by A. B. Grosart. 4 vols. 1879.

DANTE, ALIGHIERI. La Divina Commedia. Paris, 1847.

DAVIS, THOMAS. Poems. Dublin, 1846.

DAVISON, FRANCIS. Poetical Rhapsody. 2 vols. in 1. London, 1826.

DELAVIGNE, CASIMIR. Sept Messeniennes. Paris, 1828.

DENVER, J. C. and M. C., Poems by. Privately printed. New York.

DESJARDINS, G. Première Babylone, Semiramis la Grande. 2 copies.
　　Paris, 1834.

DIBDIN, CHARLES, Songs of. London, 1854.

DONOHO, T. SEATON. Mœna and Ivywall.

—— Poems of.

DOOMED RACE, The. By a Priest of the Order. [See Poetæ Min-
　　ores.]

DORAN, DR. The Bentley Ballads. London, 1858.

DRAKE, J. RODMAN. The Culprit Fay. New York.

DRUMMOND, WM., Poetical Works of. London, 1856.

DRYDEN, JOHN, Poetical Works of. 5 vols. London, Pickering,
　　1852.

Dyce, Rev. Alexander. Specimens of British Poetesses. London, 1827.

Early Popular Poetry. Utterson. 2 vols. London, 1817.
Eliot, George, Works of.
    The Legend of Jubal and other Poems. Edinburgh. No year.
    The Spanish Gypsy. Boston, 1868.
Ellis, George. Specimens of the Early English Poets. 3 vols. London, 1845.
—— Same. Metrical Romances. London, 1848.
Emerson, Ralph W., Poems of. (2 copies.) 2 vols.
Emmons, Richard, M.D. The Fredoniad, or Independence Preserved. An Epic Poem on the War of 1812. 4 vols.
—— Poem on the Battle of Bunker Hill.
English Drama and Stage, 1543 to 1644. By Wm. Carew Hazlitt. Roxburghe Library Edition, 1869.
English-Gipsy Songs, In Rommany. By Chas. G. Leland, Prof. E. H. Palmer and Janet Tuckey. London, 1875.
English Sonnets, Treasury of. David M. Main. New York, 1881.
Epic of Hades, The. By the Author of "Songs of Two Worlds." 8th Edition. Boston, 1882.

Falconer, William, Poetical Works of. London, Pickering, 1836.
Fay, Theodore S. Ulric, or the Voices. [See Poetæ Minores, Vol. II.]
Ferguson, Robert, Works of. Edinburgh, 1851.
Finlay, John. Scottish Ballads. 2 vols. Edinburgh, 1808.
Fontaine, Francis. The Exile; A Tale of St. Augustine. New York, 1878. [See Poetæ Minores, Vol. VIII.]
Fuller Worthies' Library. Edited by Dr. A. B. Grosart. Printed for private circulation.
—— Lord Brooke [Rt. Hon. Fulke Greville]. 4 vols. 1870.
—— Phineas Fletcher's Poems. 4 vols. 1869.
—— Giles Fletcher's Poems. 1868.
—— Joseph Fletcher's Poems. 1869.
—— Thomas Fuller's Poems and Epigrams. 1868.

Gascoigne, George, Poems of, Complete. By William Carew Hazlitt. 2 vols. Roxburghe Library, 1869.
Gaultier, Bon. Book of Ballads. New York, 1852.
Gay, John, Poems of. 2 vols. London, 1775.
Gilbert, W. S. Fifty "Bab" Ballads. London, 1878.
Giorgio, and other Poems. By Stuart Sterne. Boston, 1881.

GOLDSMITH, OLIVER, Poetical Works of. Large 8vo. London, Longman, 1846.
—— Same. London, Brown & Co. No year.
—— Poems. Traveller, Deserted Village, etc. London, 1826.
—— Misceilaneous Works of. Philadelphia, 1836.
GOODALE, ELAINE and DORA READ. Apple Blossoms ; Poems of Two Children. New York, Putnam.
GRAVES, MRS. ADELIA C. Filial Obedience, Jephthah's Daughter· [See Poetæ Minores, Vol. V.]
GRAY, THOMAS, Works of. 4 vols. London, Pickering, 1836.
GRISWOLD, RUFUS W. Poets and Poetry of America.

HAKE, THOMAS GORDON. New Symbols. London, 1876.
—— Legends of the Morrow. London, 1879.
—— Maiden Ecstasy. London, 1880.
HALLAM, ARTHUR HENRY, Remains in Verse and Prose of   Boston, Ticknor & Fields, 1863.
HALLECK, FITZ-GREENE, Poems of. New York.
HARRIS. A Lyric of the Golden Age. New York.
HARTE, BRET, Poems of. (3 copies.) New York.
HAYES, EDWARD. Ballads of Ireland. 2 vols. Dublin, 1856.
HAYNE, PAUL H. His Complete Poems.
—— The Mountain of the Lovers. With Poems of Nature and Tradition.
—— Legends and Lyrics.
HEBER, BISHOP REGINALD, Poetical Works of. London, John Murray, 1854.
HEMANS, MRS. FELICIA, Works of. 6 vols. Edinburgh. No year.
HERBERT, GEORGE, Works of. 2 vols. London, Pickering, 1846.
—— Poems of. London, 1844.
HERRICK, ROBERT, Poetical Works of. 2 vols. London, 1846.
HOGG, JAMES. Jacobite Relics. Edinburgh, 1819.
HOLLAND, J. G., The Complete Poetical Writings of.
HOLMES, OLIVER WENDELL, Poems of.
—— Songs of Many Seasons. Boston, Osgood & Co., 1875.
HOME-LAND, Lyrics of. By Eugene J. Hall. Chicago, 1882.
HOMEROS, ILIAS. Greek Text of Wolf. C. C. Felton, ed. Boston, 1833.
HOOD, THOMAS. Prose and Verse. New York, 1845.
—— Whims and Oddities. London, Moxon, 1857.
—— Wit and Humor. London, Moxon, 1858.
—— Poems. London, Moxon, 1858.
HORNE, RICHARD HENGIST. Orion. London, 1874.

HUNT, LEIGH. Wit and Humor. London, 1846.
—— Poetical Works of. London, Moxon, 1849.
HYMNS FOR ALL NATIONS. London, Tupper, 1851.
HYMNS, Seven Great, of the Mediæval Church. New York.
HYNEMAN, MRS. LEON H., Poems of. Philadelphia.

INGELOW, JEAN, The Poetical Works of. Boston, 1880.
—— A Story of Doom, and other Poems. Boston, 1867.

JAMES, Southern Selections by.
JAMES, RICHARD, Poems of [1592–1638]. Printed for private circula-
   tion only. By A. B. Grosart. 4to. 1880.
JAMIESON, ROBERT. Popular Ballads and Songs. 2 vols. Edinburgh
   1806.
JONES, MRS. J. CLINTON. Valhalla, the Myths of Norseland. [See
   Poetæ Minores, Vol. III.]
JOSSELYN, ROBERT. A Satire on the Times. 1873. [See Poetæ
   Minores, Vol. VII.]
JUVENALIS ET PERSII SATIRÆ. London, 1857.

KEATS, JOHN, Poetical Works of. London, Moxon, 1851.
KEMBLE, FRANCES ANNE, Poems by. Boston, 1859.
KINGSLEY, CHARLES, Poems of. London.

LA FONTAINE. Fables Inédites, des XIIᵉ, XIIIᵉ et XIVᵉ Siècles. 2
   vols. Paris, 1825.
—— Fables of. Illustrated by Grandville. Translated. New York,
   1860.
LAMARTINE, ALPHONSE DE, Œuvres de. Paris, 1801.
—— La Chute d'un Ange. Paris, 1838.
LAMB, CHARLES, Poetical Works of. London, 1841.
LANDOR, WALTER SAVAGE, Selections from the Writings of. By Sid-
   ney Colvin. London, 1852.
LARCOM, LUCY. An Idyl of Work. Boston, 1875.
LEAVITT, REV. PROF. JOHN M. Afranius and the Idumean, with the
   Roman Martyrs and other Poems. [See Poetæ Minores, Vol. IV.]
LE BRUN, PONCE DENIS (Écouchard), Works of. 4 vols. Paris,
   1811.
L'ECLAIR. Lenare. [See Poetæ Minores, Vol. II.]
LE GRAND. Fabliaux. 3 vols. London, 1815.
LELAND, CHARLES GODFREY. Music Lesson of Confucius and other
   Poems. 1872.
LINTON. Poetry of America.

LONGFELLOW, HENRY W., Poems of. 2 vols.
—— Golden Legend.
—— Ultima Thule.
—— In the Harbor.
LOWELL, J. RUSSELL, Poems of.
—— Same. [2 vols. in 1.]
LOYAL SONGS, Collection of, against the Rump Parliament. 2 vols.
   London, 1731.
LUNT, GEORGE. The Age of Gold, and other Poems.
—— Lyric Poems.
—— Poems.
—— Julia.
—— Poems. Boston, 1884.
LYRA GERMANICA. Winkworth.
LYRA URBANICA; or the Social Effusions of the Celebrated Captain
   Charles Morris, of the late Life-Guards. 2 vols. London, 1840.
LYRICS. By Daniel O'Connell. San Francisco, 1881.
LYRICS OF LOYALTY. Arranged and edited by Frank Moore. New
   York, 1864.

MACDONALD, GEORGE. Within and Without. New York, 1872.
MACKAY, CHARLES, Poetical Works of. London, 1857.
—— Poems. Boston, 1853.
—— Lump of Gold and Salamandrine. London, 1856.
—— Collected Songs. London, 1859.
—— Under Green Leaves. London, 1857.
MASSEY, GERALD, Poems by. Boston, 1866.
MCDERMOTT, HUGH F. Self-Communing. [See Poetæ Minores,
   Vol. VII.]
MELLEN, GRENVILLE. Martyr's Triumph, etc.
MESSENGER, LILLIAN R. Threads of Fate. [See Poetæ Minores,
   Vol. V.
MILLER, JOAQUIN. Songs of Italy. Boston, 1878.
—— Songs of the Sun Lands. Boston, 1873.
—— The Ship in the Desert. Boston, 1875.
—— Poems by. Boston, 1882.
MILMAN, HENRY, Works of. 3 vols. London, John Murray, 1839.
—— Samor. New York, 1818.
MILNES, RICHARD MONCKTON. Memorials of many Scenes. London,
   Moxon, 1844.
—— Palm Leaves. London, Moxon, 1844.
—— Poems of Many Years. London, Moxon, 1844.
—— Poems, Legendary and Historical. London, Moxon, 1844.

MILTON, JOHN, Works of. 3 vols. 12mo. London, Pickering, 1852.

—— Poetical Works of. Large 8vo. London, 1842.

MINSTRELSY OF THE ENGLISH BORDER. By Frederick Sheldon. London, 1847.

MIRROR FOR MAGISTRATES, The. By Joseph Hazlewood. Little & Brown's price for this and the " Palace of Pleasure," in 1882, was $135. Only 150 copies printed. 2 vols. London, 1815.

MISTRAL, FRÉDÉRIC. Mirèio ; a Provençal Poem. Translated by Harriet W. Preston. 1874. ‚

MONUMENS DE LA LITTÉRATURE ROMAINE. 4 vols. Paris and Toulouse. No year.

MOORE, THOMAS, Poetical Works of. 10 vols. New York, 1853.

MORRIS, LEWIS. Songs Unsung. Boston, 1884.

MORRIS, WILLIAM. The Earthly Paradise. 4 vols. London, 1880.

—— Love is Enough, or the Freeing of Pharamond. London. No year.

—— The Story of the Volsungs and Niblungs. London, 1870.

—— The Æneids of Virgil. London, 1876.

—— The Life and Death of Jason. London, 1882.

—— The Defence of Guenevere, and other Poems. London, 1875.

—— The Story of Sigurd the Volsung, and the Fall of the Niblungs. London, 1877.

MOTHERWELL, WILLIAM, Posthumous Poems of. Boston, 1851.

—— Narrative and Lyrical Poems. Boston, 1844.

—— Scottish Minstrelsy. Glasgow, 1827.

NARAMORE, GAY H., Poems of. [See Poetæ Minores, Vol. IV.]

NEAL, JOHN. Battle of Niagara, Goldau, etc. Baltimore, 1819.

NICHOLS, J. Collection of Poems. 8 vols. London, 1780.

NICHOLS, REBECCA S. Bernice.

NORTON, MRS. Child of the Islands. London, Chapman & Hall, 1846.

OLDHAM, JOHN, Works and Remains of. 2 vols. London, 1722.

OMAR KHAYYAM, The Quatrains of. By E. H. Whinfield. London, 1882.

OWEN MEREDITH [Robert, Lord Lytton], The Poetical Works of. Boston, 1882.

OXFORD SAUSAGE. Poetical Pieces, by Celebrated Wits of Oxford University. London, 1764.

PARNELL, THOMAS, Poetical Works of. London, Pickering, 1852.

PARNY, EVARISTE. La Guerre des Dieux. Paris, An. VII.

8

PARNY, EVARISTE, Œuvres de. 5 vols. Paris, 1808.
PARSONS, THOMAS W., Poems of. Boston.
PERCY, THOMAS. Reliques of Ancient English Poetry. London, 1840.
PERSIUS, Translation of. By Thomas Sheridan. Dublin, 1728.
PETRARCA, FRANCESCO. Le Rime. Paris, 1847.
PIERPONT, JOHN. Airs of Palestine. 3d Edition, revised. Boston, 1817.
PIERS PLOUGHMAN. Edited by Thos. Wright. 2 vols. London, 1856.
—— Folio. Printed in Colors. London, John Murray, 1813.
PIKE, ALBERT. Nugæ. Poems. Printed for private distribution. 1855.
—— Hymns to the Gods and other Poems. [Privately printed.] 1875.
—— Poems of; Collected. [Privately printed.] 1882.
PLANCHÉ, J. R. Songs and Poems. From 1819 to 1879. London 1881.
POETÆ MINORES, Americani. Poems of Various Authors. 8 vols.
POETICAL TRANSLATIONS. Homer, Pindar, Virgil, Juvenal, Persius, Lucan, etc. 2 vols. London and Edinburgh. No year.
POLLOCK, EDWARD, Poems by. Philadelphia, 1876.
POLLOCK, ROBERT. Course of Time. Edinburgh, 1858.
POPE, ALEXANDER, Poetical Works of. 3 vols. London, Pickering, 1851.
POPULAR BALLADS. English and Scottish. Edited by Francis J. Child. Part I. 4to. Boston and New York.
PRAY, ISAAC C., JR. Prose and Verse. Boston, 1836.
PRIOR, MATTHEW, Poetical Works of. 2 vols. London, Pickering, 1835.
PROCTOR, ADELAIDE-ANNE. Legends and Lyrics. London, 1859.
PROPERTIUS, Elegies of, etc. Translated. London.

QUARLES, FRANCIS. Emblems, Divine and Moral. New York, 1854.
—— Same. London, 1839.

RAMSAY, ALLAN, Works of. 3 vols. Edinburgh, 1852.
RARE POEMS, OF THE 16TH AND 17TH CENTURIES. Edited by W. J. Linton. Boston, 1883.
RAYNOUARD. Lexique Roman. 6 vols. Paris.
READ, T. BUCHANAN, Poetical Works of. Philadelphia, 1883.
RED-LETTER DAY, A, and other Poems. By Lucius Harwood Foote. Boston, 1882.
REJECTED ADDRESSES. By Horace and James Smith. Boston, 1851.
RELIQUES OF FATHER PROUT. Francis Mahoney. London, 1860.

RICHARDS, WM. C. Electron : A Telegraphic Epic. [See Poetæ
Minores, Vol. II.]

RITSON, JOSEPH. Works.

—— Robin Hood. 2 vols. London, 1832.

—— Ancient Songs and Ballads. 2 vols. London, 1829.

—— Ancient Popular Poetry. London, 1833.

ROBIN HODE, A Lytell Geste of. Edited by Gutch. 2 vols. London,
1847.

—— Songs, Ballads, etc., Relating to. By Joseph Ritson. London.
No year.

ROMAN, The. By Sydney Yendys. London, 1852.

ROMAN DE LA ROSE. 4 vols. Paris, 1814.

ROMAN DE LA VIOLETTE. Paris, 1834.

ROSE DE LA VALLÉE, La. Paris, 1808.

ROSSETTI, CHRISTINA. A Pageant, and other Poems. Boston, 1881.

ROSSETTI, DANTE GABRIEL, Poems by. London, 1881.

RYAN, FATHER. Poems : Patriotic, Religious, Miscellaneous. Baltimore, 1883.

SABRINÆ COROLLA. In Hortulis Regiæ Scholæ Salopiensis. London, 1850.

SAVAGE, JOHN. Poems : Lyrical, Dramatic and Romantic. New
York, 1870.

SAXE, JOHN G. Leisure-Day Rhymes.

—— Money King and other Poems.

—— Poems of.

SCHILLER, Poems of. Translated. London.

SCOTT, SIR WALTER, Poetical Works of. Vol. V. of Works Prose
and Poetical. Sir Tristrem. Edinburgh, 1880.

—— Poetical Works of. 8vo. Edinburgh, 1857.

—— Same. 12mo. London, 1849.

SCOTTISH BALLADS. Tragic. London, 1781.

—— Comic. London, 1781.

SCOTTISH SONGS. 2 vols. London, 1794.

SEDLEY, SIR CHARLES, Works of. 2 vols. London, 1722.

SHAKESPEARE, WM., Poems of. 2 vols. London, 1804.

SHELLEY, PERCY BYSSHE, Works of. 3 vols. London, Moxon, 1847.

SIMMS, WILLIAM GILMORE. 6 vols.

—— Atalantis.

—— Southern Passages and Pictures.

—— The Hireling and the Slave.

—— Areytos.

—— Donna Florida.

SKELTON, JOHN, Poetical Works of. 2 vols. London, 1843.

SMITH, ALEXANDER, Poems of. London, 1856.

SMITH, WM. R. The Uses of Solitude. [See Poetæ Minores, Vol. VII.]

SONGS FROM THE DRAMATISTS. By Robert Bell. London, 1855.

SONGS FROM THE SOUTH. By Ella E. Hebron.

SONGS OF LAKE GENEVA. By John Brayshaw Kaye. New York, Putnam, 1882.

SOUTHEY, ROBERT, Poetical Works of. 10 vols. London, Longman, etc., 1837.

SOUTHWELL, REV. ROBERT, Poetical Works of. London, 1856.

SPAIN, Modern Poets and Poetry in. By James Kennedy. London, Longman, etc., 1852.

SPENCER, CHAS. EDGAR. The Viking, Guy, Legend of the Moxahala, and other Poems.

SPENSER, EDMUND, Poetical Works of. 5 vols. Boston, 1842.

—— Same. 5 vols. London, Pickering, 1852.

—— Same. Large 8vo. London, 1840.

SPRAGUE, CHARLES, Works of. Boston.

STODDARD, RICHARD HENRY, Poems of. Boston, 1852.

—— Songs of Summer. Boston, 1857.

STORY, W. W. He and She, or a Poet's Portfolio. Boston, 1884.

—— Graffiti d' Italia. 2d Edition. Edinburgh. No year.

—— Nero. Edinburgh, 1875.

STREET, ALFRED B., Poems of. 2 vols. New York.

SUCKLING, SIR JOHN. Fragmenta Aurea. London, 1648.

SUFFOLK GARLAND. Collection of Poems, Songs, etc. Ipswich, 1818.

SURF AND WAVE. The Sea, as Sung by the Poets. Edited by Anna L. Ward. New York.

SURREY, EARL OF [Henry Howard], Poems of. (2 copies.) London, Pickering, 1831.

SWIFT, JONATHAN, Poetical Works of. 3 vols. London, Pickering, 1833.

SWINBURNE, ALGERNON CHARLES, Works of.

—— Poems and Ballads. New York, 1878.

—— Laus Veneris. New York, 1867.

—— Songs of Two Nations. London, 1875.

—— Heptalogia. London, 1880.

—— Studies in Songs. New York, 1880.

—— Tristram of Lyonesse, etc. London, 1882.

—— Songs of the Spring Tides. London, 1880.

—— Songs before Sunrise. London, 1880.

SWINBURNE, ALGERNON CHARLES, Works of.
—— Atalanta in Calydon. London, 1880.
—— Poems and Ballads. 2 vols. (2 copies.) London, 1880 and '82.
—— A Century of Roundels, and other Poems. New York, 1883.
SYNTAX [DOCTOR]. His Three Tours. London. No year.

TAYLOR, BAYARD, The Poetical Works of.
TENNYSON, ALFRED, Poems of. London, Moxon, 1853.
—— Same. 3 vols. Boston, 1851.
—— Idyls of the King. Boston, 1859.
—— The Princess. London, Moxon, 1854.
—— Maud. London, Moxon, 1855.
—— In Memoriam. London, Moxon, 1856.
—— Ode on the Death of Wellington. London, Moxon, 1853.
THOMPSON, MAURICE. Songs of Fair Weather. Boston, 1883.
THOMSON, JAMES, Poetical Works of. 2 vols. London, Pickering,
    1847.
TOAST, The. An Heroic Poem, in four parts. Folio. Printed, Dub-
    lin. London reprint, 1747. [By Dr. W. King, of Dublin.] A
    Bitter Satire. Privately printed. This copy presented by the
    author to the Earl of Orrery.
TOKEN, and ATLANTIC SOUVENIR, The. 2 vols. 1836 and 1837.
TOLAND, M. B. M. Sir Rae. A Poem. Illustrated.
—— Iris. Romance of an Opal Ring. Illustrated.
—— Onti Ora. A Metrical Romance. Illustrated.
TRENCH, RICHARD CHENEVIX, Poems of. New York, 1856.
TROWBRIDGE, JOHN TOWNSEND. A Home Idyl, and other Poems.
    Boston, 1881.
TUPPER, MARTIN FARQUHAR. Geraldine, etc. Boston, 1846.
—— Hymns for all Nations. London. No year.

UHLAND, Poems of.
UNION, The. Anonymous.
UNIVERSAL SONGSTER, or Museum of Mirth. 3 vols. London. No
    year.

VAUGHAN, HENRY. Sacred Poems and Private Exhortations. Lon-
    don, 1847.
VERY, JONES, Poems by, with Memoir by Wm. P. Andrews. Boston,
    1883.
VOICES FROM THE EARLY CHURCH. London, 1845.

WALKER, JOSEPH C. Irish Bards. 2 vols. (with Music) Dublin,
    1818.

Wanless, Andrew.   Poems and Songs, maistly Scotch.   [See Poetæ Minores, Vol. III.]

Ward, Samuel.   Lyrical Recollections.   [See Poetæ Minores, Vol. VI.]

Watts, Alaric A.   Lyrics of the Heart.   New York, 1852.

Weber.   Metrical Romances.   3 vols.   Edinburgh, 1810.

Wheat, John Thomas.   Reminiscences of His Pre-Nuptial Life. [See Poetæ Minores, Vol. V.]

Wheeler, Ella.   Poems of Passion.

White, Henry Kirke, Poetic Works of.   London, Pickering, 1830.

Whittier, John G., Poems of.

—— Same.

—— Same.

Wilkinson, William Cleaver.   Poems.   New York, 1883.

Wither, George.   Hymns and Songs of the Church.   London, 1856.

Wordsworth, William, Poetical Works of.   7 vols.   London, Moxon, 1836.

—— Same.   6 vols.   London.   No year.

Wotton, Sir Henry and Sir Walter Raleigh, Poems of.   Rev. John Hannah, edid.   London, Pickering, 1845.

Wright, Thomas.   Political Songs of England; John to Edward II. Camden Soc. Pub., 1839.

Wyatt, Sir Thomas, Poetical Works of.   London, Pickering, 1831.

Yosemite, The.   By Wallace Bruce.   1880.

Young, Edward, Poetical Works of.   2 vols.   London, Pickering, 1852.

DRAMA.

ANCIEN THÉÂTRE FRANÇOIS. Viollet le Duc. 9 vols. Paris, P. Jannet, 1834-1856.

AUTEURS COMIQUES, Chefs d'Œuvres des. Scarron, Montfleury, La Fontaine, Boursalt, Baron. Paris, Firmin Didot Frères, 1845.

BAILLIE, JOANNA, Dramatic and Poetical Works of. London, Longman, etc., 1853.

BEAUMONT AND FLETCHER, Works of. 2 vols. Large 8vo. London, Moxon, 1839.

BECKET, ANDREW. Dramatic and Prose Miscellanies. London, George Virtue, 1838.

BROME, RICHARD, Plays of. 2 vols. London, 1653-1659.

BULWER, SIR EDWARD LYTTON. Poetical and Dramatic Works. 5 vols. London, Chapman & Hall, 1852.

CHAPMAN, GEORGE, Dramatic Works of. 3 vols. London, John Pearson, 1873.
—— Plays. London, Chatto and Windus, 1874.

CHAVERO, ALFREDO. Comedias. Mexico, 1880.

COLERIDGE, S. TAYLOR, Dramatic Works of. London, Moxon, 1852.

DEKKER, THOMAS, Dramatic Works of. 4 vols. London, John Pearson, 1873.

DICKENS, CHARLES, Plays and Poems of. 2 vols. Edited by Richard Herne Shepherd. London, 1882.

DIDO, QUEEN OF CARTHAGE. By Marlowe and Nash. London, 1825.

DODSLEY. Old Plays. 12 vols. Old London Edition, 1825.

DRAMA AND STAGE, The English. Documents and Treatises, 1543-1664. London.

DRAMA, The British. Tragedies, Comedies, Operas, Farces. 2 vols. Philadelphia, Cowperthwaite, 1838.

ENGLISH PLAYS, Old. Continuation of Dodsley's Collection. 6 vols. London, Rodwell & Martin, 1816.

ENGLISH PLAYS, Old.   2 vols.
>   Heroick Friendship. Tragedy. Otway. London, 719.
>   Siege of Rhodes. Wm. D'Avenant. London, 1663.
>   Heroick Love. Tragedy. Mr. Granville. London.
>   The Patriot. C. Gildon. 1703.
>   The Marriage Night.—Lord Faulkland. 1664.
>   Pausanius, the Betrayer of His Country. Tragedy. Mrs. L.
>   Norten. London, 1696.
>   Princess of Parma. Tragedy. H. Smith. 1696.
>   Pyrrhus and Demetrius. Opera. 1709.
>   Hypermnestra, or Love in Tears. Tragedy. Robert Owen.
>   1703.
>   Altemira. Tragedy. Earl of Orrery. 1702.
>   Ibrahim, the Illustrious Bassa. Tragedy. Elkanah Settle.
>   1677.

ENGLISH PLAYS. 5 vols.
>   Vol. I. False Delicacy ; Henry II.; West Indian ; Benevolent
>   Tar.
>   Vol. II. Castle Spectre ; Pizarro ; Free Knights ; Germanicus.
>   Vol. III. Not at Home ; Love Chase ; Woman's Wit ; Nina
>   Sforza.
>   Vol. IV. Francis the First ; The Hunchback.
>   Vol. V. The Wife ; The Daughter ; Ion.

ENGLISH REPRINTS. Edward Arber, editor. London, 1869.
—— The Rehearsal. By George Villiers, 2d Duke of Buckingham
>   1595. Printed with
—— Works of George Gascoigne. 1596.
—— The Apologie for Poetrie. Sir Philip Sidney. 1595.
—— Table-Talk. John Selden, 1689.

GLAPTHORNE, HENRY, Plays by. London, Thomas Paine, 1639.
GREENE, ROBERT, Works of. Rev. Alex. Dyce, editor. 2 vols. Lon-
>   don, Pickering, 1831.

HEYWOOD, THOMAS, Dramatic Works of. 6 vols. London, John
>   Pearson, 1874.
HOGARTH, GEORGE. Memoirs of the Musical Drama. 2 vols. Lon-
>   don, Richard Bentley, 1838.

ITALIAN BRIDE. Play written for Eliza Logan. Savannah, John M.
>   Cooper, 1856.

JONSON, BEN, Works of. Barry Cornwall, editor. Large 8vo. Lon-
>   don, Edward Moxon, 1838.

KNOWLES, SHERIDAN, Dramatic Works of. 2 vols. London, 1856.

LEE, NATHANIEL, Dramatic Works of. 3 vols. London, 1734.

LILLY, JOHN, the Euphuist, Dramatic Works of. 2 vols. [2 copies.]
London, John Russell Smith, 1858.

MAGEN, HIPPOLYTE. Un Drame sous la Terreur Bonapartiste. London, Libraire Polonaise, 1856.

MARLOWE, KIT, Works of. 3 vols. London, Pickering, 1826.

MARSTON, JOHN, Works of. 3 vols. London, John Russell Smith, 1856.

MASSINGER AND FORD, Dramatic Works of. By Hartley Coleridge.
Large 8vo. London, Moxon, 1839.

MIDDLETON, THOMAS, Works of. Rev. Alex. Dyce. 5 vols. London, Edward Lumley, 1840.

MOLIÈRE, Works of. 2 vols. Paris, Firmin Didot Frères, 1850.

MORATIN, Comedias de. 2 vols. Paris, Baudry, 1821.

MORRIS, WILLIAM. Love is Enough. London, 1873.

NICHOLS, J. Six Old Plays. 2 vols. Old London edition. S. Leacroft. 1779.

O PEDREIRO LIVRE. Drama. By A. M. da Cunha Bellem. Lisboa, J. G. De Sousa Neves, 1877.

PEELE, GEORGE, Works of. Edited by Rev. Alex. Dyce. 3 vols
London, Pickering, 1829.

RANDOLPH, THOMAS. Poetical and Dramatic Works. Hazlitt. 2
vols. London, 1875.

REGNARD, Théâtre de. Paris, Firmin Didot Frères, 1845.

SCHILLER, FREDERICK, Works, Dramas and Romances of. London, 1853.

SHAKESPEARE, WM., Works of. Large 8vo. Boston, 1856.

—— Devonshire Hamlet, 1603–1604. London, 1860.

—— Fac-Simile of 1st Edition of Works of. J. O. Halliwell-Phillips
London, 1876.

—— The Lansdowne. Illustrated. London, 1875.

SHAKESPEARE SOCIETY PUBLICATIONS. 15 vols.
Pride of Lowliness ; School of Abuse ; Apology for Actors ;
Treatise *vs.* Dancing, Dicing, etc. London, 1841.
Ludus Coventriæ. London, 1841.

SHAKESPEARE SOCIETY PUBLICATIONS—*Continued.*

Merry Wives of Windsor; King Henry VI., 2d. and 3d Parts London, 1842.

Ben Jonson's Conversations; Riche, His Farewell; Lodge's Defence; Alarum against Usurers; Forborius and Prisceria; Remarks of M. Carl Simrock.   London, 1842.

Alleyn Papers; Memoirs of Alleyn; Revels at Court.   London, 1843.

Oberon's Vision in the Midsummer Night's Dream.   London, 1843.

The Chester Plays.   London, 1843.

Richard III.; Ghost of Richard III.; King Henry IV.; Taming of a Shrew.   London, 1844.

Shakespeare Society Papers.   London, 1844.

Tarleton's Jests, etc.; Nest of Ninnies; Pierce Penniless.   London, 1844.

Fairy Mythology of a Midsummer Night's Dream.   London, 1845.

Diary of William Henslowe.   London, 1845.

Marriage of Wit and Wisdom; Early Illustrations of Shakespeare; Wyt and Science; Early Political Miscellanies; Society Papers, Vols. III. and IV.   London, 1846.

Fair Maid of Exchange; Fortune by Land and Sea; Patient Grissell; Sir Th. More; Honour Triumphant; A Line of Life.   London, 1846.

Inigo Jones; Five Court Masques; Registers of the Stationers' Co., from 1557 to 1587.   London, 1848.

The Fair Maid of the West.   Two Comedies.   By Thomas Heywood.   London, 1850.

The Two Noble Kinsmen.   London, 1876.

William Stafford's Examination.   London, 1876.

SHERIDAN, RICHARD BRINSLEY, Dramatic Works of.   Introduction by Richard Grant White.   3 vols.   New York, 1883.

SHIRLEY, JAMES, Dramatic Works of.   6 vols.   London, John Murray, 1833.

SIX OLD PLAYS, on which Shakespeare founded Measure for Measure, etc.   2 vols.   London, 1779.

SWINBURNE, ALGERNON CHARLES.   The Queen Mother and Rosamond.   London, 1868.

—— Bothwell.   Tragedy.   London, 1884.

—— Chastelard.   Tragedy.   London, 1878.

—— Mary Stuart.   Tragedy.   London, 1881.

—— Erectheus.   Tragedy.   London, 1881.

TALFOURD, SIR THOS. NOON, Dramatic Works of. London, Moxon, 1852.

TAYLOR, HENRY. Edwin the Fair. London, Moxon, 1852.

—— Isaac Comnenus. London, Moxon, 1852.

—— Eve of the Conquest. London, Moxon, 1852.

—— Philip Van Artevelde. London, Moxon, 1852.

TAYLOR, TOM. Historical Dramas. London, 1877.

TERENCE AND PHÆDRUS. Translation. By Riley and Smith. London, 1853.

TERENTIUS. Original. J. A. Giles. London, 1837.

TOURNEUR, CYRIL, Plays and Poems of. 2 vols. By J. Churton Collins. London, 1878.

TRIBOULET, EMILE. Les Petits Grands Hommes. Comédie. Paris, Tresse, Editeur, 1878.

WEBSTER, JOHN, Works of. 4 vols. London, Pickering, 1830.

WYCHERLY, CONGREVE, VANBRUGH AND FARQUHAR, Works of. With Biographical and Critical Notices by Leigh Hunt. Large 8vo. London, Moxon, 1840.

WYNNE, JOHN. Three Original Plays, viz.:

Tricks of the Time ; Napoleon the First's Love ; The Advocate of Durango. London, Thos. Bosworth, 1853.

CLASS XII.

ARTISTIC.

CLASS XII.

AFRICA, Southern. Sketches of Classes and Tribes, and Descriptive Account of their Manners and Customs. 4to. London.

AMERICAN HISTORICAL AND LITERARY CURIOSITIES. By J. Jay Smith and John F. Watson. New York, 1852.

ANTIQUITÉS DE LA NUBIE. Par F. C. Gau, Architecte. Imperial folio. Paris, Firmin Didot, 1822.

ARAS ET IMAGINES. By Giacomo de Rossi. With Privilege of the Pope. Large folio. Rome. No date.

ARCHITECTURE, Gothic, From Ancient Edifices in England, Specimens of. By A. Pugin, Architect. 2 vols. 4to. London, J. Taylor, 1821.

ART JOURNAL, 1848 to 1854. With Catalogue of Exhibition of 1851. 8 vols. 4to. London, Chapman & Hall.

CHINESE EMPIRE. Historical and Descriptive. Illustrated. From Sketches by T. Allom. 2 vols. 4to. London and New York.

COSTUMES. Representing the Dress and Manners of Austria, China, Russia and Turkey. By Wm. Alexander. 4 vols. 8vo. London. No year.

EGYPT AND PALESTINE. Photographed and Described by Francis Frith. 2 vols. Folio. London, Jas. S. Virtue, 1857.

FOSBROKE, REV. THOS. DUDLEY. Foreign Topography of Ancient Remains in Africa, Asia and Europe. 4to. London, J. B. Nichols & Son, 1828.

GREEK VASES. In possession of Sir Wm. Hamilton. Discovered in Sepulchres in the Kingdom of the Two Sicilies. Published by Wm. Tischbein, Director of the Royal Academy of Painting at Naples. 3 vols. Large folio. 1791 and 1795.

HINDOUSTAN, De L', Ancient and Modern Monuments of. Décrits, etc., par L. Langlès. 2 vols. Folio. Paris, P. Didot l'Aîné, 1821.

HISTORICAL AND LITERARY CURIOSITIES.   By Chas. John Smith.   4to.
London, 1847.

HOLBEIN SOCIETY, The.   Fac-Simile Reprints.   Folio.   Part I.   Man-
chester, 1882.

LONDON EXHIBITION OF 1851.   [Presentation copy.]   Cost $150.   6
vols.   Royal folio.   3 vols.   Official Catalogues ; 3 vols.   Reports
by Juries.   London, Spicer Bros.

MONUMENTS, English.   By Blore.   2 vols.   4to.   London, Riphook
& Lepard, 1824-5.

MUSEUM DISNEIANUM.   Description of Ancient Marbles, Bronzes and
Vases, in possession of John Disney.   Royal folio.   London,
Longman & Brown, 1849.

MUSIC, Collection of.   For Two Violins.   From Operas and elsewhere.
By various composers.   4 vols.   Folio.

ORATIO DOMINICA.   The Lord's Prayer, in 155 Languages.   Printed
by Bodoni, at Parma, Italy, 1806, for the Private Library of
Eugène Napoleon, Viceroy ; with movable types.   Royal folio.

SCHOOLCRAFT, HENRY R.   History of the Indian Tribes.   Vols. I.,
IV. and VI.   4to.   Philadelphia, 1851.

WALES, Royal Visits and Progresses to.   From the First Invasion of
Julius Cæsar to the Friendly Visit of H.M. Queen Victoria.   By
Edward Parry.   Royal 4to.   Chester, 1850

CLASS XIII

MASONIC.

CLASS XIII.

ALPHABETS. Of High Antiquity : MSS. By Albert Pike.

CHAPTER OF ROSE CROIX, Offices of Constitution and Installation of. Published by the Sup.·. Council for the So.·. Jurisdiction.

CONSTITUTIONS OF FREE MASONRY. Ancient and Accepted Scottish Rite. Compiled by Albert Pike, 33°, Sov.·. Grand Commander. 4to. Given to and published by Robert Macoy in 1860.

FREE MASONRY IN SCOTLAND. By David Murray Lyon. Edinburgh and London, Wm. Blackford & Sons.

FUNERAL CEREMONY AND LODGE OF SORROW, of Knights Rose Croix. Published by the Sup.·. Council, So.·. Jurisdiction.

GRAND CONSISTORY, Offices of Constitution and Installation of. Published by the Sup.·. Council, So.·. Jurisdiction.

GRAND CONSTITUTIONS OF FREE MASONRY. Ancient and Accepted Scottish Rite. Compiled by Albert Pike. 8vo. Published by the Sup.·. Council, So.·. Jurisdiction.
—— Same. 4to. Full-bound, purple morocco.

KNIGHTS KADOSH, Offices of Constitution and Installation of Council of. Published by the Sup.·. Council, So.·. Jurisdiction.

LEGENDA, 32 DEG. Published by the Sup.·. Council, So.·. Jurisdiction.

LITURGY, of the Ancient and Accepted Scottish Rite. Published by the Sup.·. Council, So.·. Jurisdiction. Parts 1 to 4. 4 vols.

LODGE OF PERFECTION, Offices of Constitution and Installation of. Published by the Sup.·. Council, So.·. Jurisdiction.

MAGNUM OPUS. [100 copies privately printed in 1859, at a cost of $1,200, by Albert Pike.] Value, per copy, $100. 4to. 2 copies.

MASONIC BAPTISM, Reception of Louveteau, and Adoption ; Ceremonies of. Published by the Sup.·. Council, So.·. Jurisdiction.

MASONIC Symbolism, Lecture on.   By Albert Pike.   100 copies printed
    and plates melted down.   Value of copy, $50.   4to.   2 copies.
—— Second Lecture on.   By Albert Pike.   100 copies printed and
    plates melted down.   Value of copy, $25.   4to.
MORALS AND DOGMA.   Of Free Masonry.   Published by the Sup.˙.
    Council, So.˙. Jurisdiction.   8vo.
MUSIC.   Part I.   For the Ritual of Various Degrees, in the Ancient
    and Accepted Scottish Rite.   By Matthew Cooke, 33˙.   Published
    by the Sup.˙. Council, So.˙. Jurisdiction.

OFFICIAL BULLETIN OF THE SUPREME COUNCIL.   Vols. I. to VI.
    From 1870 to 1884.

PRINCES ˙OF JERUSALEM, Offices of Constitution and Installation of
    Council of.   Published by the Sup.˙. Council, So.˙. Jurisdiction.

READINGS OF 32D DEG.   Published by the Sup.˙. Council, So.˙. Juris-
    diction.

SEPHAR II' DEBARIM.   The Book of the Words.   Published by the
    Sup.˙. Council, So.˙. Jurisdiction.   4to.
SUPREME COUNCIL, Transactions of.   Northern Jurisdiction.   1860.
—— Southern.   1851–1860.
—— Northern.   Vol. V.   1865–1866.
—— Same.   Gourgas Body.   1813–'51.
—— Same.   Raymond Body.   1851–'60.
—— Same.   Van Rensselaer Body.   1860–'62.
—— Same.   1866–'68.
—— Southern.   1868.
—— Northern.   1869.
—— Southern.   May, 1870.
—— Northern.   June, 1870.
—— Same.   1870–1771.
—— Same.   1872–1874.
—— Same.   1875–1876.
—— Same.   1877, 1878, 1879.
—— Same.   1878–1879.
—— Same.   1880, 1881, 1882.
—— Southern.   Reprint, 1857 to 1866.
—— Same.   1860 to 1882.   5 vols.

CLASS XIV.

SUPPLEMENT.

Books presented to the Grand Commander, by Bro.·. Richard H. Hartley, of Lima, Peru, in 1883, but received after January, 1884.

CLASS XIV.

ACTA SANCTORUM MAII, DIES XXI.–XXVI. P. Godoferido Henschenio et Daniele Papebrochio e Societate Jesu. Tomus Quintus. Large folio. Bound in vellum. 1188 pp. Venetiis, apud Sebastianum Coleti et Jo : Baptistam Albrizzi Hieron. Fil., MDCCXLI.

ARRIANI. Expeditionis Alexandri, Libri Septem. Operâ Jacobi Gronovii. Large 8vo. (Greek and Latin). Excudit Petrus Vander, AA, Bibliop Lvgdvni Batavorum, MDCCIV.

BIBLIA RUSA, ó Libros del Testimonio de la Escritura de la Antigua y Nueva Revelacion, en Lengua Rusa. Square 8vo. 1204 pp. Impreso en la Ciudad de Moscovia.

BIBLIA SACRA. Vulgatæ Editionis. Sixti V., Pontificis Maximi jussu recognita ; et Clementis VIII., auctoritate edita. Large folio. Lugduni, apud Antonium Baujolin, MDCXCII.

—— Cum Glossâ ordinariâ. Primùm à Strabo Fvldensi collecta, Tomvs Quartvs. Large folio. 2523 pp. Antverpiæ, apud Joannem Mevrsivm, Anno MDCXXXIV.

BIBLIA SACRA POLYGLOTTA. Samaritanæ, Græcæ, Chaldaicæ, Syriacæ, Arabicæ, Æthiopicæ, Persicæ, Vulg. Lat. Edidit Brianus Waltonus, S.T.D. 6 vols. Large folio. Londini, imprimebat Thomas Roycroft, MDCLVII.

BIBLIORUM SACRORUM. Latinæ versiones antiquæ, seu vetus Italica. Operâ & studio D. Petri Sabatier. Tomus Secundus, Pars Secunda. Large folio. Illustrated. 466 pp. Parisiis, Franciscus Didot, MDCCLI.

—— Same. Tomus Tertius, Pars Secunda. Large folio. Without illustrations. 622 pp.

—— Cum Glossâ Ordinariâ. Primùm à Strabo Fvldensi collecta. Tomvs Tertivs. Large folio. 2232 pp. Parisiis, MDXC.

CICERONIS, MARCII TULLII. Opera. Volumen Primum, 849 pp.; Volumen Secundum, 1051 pp., cum Indice, pp. 104. 2 vols. Large folio. Amstelædami, apud Rod. & Gerh. Wetstenios. MDCCXXIV.

HEBRAICORUM BIBLIORUM. Veteris Testamenti Hebraici, cum Latinâ interpretatione. Operâ olim Xantis Pagnini Lucensis, nunc verò Benedicti Ariæ Montani Hispalensis et aliorum. Cum censurâ Doctorum Parisiensium, datum Parisiis, Anno 1569, die 8 Martij. Large folio. Bound in vellum. Imprim. Christophorus Plantinus, Antverpiæ, 1571.

HERODOTI HALICARNASSEI. Historiarum, Libri IX. Folio. 708 pp. Oliva Pauli Stephani. MDCXVIII.

LA SACRA BIBLIA. Tradotta in Lingua Italiana da Giovanni Diodati. 2ᵉ Editione. Testamente Antico e Nuevo, colle Libri Apocrifi ed I Sacri Salmi messi in rime. PP. 331, 143-68. Square 8vo. Per Pietro Chorët. MDCXL.

LA SAINTE BIBLE. Qui contient le vieux et le nouveau Testament, faite sur la version de Genêve. 2 vols. Large folio. Illustrated with maps, etc. À Amsterdam, chez Louys & Daniel Elzevier, CIƆ IƆ C LXIX.

LEXICON GRÆCO-LATINUM. P. Ioannis Scapulæ. Folio. 1790 pp., cum Indice, et Jacobi Zvengeri Græcorum Dialectorum Hypotyposi, 354 pp. Sumptibus Joannis Antonii Hvgvetan & Marci Antonii Ravavd. Lvgdvni, MDCLXIII.

LEXICON HEPTAGLOTTON. Hebraicum, Chaldaicum, Syriacum, Samaritanum, Æthiopicum, Arabicum et Persicum. Authore Edmundo Castello, S.T.D. Tom. I. Large folio. 1654 pp. Londini, Thomas Roycroft, CIƆ DC LXIX.

LEXICON LATINUM. Jacobi Facciolati Calepinus. Operâ et studio Johannis Baptistæ Gallicciolli. i., pp. 984. Large folio. Venetiis, à Typ. Johannis Gatti, MDCCLXXVIII.

NOVVM TESTAMENTVM GRAECÈ. Large folio. Bound in vellum. 191 pp. Antverpiæ, Christoforus Plantinus, MDLXXII.

PHOTII, MYRIOBIBLON SIVE BIBLIOTHECA. Librorum quos Photius Patriarcha Constantinopolitanus legit & censuit. Græcè, edidit David Hoeschelivs; Latinè, reddidit Andreas Schottus. Tom. III. 1728 pp. Folio. Bound in vellum. Oliva Pavli Stephani. Antverpiæ, MDCXI.

PLINIJ, C. SECUNDI HISTORIÆ MUNDI. Libri XXXVII. Folio. Bound in vellum. 746 pp., and Index, 173 pp. Sumptibus Jacobi Crispini. Genevæ, Anno MDCXXXI.

POETÆ GRÆCI VETERES. Tragici, Comici, Lyrici, Epigrammatarii. 2 vols. in 1. Thick folio. Vol. I., 1022 pp.; Vol. II., 753 pp., and Index. Coloniæ Allobrogvm. Typis Petri de la Rouière. Anno CIƆ IƆC XIV.

PSALTERIUM. Hebraicum, Græcum, Arabicum & Chaldaicum, cum tribus Latinis interpretationibus & glossis. Genuæ, MDXVI.

THEATRUM TERRÆ SANCTÆ et Bibliarum Historiarum, cum tabulis geograficis ære expressis. Avttore Christiano Adrichomio Delpho. Folio. 286 pp. Bound in vellum. Coloniæ Agrippinæ. Birckmann, Anno CIƆ IƆC.

THUCYDIDES DE BELLO PELOPONNESIACO. Libri Octo. Large folio. 728 pp.; Index, et Apparatus ad Annales, 171 pp. Amstelædami, apud R. & J. Wetstenios & Gul. Smith, MDCCXXXI.

VIRGILII MARONIS, P. Opera. Tomi duo in uno. Tom. I., 340 pp.; Tom. II., 296 pp. Large folio. Full bound in red morocco, gilt edges, etc. Parmæ, in Aedibus Palatinis, CIƆ IƆCC XCIII. Typis Bodonianis.

XENOPHONTIS PHILOSOPHI Imperatoris Clarissimi, quæ exstant opera in duos tomos divisa. Opera Joannis Levnclavii Amelbvrni. Large folio. Bound in vellum. 1213 pp., and Index. Francofvrti, apud Andreæ Wecheli heredes, MDXCVI

LIBRARY B.

THE GENERAL LIBRARY

OF THE

SUPREME COUNCIL.

CLASS I.

HISTORICAL AND BIOGRAPHICAL.

CLASS I.

Actes et Gestes Merveilleux, Les, de la Cité de Genève. Anthoine Fromment. Reprint by Gustave Revilliod. Genève, 1854.

Alabama, History of. By Albert James Pickett. 2 vols. 1851.

Albany City and County, and Colony of Rensselaerswyck, Early Records of, 1656-1675. Jonathan Pearson.

American Revolution in the South, Reminiscences of the. By Jos. Johnson. 1851.

Ancient Geography, Lectures on. By Niebuhr. 2 vols.

Ancient Monarchies. By George Rawlinson, M.A. 3 vols. New York, 1873.

Anecdotes. Poetry and Incidents of the War, North and South, 1860-'65. By Frank Moore. New York, 1882.

Arkansas, Report of the Secretary of State of. 1882.

—— Journal of the Convention, held in March, 1861.

Army of the Potomac, 1861-'65. By Wm. Swinton.

Ashburnham's Narrative. Time of Charles the First. John Ashburnham. Never before printed. 2 vols. London, 1830.

Ashby and His Compeers. By James B. Avirett. 1867.

Attakapas, Histoire des Comités de Vigilance aux. Par Alexandre Barde. Louisiane, 1861.

Autobiography of Stilling. Translated by S. Jackson. New York, 1844.

Babeuf's Conspiracy, Buonarroti's History of. By Bronterre. London, 1836.

Baltimore in the Revolutionary War. By Robert Purviance. 1849.

Bancroft, Hubert Howe, Works of. Native Races, Central America, etc. 12 vols. 1882-1884.

Boston, Its History and Antiquities. By Samuel G. Drake, A.M. 1856.

Brant, Joseph, "Thayendanegea," Life of. By W. L. Stone. 2 vols. New York, 1838.

BRAZILIAN BIOGRAPHICAL ANNUAL.   By J. M. de Macedo.   3 vols.
Rio de Janeiro, 1876.

BUNSEN, BARON, Memoir of.   By Frances, Baroness Bunsen.   2 vols.
London, 1868.

BURNHAM FAMILY, Genealogy of the.   Roderick H. Burnham.   1869.

CALIFORNIA AND OREGON, Capture of, by the Chinese, in 1899.   By
Robert Wolter, a Survivor.   1882.

CALIFORNIA, History of.   Translated from the Spanish of Miguel
Venegas, a Mexican Jesuit.   2 vols.   1758.

—— Same.   By Franklin Tuthill.   San Francisco, 1866.

—— Convention of 1849, Debates in the.   J. Ross Browne.   1850.

CAMP, MARCH AND BATTLE-FIELD.   Army of the Potomac.   By Rev.
A. M. Stewart.   1865.

CAMPAIGNS OF A NON-COMBATANT.   By Geo. Alfred Townsend.
1866.

CAMPAIGNS OF THE CIVIL WAR.   13 vols.   Scribner.   1882.

CARLYLE, THOMAS, Life of.   By Richard Herne Shepherd.   2 vols.
1795–1846.

CAROLINA AND GEORGIA, Revolution in.   By Wm. Moultrie.   2 vols.
1802.

CHANCELLORS, Campbell's Lives of the.   10 vols.

CHATHAM ARTILLERY OF GEORGIA, Historical Sketch of, during the
Civil War.   By Charles C. Jones, jr.   1867.

CHIEF JUSTICES OF ENGLAND, Lives of the.   Campbell.   6 vols.

CHRONICLES OF THE LAND OF COLUMBIA.   By the Prophet James.
Book I.   Milwaukee, 1876.

CHRONIQUES DE GENÈVE.   Par François Bonivard, Prieur de St. Victor.   Reprint by Gustave Revilliod.   2 vols.   Genève, 1867.

CITIES AND CEMETERIES OF ETRURIA.   2 vols.   London, Dennis,
1878.

CIVIL WAR, Our, A Bird's-Eye View of.   By Theodore Ayrault Dodge,
U. S. Army.   1883.

—— Anecdotes of the.   By Maj. Gen. E. D. Townsend.   New York,
1884.

CLARK'S HISTORY OF KNIGHTHOOD.   2 vols.   London, 1874.

COBBETT'S LETTERS, on the Late War between the U. S. and Great
Britain.   Wm. Cobbett.   1815.

COLLINS' PEERAGE.   4 vols.   London, 1741.

CONFEDERATE HISTORY OF THE REBELLION.   H. C. Clarke.   Augusta,
Ga., 1862.

CONFEDERATE STATES OF AMERICA, Statutes at Large of the.   From
February 8, 1861, to February 18, 1862.

CONFUSIONS AND REVOLUTIONS OF GOVERNMENTS. Ant. Ascham, Gent. London, 1649.

CONSTANTINE, Life of. By Eusebius Pamphilus. Translated. London, 1874.

CONSTITUTIONAL CONVENTION, The. John Alexander Jameson. Chicago, 1873.

CROMWELL, OLIVER. The Man and His Mission. By J. Alanson Picton.

CRUSADES, History of the. By Major Procter. London, 1884.

DANUBE, The. By Michael J. Quin. New York, 1837.

DELAWARE, Original Settlements on the. By Benj. Ferris. 1846.

DIARY AND CORRESPONDENCE. Amos Lawrence.

EGYPT, History of the British Expedition to. By Robt. Thos. Wilson. 4to. London, 1803.

ELLIS' ORIGINAL LETTERS, Illustrative of English History. Sir Henry Ellis. 4 vols. London, 1846.

ENGLAND, The History of. By M. Rapin de Thoyras. 2 vols. London, 1757.

ETRURIA, The History of. Mrs. Hamilton Gray. 2 vols. London, 1844.

FALL OF THE CRIMEA. Spencer. London, 1854.

FEDERAL DEAD, Record of the. War Dept. 1866.

FLORIDA. History of the War in West Florida. With Atlas. Maj. A. Lacarrière Latour. 2 vols. 1816.

FLORENTINE HISTORIES. Machiavelli. Translated by Lester. [2 vols. in 1.]

FOUR YEARS WITH GENERAL LEE. By Walter H. Taylor. 1878.

FRANCE, Guizot's History of. Estes and Lauriat. 6 vols.

—— Same. Martin's Continuation of. 3 vols.

GALILEO GALILEI, and the Roman Curia. Carl von Gebler. Translated by Mrs. George Sturge. London, 1879.

GENERAL ORDERS. Headquarters, Dept. of the Cumberland, January 7th to December 5th, 1863.

GEORGIA, The Dead Towns of. By C. C. Jones, jr. Savannah, 1878.

—— Stevens's History of. By Wm. Bacon Stevens. 2 vols. 1847.

—— Statistics of. By George White. 2 copies. 1849.

—— The History of. By Capt. Hugh McCall. Vol. I. 1811.

—— Collections of the Historical Society of. 2 vols. 1840–1842.

10

GETTYSBURG TO THE RAPIDAN.   The Army of the Potomac, July, 1863 to April, 1864. A. A. Humphreys.

GREECE, TURKEY, EGYPT AND THE HOLY LAND. Mrs. Damer. 2 vols. London, 1842.

GREECE, TURKEY, RUSSIA AND POLAND. New York, 1843.

HARTFORD CONVENTION, History of the. By Theodore Dwight, Sec. of the Convention. 1833.

HEBREW HEROES. Tale founded on Jewish History. By A. L. O. E. 1869.

HEBREWS' SECOND COMMONWEALTH, History of the. By I. M. Wise. 1880.

HENNINGSEN, CHARLES FREDERICK. A Campaign with Zumalacarregui. London, 1836.

—— Revelations of Russia, in 1846. 3d Edition. 2 vols. London, 1846.

HIGHLAND CLANS, History of the. John S. Keltie. 4 vols. London, 1882.

HISTOIRE DES ORDRES DE CHEVALERIE. Par Auguste Wahlen. Bruxelles, 1844.

HISTORIA DES PERSEGUIÇÃOES. F. Garrido. 3 vols. Lisboa, 1881.

HISTORICAL POETRY OF THE ANCIENT HEBREWS. 2 vols. By Michael Heilprin. New York, 1879.

HISTORY OF FLORENCE, AND THE PRINCE. Machiavelli. London, 1851.

HISTORY OF TEN YEARS. By Louis Blanc. 2 vols. London, 1844.

HISTORY OF THE UNITED STATES. By Alex. H. Stephens. 1852.

—— By Richard Hildreth. Revised Edition. 6 vols. 1880.

HUNGARY, War in. By General Klapka. 2 vols. London, 1850.

ILLINOIS, History of, from its First Discovery. By Henry Brown. 1844.

—— Same. From 1818 to 1847. By Thomas Ford. 1854.

INDIANA IN THE REBELLION. Report of W. H. H. Terrell, Adjt. General. 1869.

INDIANS, Speeches on the Removal of the. April and May, 1830.

IRELAND, History of, Ancient and Modern. By the Abbé MacGeohegan. 1851.

IROQUOIS, League of the. By Lewis H. Morgan. 1851.

JACKSON, ANDREW, Life of. By Maj. John Reid. Completed by Gen. J. H. Eaton. 1817.

JACKSON, LIEUT.-GEN. T. J. [Stonewall], Life and Campaigns of. By R. L. Dabney, D.D. 1866.

Jacques Cœur. The French Argonaut. By Costello. London, 1847.

Johns Hopkins University Studies, In Historical and Political Science. Vol. I. 1883.

Johnston, Albert Sidney, Gen., Life of. By Wm. Preston Johnston. 1878.

Johnston, Joseph E., Gen. Narrative of Military Operations directed by him during the War.

Jomini. Traité des Grandes Opérations Militaires. 2 vols. Bruxelles, 1842.

—— Guerres de la Révolution. 4 vols. Bruxelles, 1842.

—— Principes de la Stratègie. Bruxelles, 1840.

—— Atlas, Ouvrages de.

—— Légendes pour l'intelligence de l'Atlas des Guerres de Sept Ans.

Jones, John Paul, Life of. By Col. John Henry Sherburne. Washington, 1825.

Josephus, Flavius, Genuine Works of. By Wm. Whiston. Folio London, 1737.

Journal de Las Cases, De la Vie Privée de l'Empereur Napoléon. 4 vols. Londres, 1823.

Kansas. Reports of the Special Committee on Troubles in. House of Reps., XXXIVth Congress, 1st Session. 1856.

—— War in. By G. Douglass Brewerton. 1856.

Kansas and Nebraska, History of, etc. Edward E. Hale. 1854.

Kentucky, History of. By Mann Butler. 1834.

Kentucky Volunteers and Regulars. Commanded by Gen. Winchester, in War of 1812, Account of. By Elias Darnell.

King Philip's War. Narrative History. By Richard Markham.

Knights of Malta, Achievements of the. By Alex. Sutherland. 2 vols. Edinburgh, 1831.

—— Same. By Alex. Sutherland. Philadelphia, 1846.

Land of Bolivar, The. Spence. 2 vols. London, 1878.

Lanman's Dictionary of Congress. [2 copies.] 1864.

Lawrence, Amos, Extracts from Diary and Correspondence of. Boston, 1855.

Letters on Livonia and other States. London, 1701.

London. New Remarks of. By the Company of Parish Clerks. 1732.

—— A History of. By W. J. Loftie, B.A., F.S.A. Maps and Illustrations. 2 vols. London, 1883.

Lorenzo dei Medici. London, Roscoe, 1851.

Los Gringos. By Lieut. Henry A. Wise, U. S. Navy. New York, 1850.

Louisiana. Histoire de la Louisiane. Du Pratz. 3 vols. 1758.

LOUISIANA, Sketches of.   By Major Amos Stoddard.   1812.
—— Historical Memoirs of.   By B. F. French.   1853.
—— History of.   The Spanish Domination.   Charles Gayarre.   1854.
—— Same.   The French Domination.   Charles Gayarre.   2 vols.
    1854.
—— Same.   The American Domination.   Charles Gayarre.   1866.
—— Historical Collections of.   By B. F. French.   In 3 parts.   3 vols.
—— and Florida, Historical Collections of.   By B. F. French.   [2 cop-
    ies.]   2 vols.   1869.
LYNAM'S ROMAN EMPERORS.   2 vols.   London, 1850.

MAINE HISTORICAL SOCIETY, Collections of the.   3 vols.   1831, 1847,
    1853.
MARTYRS OF SPAIN, The.   New York, 1865.
MARYLAND, History of, from 1634 to 1848. By James McSherry.   1849.
—— Same.   From 1633 to 1660.   By John Leeds Bozman.   2 vols.
    1837.
—— The Founders of.   By Rev. Edward D. Neill.   1876.
—— Conventions of.   1774-'75-'76.   Baltimore, 1836.
MEMOIRS OF THE WAR, in the Southern Department of the U. S.   By
    Henry Lee.
MEXICO [OLD] AND HER LOST PROVINCES.   By William Henry Bishop.
MEXICO AND THE MEXICAN WAR, Pictorial History of.   John Frost.
    1851.
MEXICO, The War With.   By Horatio O. Ladd.   New York, 1882.
—— The Republic of, in 1876.   By Antonio Garcia Cubas.   Trans-
    lated by Geo. F. Henderson.
MILITARY AND NAVAL LETTERS, of Officers, during the War with
    Great Britain.   By John Brannan.   1823.
MILLS, CHARLES, Works of.   Crusades.   2 vols.
—— Chivalry.   2 vols.
—— Muhammedism.
MILWAUKEE, Pioneer History of.   By James S. Buck.   1876.
MINNESOTA HISTORICAL COLLECTIONS.   Vol. I., 1850-'56.
MISSION OF THE UNITED BRETHREN AMONG THE INDIANS OF NORTH
    AMERICA.   By George Henry Loskiel.   1794.
MISSOURI, Gazetteer of the State of.   Compiled by Alonzo Wetmore.
    1837.
—— Illustrated History of.   By Davis and Durrie.   1876.
—— History of, from 1541 to 1877.   Switzler, 1879.
—— The 1st and 2d Confederate Brigades of, History of.   By R. S.
    Bevier.   1879.
MNEMONIKA, or Chronological Tablets.   Philadelphia, 1812.

MONROE'S MISSION. By James Monroe. 1797.

MONTANA, The Vigilantes of. By Prof. Thomas J. Dinsdale. 1882.

MOUNTAIN AND FRONTIER. The Sioux War, and Life of Gen. Geo. A. Custer. By Frances F. Victor. Illustrated.

NANTUCKET, History of. Events from 1835 to 1880. Obed Macy.

NAVY IN THE CIVIL WAR, The.

    The Gulf and Inland Waters. A. T. Mahan.

    The Atlantic Coast. Daniel Ammen.

    The Blockade and the Cruisers. J. R. Soley.

NELL GWYN, The Story of, and Sayings of Charles II. By Peter Cunningham, F.S.A. New York, 1883.

NEWBURY, NEWBURYPORT AND WEST NEWBURY, from 1635 to 1845, History of. By Joshua Coffin.

NEW ENGLAND, History of. By John Gorham Palfrey. 3 vols. Boston, 1859.

—— A Compendious History of. By Jedediah Morse and Elijah Parish. 1809.

NEW JERSEY, History and Gazetteer of. By Thomas F. Gordon. 2 vols. [1 vol. 2 copies.] 1834.

—— History of. Mulford.

—— Same. John O. Raum. 2 vols.

—— Provincial Courts of. Richard S. Field. 1849.

—— Historical Society Collections. The Life of Lord Stirling.

—— The Papers of Lewis Morris, Governor of Province of New Jersey. 1738–1746.

—— Record of the Governor and Council of East Jersey. 1682–1703.

—— Journal and Votes of the House of Representatives of. 1703.

—— Minutes of the Council of Safety of. 1777.

—— Contributions to East Jersey History. Whitehead.

NEW YORK. Documents Relating to the Colonial History of the State. Vols. I. to X.

—— Historical Collections of the State. By Barber and Howe. 1841.

—— Historical Society Collections, 1868 to 1873. 6 vols. Large 8vo.

NORTH CAROLINA, History of. Maps and Illustrations. By Francis L. Hawks. 2 vols. 1859.

—— Same. By Hugh Williamson. [2 copies.] 2 vols. 1812.

—— Same. By John H. Wheeler. 1851.

—— Same. By John Lawson. 1860.

NORTH CAROLINA.   Defense of its Revolutionary History from asper-
sions of Mr. Jefferson.
—— Chronology of.   By D. K. Bennet.   1858.
·—— Revolutionary History of, in 3 Lectures.   By F. L. Hawks,
D. L. Swain, William A. Graham.
—— Sketches of.   By William Henry Foote.   1846.

OFFICIAL CORRESPONDENCE WITH WAR DEPARTMENT, IN 1814–1815,
Relative to Operations under Maj.-Gen. Izard.   1816.
OREGON, A History of.   By W. H. Gray, of Astoria.   1870.
OREGON AND CALIFORNIA, History of.   By Robert Greenhow.   [1 vol.
2 copies.]   2 vols.   1845.
ORIENTAL MONARCHY, The Sixth.   By Prof. George Rawlinson.
London, 1873.
—— The Seventh.   By Prof. George Rawlinson.   London, 1875.
OUR LIVING REPRESENTATIVE MEN   John Savage.   Philadelphia,
1860.
OUR COUNTRY, History of.   Illustrated.   By B. J. Lossing.   3 vols.

PALESTINE, The History of.   By John Kitto.   1883.
PALMERSTON, The Life of Henry John Temple, Viscount.   By Sir
Henry Lytton Bulwer.   2 vols.
PENNSYLVANIA, An Historical Review of, from its Origin.   By Benj.
Franklin.
—— History of the Whiskey Insurrection.   By H. M. Brackenridge.
—— Archives.   12 vols.   1664–1790.
—— Minutes of the Provincial Council of.   16 vols.   1683–1790.
PERU AND MEXICO, Historical Researches on the Conquest of by the
Mongols.   London, 1827.
PICTORIAL HISTORY OF THE MIDDLE AGES.   John Frost.   1846.
PIONEER HISTORY OF MILWAUKEE.   Buck.   Milwaukee, 1876.
POLYNESIAN RACE, Account of the.   By Abraham Fornander.   Lon-
don, 1878.
PONTIAC, The Conspiracy of.   By Fr. Parkman, jr.   1851.

REVOLUTION FRANÇAISE   Cabet.   4 vols.   Paris, 1845.
—— Par M. Jules Janin.   2 vols.   Folio.   Paris, 1862–1865. •
REVOLUTIONARY WAR.   Records, Correspondence, etc.   W. T. R.
Saffell.   New York, 1858.
REVOLUTION, The American.   Written in Scriptural or Historical
Style.   By Richard Snowden.   Baltimore.
RUSSIA AS IT IS.   By Count Gurowski.   New York, 1854.

Russian Invasion of Poland in 1563. Exact Fac-Simile and Translation of the published account of, at the time.

San Francisco, History of. By John S. Hittell. 1878.
—— Vigilance Committee of. 1856.
—— The Annals of. Illustrated. 1855.
Scotland in Early Christian Times. By Joseph Anderson. 2 vols. Edinburgh, 1881.
Sherman, Gen. Wm. T., and His Campaigns. A Military Biography. By Bowman and Irwin. 1865.
—— Memoirs of. Written by Himself. 2 vols. 1875.
Sicily, The History of, to the Athenian War. By W. Watkiss Lloyd. London, 1872.
Simcoe's Military Journal. History of the Queen's Rangers ; War of the Revolution. 1844.
Skobeleff and the Slavonic Cause. By O. K. London, Longmans, 1883.
South Carolina, The History of, from its First Settlement, in 1670 to 1808. 2 vols. By David Ramsay.
—— History of the Upper Country of. John H. Logan. Vol. I. 1859. No more published.
—— History of the Protestant Episcopal Church in. Rev. Frederick Dalcho. Charleston, 1820.
—— Historical Collections of. B. R. Carroll. 2 vols. 1836.
—— Same. By the Historical Society. 3 vols.
—— Documentary History of. By R. W. Gibbs. 4 Vols. 1764-1766, 1781, 1782.
—— History of. By W. Gilmore Simms. [2 copies.] 2 vols. 1860.
—— Annals of Newberry. By John Belton O'Neall. 1859.
—— Historical Account of Protestant Episcopal Church in. Dalcho.
—— Bench and Bar of. By John Belton O'Neall. Vol. II. 1859.
—— Same. By John Belton O'Neall. 2 vols. 1859.
—— Historical Sketches of, to close of Revolution of 1719. 1856.
—— In the Revolutionary War. 1853.
Southern Historical Society Collections. 10 vols.
Southern States. Compiled from De Bow's Review.
Southwestern History, Romantic Passages in. By A. B. Meek. 1857.
Stories from the State Papers. By Alex. Chas. Ewald, F.S.A. 2 vols. London, 1882.
Stuart, Prince Charles, Life and Times of. By A. C. Ewald, F.S.A. London, 1883.

Tarleton, Lieut.-Col., History of His Campaigns of 1780-1781 in the Southern States. Cost $18. 4to. London, 1787.

TECUMSEH, Life of, and of his brother, the Prophet.   By Benjamin Drake. 1856.

TENNESSEE, McNairy County, Reminiscences of the Early Settlement and Settlers of.   By Marcus J. Wright.   [2 copies.]   1882.

—— Annals of.   J. G. M. Ramsey.   1853.

—— Old Times in West Tennessee.   Memphis, 1873.

—— Battle of Murfreesboro', Report of the.   By Maj.-Gen. Rosecrans.   1863.

TEXAS, The Rise, Progress and Prospects of.   Wm. Kennedy.   2 vols. 1841.

TEXAS LETTERS, from an Early Settler.   By W. B. Dewees.   1854.

TOMO-CHI-CHI, Micco of the Yamacraws.   By Chas. C. Jones, jr.   Albany, Ga., 1868.

TURKESTAN.   Eugene Schuyler.   2 vols.   New York, 1876.

UNDERGROUND RUSSIA.   By Stepniak.   1883.

UNITED STATES, Governmental History of.   Henry Sherman.   Hartford, 1860.

VERMONT, The Natural and Civil History of.   By Samuel Williams. 1794.

—— Governor and Council.   4 vols.   1775-1804.

—— State Papers 1779-1786.   Wm. Slade, jr., Secretary of State.   1828.

VIRGINIA, The State of, Its History.   . By Chas. Campbell.   1860.

—— History of.   By Henry Howe.   1845.

—— Illustrated.   By " Porte Crayon " [D. H. Strother].   1857.

—— Calendar of State Papers.   2 vols.   Vol. I., 1652 to 1781 ; Vol. II., April 1st to December 31st, 1781.

—— History of.   By Robert Beverley.   1855.

—— Historical Reporter for 1833, and 1851 to 1860.

—— History of the Valley of.   By Samuel Kercheval.   1833.

—— Historical Register for 1848 to 1853, inclusive.   6 vols.

—— History of.   By Robert H. Howison.   2 vols.   1846.

—— History of the College of William and Mary, from 1660 to 1874.

—— Historical and Biographical Sketches of.   By Rev. W. H. Foote. 1850.

—— Same.   By Rev. W. H. Foote.   [2d Series.]   1855.

—— History of its Early Settlement and Indian Wars.   By W. De Hass.

—— Colonial Records of.   4to.

—— History of.   By John Burke.   4 vols.   1804.

—— Journal of Major George Washington.   1754.

—— History of.   By Capt. John Smith.   1593 to 1629.   2 vols.

VIRGINIA, A Geographical and Political Summary of. 1876.
—— Gazetteer History of. By Joseph Martin. 1835.
—— The Present State of. By Hugh Jones, A.M. New York, 1865.
—— Notes on the State of. By Thomas Jefferson. 1853.
—— Historical Society of, Publications of the. New Series, No. 1. 4to.
—— Historical Society, Collections. [Spotswood Letters.] No. 1.
—— Old Churches and Families of. By Bishop Meade. 2 vols. 1878.
—— The "Bland Papers." From Manuscripts of Theodore Bland. 2 vols. 1840.
—— History of the Line between Virginia and North Carolina. Byrd Manuscripts. 2 vols. Westover, Va., 1728.
—— History of the First Discovery and Settlement of. Wm. Stith. 1748.
—— The First Settlers of. An Historical Novel. 1806.
—— History of the People. By John Esten Cooke. Boston, 1883.
—— Notes on the Settlement, and Indian Wars of Western Parts of Virginia and Pennsylvania.
—— History of Augusta County. By J. Lewis Peyton. Staunton, 1882.
—— History of Western Virginia. By W. De Hass. 1851.

WAR IN THE UNITED STATES, The. By Ferdinand Lecomte. New York, 1863.
WAR DEPARTMENT. Report of Judge Advocate Gen. on the "Order of American Knights," or "Sons of Liberty." Pamphlet. 1864.
—— Official Army Register of Volunteer Force of U. S. Army, 1861, 1862, 1863, 1864, 1865. 8 vols.
—— Report of the Provost Marshal General. Parts I. and II. 2 vols. 1866.
WAR PICTURES FROM THE SOUTH. Estvan. New York, 1864.
WASHINGTON, The Invasion and Capture of, History of. By John S. Williams. New York, 1857.
WASHINGTON FAMILY, Story of the. By Albert Welles.
WASHINGTON'S ACCOUNT AS COMMANDER-IN-CHIEF, from 1775 to 1783. Fac-simile.
WASHINGTON'S WILL AND TESTAMENT. Mount Vernon, July 9, 1799.
WATSON'S ANNALS OF PHILADELPHIA. 2 vols. Edition of 1850.
WENTWORTH, THOMAS, Earl of Strafford, The Life of. By Elizabeth Cooper. 2 vols. London, 1874.
WESTERN ANNALS. From the Discovery of the Mississippi Valley to the year 1845. James H. Perkins.

Western Antiquary, The, or Devon and Cornwall Note-Book. May, 1882 to October, 1883.

Western States, Geography and History of the.   By Timothy Flint. 2 vols.   Cincinnati, 1828.

Wisconsin ; Its History, Geography, etc.   By J. A. Lapham, 1846.

—— Illustrated History of.   By C. R. Tuttle.   1875.

—— Collections of the State Historical Society.   8 vols.   1855–1879.

—— History of, Historical, Documentary and Descriptive.   By Wm. R. Smith.   [Vols. I. and III.]   2 vols.   1854.

World, The, General History of.   Charles von Rotteck.   [4 vols. in 2.]   2 vols.

CLASS II.

PHILOSOPHICAL AND RELIGIOUS.

CLASS II.

A EGREJA E O ESTADO. Saldanha Marinho. 3 vols. Rio de Janeiro, 1874–'75.
ANALYTICAL CONCORDANCE TO THE BIBLE. By Robert Young, LL.D. 4to.
ANCIENT PAGAN AND MODERN CHRISTIAN SYMBOLISM. Inman. New York, 1880.
AZOTH SIVE AVRELIÆ OCCULTÆ PHILOSOPHORUM. Francoforti, 1613.

BAGSTER'S GEOGRAPHICAL AND CHRONOLOGICAL ILLUSTRATIONS OF THE HOLY SCRIPTURES. London.
BIBLE MYTHS AND THEIR PARALLELS IN OTHER RELIGIONS. J. W. Bouton.
BIBLE, Right and Wrong Uses of the. By R. Heber Newton, Rector of All Souls' Church, New-York.
BIBLE TEACHINGS IN NATURE. Rev. Hugh McMillan.
BIBLICAL LEGENDS OF THE MUSSULMANS. Weil. London, 1846.
BISHOP COLENSO on the Pentateuch. 4 vols. London, 1862.
BOOK OF ENOCH, The. Translated by the Archbishop of Cashel. Oxford, 1833.
BRAZIL, Anti-Jesuitismo. Izatadores. 1873.
BUDDHISM, Esoteric. By A. P. Sinnett. London, 1883.
—— Same. By A. P. Sinnett. Boston, 1883.
—— History and Doctrines of. Upham. Folio. London, 1829.
BUDDHIST BIRTH STORIES. V. Fausböll. Boston, 1880.

CABINET OF CHOICE JEWELS, A. By Rev. Thomas Brooks. Rothesay, 1854.
CATALOGUE OF FOREIGN THEOLOGY. Nutt. 8vo. London, 1837.
CHRISTIANITY AND ITS CONFLICTS. Marcy. 1867.
CHRISTIAN PHILOSOPHER. Thomas Dick. 12mo.
CIVILIZATION, The Factors of ; Real and Assumed. By J. H. Bailey. Vol. II. 1882.
CLARK'S FOREIGN THEOLOGICAL LIBRARY, viz.: The Life of Christ,

Vol. I.; Biblical Theology of the New Testament, Vols. I. and II.
Weiss. 3 vols.
COMING WONDERS EXPECTED, between 1867 and 1875. Baxter.
COMPITUM, or the Meeting of the Ways at the Catholic Church.
Kenelm Henry Digby. 7 vols. London, 1848.
COSMIC GOD, The. A Fundamental Philosophy in Popular Lectures.
1876.

DIE GEBROCHNE MACHT DER FINSTERNÜK, oder Zerstörte Geuftische
Bunds. Gottlieb Spikeln. 1687.
DISCURSOS E PROJECTOS. Saldanha Marinho. Rio de Janeiro, 1879.
DIVINE LEGATION OF MOSES. Warburton. 3 vols. London, 1846.

EIGHTH COMMANDMENT, The. By Charles Reade. Boston, 1860.

FAITH, The Way of. By Dr. Amilie Büdinger, 1847.
FALSE GODS, or the Idol Worship of the World. By Frank S. Dob-
bins.
FREEDOM OF FAITH, The. By Theodore T. Munger. Boston, 1883.

GEOMETRIA (Symbolism of). Domenico Angheri. Napoli, 1861.

HEBREW TRACTS. By Wise, Cohn and Graetz.
HIPPOLYTUS AND HIS AGE. Bunsen. 2 vols.
HOLY BIBLE, The. 4to. London, 1706.
—— Complete Analysis of the. Rev. Nathaniel West. 4to. New
York, 1854.
HOURS WITH THE MYSTICS. Robert Alfred Vaughan. 2 vols. Lon-
don.
HUSBANDRY SPIRITUALIZED. John Flavel. Small 4to. London,
1684.

IAMBLICHUS. Life of Pythagoras. Translated by Thomas Taylor.
London, 1818.
INTELLECTUAL POWERS. Abercrombie.

JESUS OF HISTORY, The. Geo. Solomon. New York, 1880.
JESUS OF NAZARETH, The Martyrdom of. I. M. Wise.
JEWS, Philosophy and Philosophical Authors of the. By S. Munk.
JOURNAL OF SACRED LITERATURE. 1852-'53-'54. London.

KABALAH, The, Extracts from, and Comments on. By the Grand
Commander. [MSS.]

KINDERGARTEN HOMES. The Plans of Mrs. Elizabeth Thompson. 1882.

LEVITIKON OU EXPOSÉ DES PRINCIPES FONDAMENTAUX DE LA DOCTRINE DES CHRÉTIENS CATHOLIQUES PRIMITIFS. Paris, 1831.
LIBERAL TRACTS.
LIFE AND OPINIONS OF SIR RICHARD MALTRAVERS. 2 vols. London, 1822.
LIFE OF TRUST, The. Müller. By Wayland.

MAN AND ANIMALS, The Expression of the Emotions in. Darwin. 1873.
MARROW OF SACRED DIVINITY. By Wm. Ames, D.D. London, ante 1735.
MASTERPIECES OF PULPIT ELOQUENCE. Fish. 2 vols.
MEMORIAL OF EARLY CHRISTIANITY. Miall. 1853.
METAPHYSICAL TRACTS. Dr. Samuel Parr. London, 1837.
MONUMENTAL CHRISTIANITY. John P. Lundy. New York, 1882.
MORES CATHOLICI, or Ages of Faith. By Kenelm Henry Digby. 3 vols. 8vo. London, 1844.
MYTHOLOGIC PHILOSOPHY. An Address by J. W. Powell, at Saratoga, N. Y., August, 1882. Pamphlet.

NATURAL RELIGION. By J. R. Seeley. 1882.
NATURE, On the Various Forces of. M. Faraday. London.

OAHSPE. The New Bible. 4to. New York and London, 1882.
OUVRAGES DE MONS. LE COMPTE DE PAGAN [Hugues des Païens]. Paris, 1669.

PANATHENÆA. Johannes Mevrsius. Leyden, 1719.
PARALLEL NEW TESTAMENT, The. Oxford, 1882.
PASSOVER, Form of Service for the Feast of the. New York, 1869.
PILATE AND HEROD. Tale of the Early History of the Church of England in Maryland. By Rev. H. Stanley. 2 vols. Philadelphia, 1853.
PILGRIM'S PROGRESS, The. By John Bunyan. Original Notes. By Rev. Thomas Scott. London, 1856.
PRAYERS OF ISRAEL. With English translation. L. H. Frank. New York, 1871.
PRIMITIVE SUPERSTITION, Origin of. Dorman. Philadelphia, 1881.
PULPIT ELOQUENCE OF THE XIXth CENTURY.

RABBINICAL DIALECTICS, The, of the Mishna and Talmud. By Aaron Hahn.

RECHERCHES SUR LES MYSTÈRES DU PAGANISME.   Par Saint Croix
Paris, 1817.
RELIGION IN AMERICA.   Dr. Baird.
RELIGION, Discourses on.   Theodore Parker.   1842.

SCRIPTURE PARADOXES; Their True Explanation.   By the Rev. Dr.
Bayley.   London, 1868.
SECRETS D'ALBERT LE GRAND.   À Lyon, 1783.
SEPHER YEZIRAH, and Sketch of the Talmud.   Kalisch, 1877.
SERPENT AND SIVA WORSHIP.   Clark and Wake.
SUPERNATURAL RELIGION.   6th edition.   2 vols.   Toronto and De-
troit, 1879.
SUPERSTITION IN ALL AGES.   By John Meslier, a Roman Catholic
Priest.
SWEDENBORG.   Divine Attributes.
—— Heaven and Hell.

TUSCULAN QUESTIONS.   Cicero.   Translated by Otis.   Boston, 1839.

VOLNEY'S RUINS.   2 vols.   Paris, 1817.

CLASS III.

ANTIQUITIES.

CLASS III.

ADVIS ET DEVIS DE L'ANCIENNE ET NOUVELLE POLICE DE GENÊVE. Svivis des Advis et Devis de Noblesse et de ses Offices ou Degréz. Par F. Bonivard. Reprint. Genève, 1865.

ADVIS ET DEVIS DE LA SOVRCE DE L'IDOLATRIE ET TYRANNIE PAPALE. Par F. Bonivard. Reprint. Genève, 1856.

AMERICAN ANTIQUITIES. Josiah Priest. Albany, 1834.

ANCIENT ATHENS. Thomas Henry Dyer. London, 1873.

ANCIENT BRONZE IMPLEMENTS OF BRITAIN AND IRELAND. Evans. New York, 1881.

ANCIENT EGYPTIANS, The. Wilkinson. 2 vols. 1864.

ANCIENT MYSTERIES EXPLAINED. Hone. London, 1823.

ANCIENT POTTERY. Birch. London, 1873.

ANTIQUITIES DE LA NUBIE. By F. C. Gau. Super-Imperial folio. Stuttgart and Paris.

ANTIQUITIES OF THE ORIENT UNVEILED. By M. Walcott Redding.

ANTIQUITIES OF THE SOUTHERN INDIANS. Particularly of the Georgia Tribes. Charles C. Jones, jr. 1873.

ARMS AND ARMOUR. Demmin. London, 1877.

ASGARD AND THE GODS. Wagner and McDowall. London, 1880.

ASIATIC RESEARCHES. 1798 to 1818. 12 vols. 12mo. London Reprint of Calcutta original edition.

—— 1799 to 1803. 7 vols. 4to. London Reprint of Calcutta edition.

ASSYRIAN CANON, The. By Smith. London.

ATLANTIS; the Antediluvian World. Donnelly.

BARRETT'S MAGUS, or Celestial Intelligencer. Being a Complete System of Occult Philosophy. By Francis Barrett. 4to. London, 1801.

BHAGAVAD-GÎTÂ, A Commentary on the Text of the. By Hurrychund Chintamon. London, 1874.

CAYLUS. Antiquités Egyptiennes, etc. 7 vols. 4to. Paris, 1756.

CHALDEAN MAGIC. Lenormant. London, 1847.

CILICIA.   Wm. Burckhardt Barker, M.R.A.S.   London, 1853.
CRATA REPOA.   Paris.   Ant. Bailleul.   1821.

DISSERTATION SUR LE PÉRIPLE de Scylax, et Recherches sur le Nature
ou Culte de Bacchus en Gréce.   Le Philologue.   Tome XVII.
Par Gail.   Paris, 1821.
DRUSES OF THE LEBANON, The.   By George W. Chasseaud.   London,
Bentley, 1855.

EARLY MAN IN BRITAIN.   W. Boyd Dawkins.   London, 1880.
EARTH AND MAN, The.   Arnold Guyot.
EGYPT, The History of.   From Earliest Times till the Conquest by
the Arabs, A.D. 640.   By Samuel Sharpe.   1846.
—— Ancient History of.   By George Rawlinson, M.A.   2 vols.   Lon-
don, 1881.
—— Under the Pharaohs.   By Dr. Henry Brugsch.   2 vols.   London,
1881.
—— Ancient History of.   From the Monuments.   By S. Birch, LL.D.
London, 1880.
EGYPTIAN OBELISKS.   Gorringe.   Folio.   :882.
ENGLAND AND WALES, The Beauties of.   Topographical, Historical
and Descriptive.   Illustrated.   26 vols.   8vo.   London, 1815–18.
Introduction.   J. Norris Brewer.
Vol. I. Bedfordshire, Berkshire, Buckinghamshire.   John Brit-
ton and Edward Wedlake Brayley.
Vol. II. Cambridgeshire, Cheshire, Cornwall.   John Britton and
Edward Wedlake Brayley.
Vol. III. Cumberland, Isle of Man, Derbyshire.   John Britton
and Edward Wedlake Brayley.
Vol. IV. Devonshire, Dorsetshire.   John Britton and Edward
Wedlake Brayley.
Vol. V. Durham, Essex, Glocestershire.   John Britton and Ed-
ward Wedlake Brayley.
Vol. VI. Hampshire, Isle of Wight, Herefordshire.   John Brit-
ton and Edward Wedlake Brayley.
Vol. VII. Hertfordshire, Huntingdonshire, Kent.   Edward
Wedlake Brayley.
Vol. VIII. Kent.   Edward Wedlake Brayley.
Vol. IX. Lancashire, Leicestershire, Lincolnshire.   John Brit-
ton.
Vol. X., Parts I.–V. Middlesex.   Edward Wedlake Brayley.
Vol. XI. Monmouthshire, Norfolk, Northamptonshire.   Rev. J.
Evans and John Britton.

ENGLAND AND WALES, The Beauties of—*Continued.*
    Vol. XII., Part I. Northumberland, Nottinghamshire. Rev. J Hodgson and T. C. Laird.
    Vol. XII., Part II. Oxfordshire, Rutlandshire. Rev. J. Hodgson and T. C. Laird.
    Vol. XIII., Part I. Shropshire, Somersetshire. Rev. J. Nightingale.
    Vol. XIII., Part II. Staffordshire. Rev. J. Nightingale.
    Vol. XIV. Suffolk, Surrey, Sussex. Frederic Shoberl.
    Vol. XV., Part I. Wiltshire, Westmoreland. John Britton.
    Vol. XV., Part II. Warwickshire, Worcestershire. John Britton.
    Vol. XVI. Yorkshire. John Bigland.
    Vol. XVII. North Wales. Rev. J. Evans.
    Vol. XVIII. South Wales. Thomas Rees.
ESSAY ON THE MYSTERIES OF ELEUSIS. Ouvaroff. Translated by Price. [2 copies.] 2 vols.
ETRUSCAN RESEARCHES. Taylor. London, 1874.

FLINT CHIPS. A Guide to Pre-Historic Archæology. By Edward T. Stevens. London, 1870.
FOOT-PRINTS OF VANISHED RACES IN THE MISSISSIPPI VALLEY. By A. J. Conant, A.M. 1879.
FOSBROKE'S ENCYCLOPEDIA OF ANTIQUITIES. 2 vols. 4to. London, 1825.

GAIL. Le Philologue. Année 1825, Nos. I. and II. Les Mystères d'Eleusis. Paris.
GALÉRIE MYTHOLOGIQUE. Par A. L. Millin. 2 vols. À Paris, 1811.
GEOGRAPHY OF HERODOTUS. By James Rennell. 2 vols. London, 1830.
GLASGOW ARCHÆOLOGICAL SOCIETY, Transactions of the. Part I., Vol. II.; Part II., Vol. II.
GREAT PYRAMID, Our Inheritance in the. By G. Piazzi Smith. London, 1880.
GREEKS AND ROMANS, The Life of the. Guhl and Koner. London.
GRONOVIUS, JACOBUS. Thesaurus Græcarum Antiquitatum. 13 vols. Folio. 1699.
GRUTERUS, JANA. Corpus Inscriptionum. 4 vols. Folio. Amstelædami, 1707.

HERCULANÆUM ET POMPÉII. Recueil Général des Peintures, Bronzes, Mosaïques, etc. Par H. Roux, ainé. 8 vols. Paris, 1875.

HOLLOWAY'S ORIGINALS. 2 vols. Oxford, 1751.
HONE'S WORKS. Every Day Book. 2 vols. London
 Year Book. London.
 Table Book. London.

IAMBLICHUS. On the Mysteries. Thomas Taylor. Chiswick, 1821.
IBERNIA PHŒNICEA. By Dr. Joachimo Laurentio Villanueva. Dublin,_1831.
ILIOS. City and Country of the Trojans. Schliemann. London, 1880.
INCAS, Histoire des. Par Jean Baudoin. 2 vols. Amsterdam, 1715.

JAPANESE MARKS AND SEALS. By James Lord Bowes. London, 1882.

LETTERS CONCERNING MYTHOLOGY. London, 1748.

METAMORPHOSIS, or the Golden Ass, and other Works of Apuleius. Thomas Taylor. London, 1822.
MIDDLE AGES, Military and Religious Life in the. By Paul Lecroix. London edition.
—— Same. By Paul Lecroix. New York edition.
—— A Literary History of the. Rev. Joseph Berington. London, 1814.
MILLS, CHARLES, Works of. Travels of T. Ducas. 2 vols.
MONTFAUCON. Antiquity Explained. 7 vols. Folio. London, 1721.
MYCENÆ AND TIRYNS. Schliemann. London, 1878.
MYSTERIES OF THE CABIRI. Faber. 2 vols. Oxford, 1803.
MYSTÈRES DE ISIS. Par J. P. Boulage. Paris,.1820.
MYTHS AND SONGS FROM THE SOUTH PACIFIC. Rev. M. W. Gill. London, 1876.

NEW RESEARCHES IN ANCIENT HISTORY. By C. F. Volney. New York, 1856.
NINEVEH AND BABYLON. Layard. 1869.

ŒUVRES DU ROI RÉNÉ. Quatrebarbes. Royal Folio. Angers, 1845.
OLD JAPAN, Tales of. By A. B. Mitford. London, 1876.
ORIGIN OF LANGUAGE AND MYTHS. Kavanagh. London, 1871.
ORKNEYINGA SAGA, The. Anderson. Edinburgh, 1873.

PITISCUS, SAMUEL. Lexicon, Antiquitatum Romanarum. 3 vols. Folio. 1737.
POPULAR ANTIQUITIES, Observations on. By John Brand. London

PRE-HISTORIC MAN. Dr. Daniel Wilson. 2 vols. London, 1876.
PRE-HISTORIC EUROPE. James Geikie. London, 1881.
PRE-HISTORIC PHASES. Westropp. London, 1872.
PRIMITIVE MANNERS AND CUSTOMS. J. A. Farrar. London, 1879.

RECORDS OF THE PAST. Being English translations of Assyrian and Egyptian Monuments. 12 vols. London.
ROMAN AND GREEK ANTIQUITIES, Dictionary of. Rich. London 1874.
ROYAL ASIATIC SOCIETY OF GREAT BRITAIN AND IRELAND, Journal of the. Parts I. and II. Vol. XIX.
RUDE STONE MONUMENTS. Fergusson. London, 1872.

SACRED BOOKS OF THE EAST. Edited by F. Max Müller.
Vol. I. Upanishads. Part I. F. Max Müller.
II. The Sacred Laws. Part I. Apastamba Gautama. By George Bühler.
III. Shu king, Shih king-Hsiâo. James Legge.
IV. The Zend Avesta. Part I. J. Darmesteter.
V. Pahlavi Texts. Part I. E. W. West.
VI. The Qur'Ân. Part I. E. H. Palmer.
VII. The Institutes of Vishṇu. By Julius Jolly.
VIII. Bhagavadgîtâ Sanatsugâtîya and Anugîtâ. K. T. Telang.
IX. The Qur'Ân. Part II.
X. Dhammapada. Müller.
Sutta-Nipata. V. Fausböll.
XI. Buddhist Suttas. T. W. Rhys Davids.
XII. Satapatha Brâhmanya. Part I., Books I.–II. Julius Eggeling.
XIII. Vinaya Texts. Part I. The Patimokka. By T. W. Rhys Davids and H. Oldenburg.
——— The Mahâvagga. I.–IV. By the same.
XIV. The Sacred Laws. Part II. Vasishtha Bandhâyara. By George Bühler.
XVI. The Yi King. James Legge.
XVII. Vinaya Texts. Part II. The Mahâvagga. V.–X. By T. W. Rhys Davids and H. Oldenburg.
The Kullavagga. I.–III. By the same.
XVIII. Pahlavi Texts. Part II. E. W. West.
XIX. The Fo-Sho-Hing-Tsan-King. Samuel Beal.
XXIII. The Zend Avesta. Part II. J. Darmesteter.
SANTA FÉ AND NEW MEXICO. By Simpson. Washington, 1852.

Scotland, Society of Antiquaries of, Proceedings of.   12 vols.   1851–1878.   Edinburgh.
—— Second Series.   5 vols.   1878 to 1883.   Edinburgh.
Scottish Monuments and Tombstones.   Charles Rogers.   2 vols.   London, 1871.
Sethos.   Par l'Abbé Terrasson.   6 vols.   Paris, 1813.
Sports and Pastimes.   Strutt.   2 vols.   [1 vol.   2 copies.]   London.
Symbolica Dianæ Ephesiæ Statua.   Folio.   Romæ, 1688.

Traditions of the Most Ancient Times.   By Wm. Howitt.   2 vols.   London, 1839.

World Before the Deluge, The.   By Louis Figuier.

CLASS IV.

TRAVELS.

.

.

CLASS IV.

ADIRONDACK, The, or Life in the Woods. J. T. Headley. New York, 1849.

ANACHARSIS'S TRAVELS IN GREECE. By the Abbé Barthelémy. 8 vols. London, 1798.

ARCTIC EXPEDITION, Narrative of C. F. Hall's Second. 1864–'69.

ARCTIC EXPLORATIONS. Dr. Kane. Second Grinnell Expedition. 2 vols. 1857.

ATLANTIC AND TRANS-ATLANTIC. By Capt. MacKinnon, R.N. 1852.

CALIFORNIA AND OREGON, Pictorial Travels in. Farnham, 1852.

CAROLANA, Called Florida by the Spaniards, Description of. By Daniel Coxe. London, 1722.

CHURCHILL'S MOUNT LEBANON. 3 vols.

CLOUDS IN THE EAST. By Valentine Baker. London, 1876.

COLUMBIA RIVER. Scenes and Adventures. By Ross Cox. 2 vols. London, 1832.

EGYPT, ARABIA PETRÆA AND HOLY LAND. By an American. [2 vols. in 1.] New York, 1844.

EL-MEDINAH AND MECCAH. Burton. New York, 1856.

ENGLISHWOMAN IN AMERICA. By Sarah M. Maury. London, 1848.

EXPEDITION TO AFRICA. Alexander. [2 vols. in 1.] Philadelphia, 1838.

EXPEDITION DOWN THE ZUNI AND COLORADO. Sitgreaves. Central Route to the Pacific. Beale. 1854.

FAR WEST, The, or a Tour beyond the Mountains. By Edmund Flagg. 2 vols. New York, 1838.

HOCHELAGA, or England in the New World. Eliot Warburton. London, 1854.

HUNTER'S LIFE IN SOUTH AFRICA. Cumming. 2 vols. New York, 1850.

IRELAND, The Stranger in. A Tour in the year 1805. By John Carr.

LAMARTINE'S NARRATIVE.   Philadelphia, 1836.
LAND OF THE MIDNIGHT SUN.   Du Chaillu.   2 vols.   New York, 1882
LIFE OF GERMANY.   Wm. Howitt.   Philadelphia, 1843.
LIFE ON THE LAKES.   [2 vols. in 1.]   New York, 1836.

MAHMOUD.   Narrative of Eastern Life.   [2 vols. in 1.]
McLELLAN'S JOURNAL.   Isaac McLellan, jr.   Boston, 1834
MISSISSIPPI VALLEY, Travels in Central Portions of the.   H. R. Schoolcraft.

NEWFOUNDLAND, in 1842.   Bonnycastle.   2 vols.   London.
NILE BOAT, The.   By Wm. H. Bartlett.   New York.

OLD AND NEW ENGLAND.   Alfred Bunn.   London, 1853.

PACIFIC TOURIST AND GUIDE.   Henry T. Williams.   New York.
PICTURES OF SCANDINAVIA, in 1859.   Wm. Hurton.

RAMBLES IN CANADA.   Mrs. Jameson.   2 vols.   New York, 1839.
ROCKY MOUNTAINS.   Oregon and California.   Fremont.   1845.
—— By Washington Irving.   Philadelphia, 1837.

SANTA FÉ.   Kendall.   2 vols.   New York, 1844.
SCOTLAND, A Tour Through, or Caledonian Sketches.   By John Carr. 1809.
SIBERIA, ORIENTAL AND WESTERN.   By Thomas William Atkinson. London, 1858.
SPORT AND TRAVEL, or the Two Americas.   By Major Sir Rose Lambert Price, Bart.   Illustrated.
ST. PETERSBURG, etc., by Von Tietz.   New York, 1836.
SYRIA, HOLY LAND, ASIA MINOR.   Illustrated.   4to.

THROUGH THE DARK CONTINENT.   Stanley.   2 vols.   New York, 1879.
TRAITS OF TRAVEL.   Grattan.   [2 vols. in 1.]   New York, 1829.
TRAVELS IN THE CHINESE EMPIRE.   M. Huc.   2 vols.   1856.
TRAVELS TO THE CITY OF THE CALIPHS.   Wellsted.   Philadelphia, 1841.
TRAVELS RELATING TO PARTS OF BARBARY AND THE LEVANT.   Thos. Shaw.   1757.
TWELVE YEARS IN CANTERBURY, NEW ZEALAND.   Mrs. Charles Thomson.

VOLNEY, C. H.   Climate and Soil of the U. S.   Account of Florida, etc.; Maps, etc.   London, 1804.

CLASS V.

LITERATURE.

CLASS V.

ADVENTURES OF A YOUNGER SON. By Trelawney. New York, 1832.

ADVERTISING, A History of, from the Earliest Times. Henry Sampson. London, 1874.

À L'ABRI. N. P. Willis. New York, 1839.

ALPHABET, The Landa. A Spanish Fabrication. By Philipp J. J Valentine. Pamphlet. 1880.

AMBROSIO DE LETINEZ, or the First Texan Novel. By A. T. Myrthe. 2 vols. 1842.

ASMODEUS AT LARGE. By Bulwer. Philadelphia, 1883.

AUGUSTUS, Memoirs of the Court of. Thomas Blackwell. 3 vols. 1753.

AUTOCRAT OF THE BREAKFAST TABLE. Holmes.

BACKBONE. By Edward H. Dixon, M.D. New York.

BENCH AND BAR [The]. [2 vols. in 1.]

BLIND MAN'S OFFERING. By B. B. Bowen. New York, 1855.

BRITISH SENATE. Philadelphia, 1838.

BRITISH SPY. William Wirt.

BURNT NJAL, The Story of, or Life in Iceland in the 10th Century G. W. Dasant. 2 vols.

CALIFORNIA SKETCHES. By O. P. Fitzgerald. 5th edition. Nashville, Tenn., 1882.

CAPTAIN CANÒT. By Brantz Mayer. 1854.

CAPTAINS OF THE ROMAN REPUBLIC. By H. W. Herbert.

CARLETON'S WORKS. By William Carleton. Collier's unabridged edition. Illustrated. 3 vols.

CASKET OF REMINISCENCES. By Henry S. Foote.

CAVALIERS OF VIRGINIA, or the Recluse of Jamestown. 2 vols.

CHAMBERS' ENCYCLOPÆDIA. 10 vols.

CHAP-BOOKS OF THE EIGHTEENTH CENTURY. By John Ashton. London, 1882.

CHEVALIERS DES SEPT MONTAGNES. By De Bock. Translated from the German. 3 vols. Metz, 1800.

CITIZEN OF A REPUBLIC.   Translated and edited by C. Edwards Lester.   New York, 1845.

CIVILIZATION AND PRIMITIVE CONDITION OF MAN, Origin of.   Sir J. Lubbock.   1882.

COMPANION OF THE TOUR OF FRANCE.   By George Sand.   Translated by Matilda M. Hays.   2 vols.   1847.

COOPER, J. FENNIMORE, Complete Works of.   32 vols.

Precaution.	Lionel Lincoln.	Deerslayer.
The Spy.	Mercedes of Castile.	Mohicans.
The Pilot.	The Bravo.	Pathfinder.
Red Rover.	Headsman.	Pioneers.
Water-Witch.	Heidenmauer.	The Prairie.
Wing and Wing.	Ways of the Hour.	Wyandotte.
Two Admirals.	Afloat and Ashore.	Red Skins.
Sea Lions.	Homeward Bound.	Wish-ton-Wish.
Jack Tar.	Home as Found.	Oak-Openings.
Crater.	Monikins.	Satanstoe.
Miles Wallingford.	Chainbearer.	

CORINNE, ou l'Italie.   Par Mme. La Baronne de Staël.   2 vols.   Paris, 1831.

CREDULITIES, Past and Present.   By William Jones, F.S.A.   London, 1880.

CURIOSITIES OF STREET LITERATURE.   4to.   London, Reeves & Turner, 1871.

DAY-SPRING, or Diurnal of Youth.   Dobbin.   Liverpool, 1852.

DE BALZAC, H.   Les Contes Drolatiques.   3 vols.   Paris, 1879.

DICKENS, CHARLES, Works of.   Carleton's illustrated edition.   15 vols.

Pickwick Papers.	Bleak House.	Hard Times.
Expectations.	Dombey & Son.	David Copperfield.
Italy.	Christmas Books.	Barnaby Rudge.
Little Dorrit.	Tale of Two Cities.	Edwin Drood.
Martin Chuzzlewit.	Oliver Twist.	Old Curiosity Shop.
Nicholas Nickleby.	England.	Uncommercial Trav'r.
Our Mutual Friend.	Sketches.	Miscellaneous.

DICK SANDS.   By Jules Verne.

DISRAELI, BENJAMIN [Lord Beaconsfield], Works of, viz.:

Lothair.   New York, 1870.

Tancred ; the Wondrous Tale of Alroy.   The Rise of Iskander.   London, 1859.

Venetia.   Philadelphia, 1837.

Vivian Grey ; Ixion in Heaven ; The Infernal Marriage ; Popanilla ; Count Alarcos.   London, 1859.

DOMINIE'S LEGACY, The. By John Galt. [2 vols. in 1.]
DREAM GOD, The. By John Cunningham.
DRUSES OF THE LEBANON, The. By George W. Chasseaud. London,
Bentley, 1855.

EAST, The. A paper read before the Washington Literary Society.
By M. F. Morris.
EIGHTEENTH CENTURY STUDIES. Essays. By Francis Hitchman.
London, 1881.
ELIOT, SIR JOHN, The Works of. 1590–1632. Printed for private cir-
culation only, for Dr. A. B. Grosart, by Elliot Stock. London.
An Apology for Socrates and Negotium Posterorum. 2 vols.
De Jure Majestatis. The Letter Book. 2 vols.
The Monarchie of Man. 2 vols. 2 copies. 1879–1882.
EMANUEL PHILIBERT. Alexander Dumas.
ENGLAND AND ITS PEOPLE, First Impressions of. Hugh Miller.
ENGLISH LITERATURE, History of. By H. A. Taine. 4 vols. Lon-
don, 1880.
—— Same. By H. Van Laun. 2 vols. London.
ENGLISH MEN OF LETTERS. Edited by John Morley. 5 vols.
ERRATA. John Neal. [2 vols. in 1.] 1823.
EVENINGS ON THE THAMES, or Serene Hours. By Kenelm Henry
Digby. 2 vols. London, 1864.
EXPERIENCES OF A BARRISTER. By Warren Warner. New York,
1852.

FACTS, The. By George Francis Train. 1860.
FINGER-RING LORE. By William Jones, F.S.A. London, 1877.
FLOWERS AND FRUITS FROM THE WILDERNESS, or 36 years in Texas.
By Z. N. Morrell. 1872.
FORREST, EDWIN, Life of. Reminiscences, etc. By James Rees.
[Colley Cibber.]
FUN, Ancient and Modern. By Dr. Maurice Davies. 2 vols. Lon-
don, 1878.

GADDINGS WITH PRIMITIVE PEOPLE. By W. A. Baillie Grohman. 2
vols. London, 1879.
GLEANINGS IN EUROPE. By an American. Philadelphia, 1837.
GOLDEN DREAMS AND LEADEN REALITIES. By Ralph Raven. New
York, 1853.
GREENE, ROBERT, Works of. [The Huth Library. By Dr. A. B. Gro-
sart. For private circulation only.] 12 vols. [Vol. I. not yet
out.] Elliott Stock. London.

GREENE, ROBERT, Works of—*Continued.*

Vol. II. Mamillia, Parts I. and II., and Anatomie of Flatterie.
1583-1593.

III. Myrrovr of Modestie; Morando; The Tritameron of
Loue [Parts I. and II.], and Arbasto; The Anatomie of Fortune. 1584-1587.

IV. The Carde of Fancie; The Debate betweene Follie and
Loue; Pandosto; The Triumph of Time, 1584-7.
Notes and Illustrations, etc.

V. Planetomachia; Penelope's Web; The Spanish Mas-
querado, 1585-9; Notes and Illustrations, etc.

VI. Menaphon; Camillus Alarum to Slumbering Euphues;
Euphues, His Censure to Philautus, 1587-9; Notes
and Illustrations, etc.

VII. Perimedes, the Blacke-smith; Ciceronis Amor, or Tul-
lies Loue; and the Royal Exchange. 1589-90.

VIII. Greene's Neuer Too Late, and Francesco's Fortunes.
1590.

IX. Alcida; Greene's Metamorphosis; Greene's Mourning
Garment; Greene's Farewell to Folly. 1588-91.

X. A Notable Discouery of Coosnage; The Second Part
of Conny-Catching; The Thirde and Last Parte of
Conny-Catching; A Disputation between a Hec
and Shee Conny-Catcher. 1591-2.

XI. The Black Booke's Messenger; The Defence of Conny-
Catching; Philomela; The Lady Fitzwater's Night-
ingale; A Quippe for an Upstart Courtier. 1592.

XII. Orpharion; Greene's Groatsworth of Wit; The Re-
pentance of Robert Greene; Greene's Vision.
1592-1599.

GRÈVES OUVRIÈRES, Des. By J. Danby. Bruxelles, 1879.

GROTESQUE AND ARABESQUE, Tales of the. By Edgar A. Poe. 1840.

GULLIVER'S TRAVELS. By Dean Swift. And Life of the Author, by
W. C. Taylor, LL.D.

HANSFORD. A Tale of Bacon's Rebellion. By St. George Tucker.
1857.

HAW-HO-NOO, or Records of a Tourist. The Prairie Scout. [2 vols.
in 1.] Charles Lanman.

HEINRICH HEINE'S PICTURES OF TRAVEL. Translated from the German, by Charles Godfrey Leland.

HERBERT, HON. and REV. WILLIAM, The Works of. H. G. Bohn. 2
vols. London, 1842

HOMO SUM. By Georg Ebers. From the German. By Clara Bell. [2 vols. in 1.]

HORSESHOE ROBINSON. By J. P. Kennedy.

HOWARD QUEEN, The. A Romance of History. By Edmund Flagg.

HYPATIA, or New Foes with an Old Face. By Charles Kingsley, jr.

IMPRESSIONS OF AMERICA. By Tyrone Power. Philadelphia, 1836.

IRVING, WASHINGTON, Complete Works of. Edition of 1881. 12 vols.

Alhambra.	Knickerbocker.
Astoria.	Salmagundi.
Bonneville's Adventures.	Spanish Papers.
Life of Columbus.	Sketch Book.
Crayon Sketches.	Tales of a Traveller.
Life of Goldsmith.	Life of Washington.
Mahomet.	Wolfert's Roost.

JEAFFRESON'S BOOK ABOUT THE TABLE. John Cordy Jeaffreson. [2 vols. in 1.] London, 1875.

JONSON, BEN, Works of. By William Gifford.

KEEP COOL. By John Neal. 1817.

KNAVES AND FOOLS. By Edward M. Whitty. New York, 1857.

KONINGSMARK. Paulding. [2 vols. in 1.]

LAVENGRO. George Borrow.

LEAVES FROM MARGARET SMITH'S JOURNAL, in 1778–'79. Boston, 1849.

LEISURE-TIME STUDIES. Chiefly Biological. By Andrew Wilson.

LES MISÉRABLES. By Victor Hugo. Complete.

LINCOLN, ABRAHAM, Tributes of the Nations to. Washington, D. C., 1866.

LOS PURITANOS DE ESCOCIA. Scott; en Castellano. 1838.

LOST LEONORE. A Novel. Mayne Reid.

LOW LIFE DEEPS. By James Greenwood. London, 1876.

MARRYAT'S DIARY. First series, 1839. Second series, 1840. 2 vols.

MEMOIRS OF ARTHUR COLLIER. London, Benson, 1837.

MISCELLANEA CURIOSA. 3 vols. London, 1708.

NASHE, THOMAS, Works of. [The Huth Library. By Dr. A. B. Grosart. For private circulation only.] Elliott Stock. London.

Vol. I. Memorial Introduction—Biographical: Anatomie of Absurditie: Martin Mar-Prelate Tractates: i. A Counter-Cuffe to Martin Junior; ii. The Returne of the Renowned Cavaliere Pasquill; iii. The Month's Mind; iv. The First Part of Pasquil's Apologie. 1589–90.

NASHE, THOMAS, Works of—*Continued*.
>   Vol. II. Pierce Penilesse, His Supplication to the Diuell. Harvey-Greene Tractates : i. A Wonderfull, Strange, and Miraculous Astrologicall Prognostication; ii. Strange Newes of the Intercepting Certaine Letters. 1592.
>   Vol. III. Haue with you to Saffron-Walden ; Terrors of the Night. 1594–96.
>   Vol. IV. Christ's Teares ouer Ierusalem. 1593.
>   Vol. V. The Vnfortvnate Traveller : Nashes Lenten Stuffe. 1594–9

NEW AMERICA. Hepworth Dixon. 1867.

NEW ENGLAND LEGENDS AND FOLK LORE. Samuel Adams Drake. Boston, 1884.

NEW REMARKS ON LONDON, or a Survey of the Cities of London and Westminster. London, 1732.

NICK OF THE WOODS. By Dr. Robt. M. Bird. [2 copies.]

NOTIONS OF THE AMERICANS. By a Traveling Bachelor [James Fenimore Cooper]. Philadelphia, 1833.

O'FLANAGAN'S IMPRESSIONS. 2 vols. London, 1837.

OLD BOOK COLLECTOR'S MISCELLANY. Vol. I. London, 1871.

OLD ROME AND NEW ITALY. Castelar. Translated by Mrs. Arnold.

OLD TONY AND HIS MASTER. By Desmos.

PERSONAL PORTRAITS. Scenes and Adventures. By John Esten Cooke.

PETER SIMPLE. By Capt. Marryatt.

. PILGRIMS OF WALSINGHAM. Agnes Strickland. [2 vols. in 1.]

PRENTICEIANA. From writings of George D. Prentice. Edited by G. W. Griffin. Philadelphia, 1871.

PRINTZ HALL. A Record of New Sweden.

PROBUS. By Dr. Ware. [2 vols. in 1.]

PROGRESS AND POVERTY. By Henry George. New York.

PUBLIC CHARACTERS. By Lord Brougham. 1839. [2 vols. in 1.]

QUEEN ANNE, Social Life in the Reign of. By John Ashton. 2 vols. London, 1882.

QUODLIBET, Annals of. By John P. Kennedy. Philadelphia, 1840.

RAILTON, JOHN, or Read and Think. By Wm. Robson.

RANDOLPH. By John Neal. [2 vols. in 1.] 1823.

RANDOM SHOTS FROM A RIFLEMAN. Capt. J. Kincaid.

RECOLLECTIONS OF ALCOBAÇA AND BATALHA. Beckford. Philadelphia, 1835.

RECOLLECTIONS OF A LITERARY LIFE. By Mary Russell Mitford. New York, 1852.

REMINISCENCES OF A NONAGENARIAN. Sarah Anna Emery [of New-
bury, Massachusetts.] 1879.
REMINISCENCES OF A RANGER, or Early Times in Southern California.
By Major Horace Bell. 1881.
ROB OF THE BOWL. A Legend of St. Inigoes. By John P. Ken-
nedy. 2 vols.
ROMANCES OF THE EAST. Comte de Gobineau.

SABLE CLOUD, The. Adams. 1861.
SALATHIEL THE IMMORTAL. By Rev. George Croly. London.
SCHOOL DAYS AT RUGBY. By an Old Boy. Boston, 1858.
SCRAPS AND SKETCHES GATHERED TOGETHER. By Sir Lascelles
Wraxall, Bart. 2 vols. London, 1865.
SEVEN CHAMPIONS OF CHRISTENDOM, The Renowned History of.
London, 1808.
SIGN BOARDS, History of. By Larwood and Hotten. London, 1866.
SIMMS, W. GILMORE, Prose Works of. 10 vols. New York, 1882.

Eutaw.	Vasconselos.	Westward Ho.
The Partisan.	Wigwam and Cabin.	Guy Rivers.
Mellichampe.	Beauchampe.	Richard Hurdis.
Katherine Walton.	Confession.	Border Beagles.
The Scout.	Yemassee.	Charlemont.

SKETCH BOOK OF CHARACTER. [2 vols. in 1.] Philadelphia, 1835.
SOCIETY IN AMERICA. By Harriet Martineau. New York, 1837.
SOUTHBROOKE. By Sutton S. Scott. Columbus, Ga., 1880.
SPARE HOURS. By John Browne. 1864.
STANLEY, or The Recollections of a Man of the World. [2 vols. in one.]
STATESMEN OF AMERICA IN 1846. By Sarah Mytton Maury. London.
1847.
STERNE, LAURENCE, Works of.
STUDIES IN LITERATURE. By G. W. Griffin. Philadelphia, 1871.
SWALLOW BARN. By John P. Kennedy.

TALES, ESSAYS AND SKETCHES. By Robert Macnish. 2 vols. Lon-
don, 1844.
TALES OF A VOYAGER TO THE ARCTIC OCEAN. [2 vols. in 1.] Phila-
delphia, 1827.
TAMAR AND THE TAVY, The Borders of the. Their Natural History,
Customs, etc. By Mrs. Bray. 2 vols.
THEATRES OF PARIS, The. By J. Brander Matthews. London, 1880.
THREE ERAS OF NEW ENGLAND. George Lunt. 1857.
THUGS OF INDIA, The. By Capt. Sleeman. Philadelphia, 1839.
TRAITS AND STORIES OF THE IRISH PEASANTRY. By William Carle-
ton. London.

TROUBADOURS, The. By Francis Hueffer. London, 1878.

VILLA EDEN. The Country House on the Rhine. Auerbach.

VOICE TO AMERICA. Edward Walker. New York, 1855.

WALTON AND COTTON'S ANGLER. Notes by Sir Harris Nicolas. London, 1875.

WAR OF THE BACHELORS. A Story of the Crescent City. 1882.

WARNER'S LITERARY RECOLLECTIONS. 2 vols. London, 1830.

WARNER'S TOPOGRAPHICAL WORKS. 5 vols. London, 1793–1802.

> Vol. I. Tour through Hampshire.
> II. Western Counties and Cornwall.
> III. Tour in the Northern Counties.
> IV. Walks through Wales.
> V. Isle of Wight. Excursions to Bath.

WAVERLEY NOVELS. Routledge Edition. 13 vols. London.

Waverley.	Tales of a Grandfather.	Kenilworth.
Antiquary.	Fortunes of Nigel.	Pirate.
Heart of Mid-Lothian.	Anne of Geierstein.	Peveril of the Peak.
Woodstock.	St. Ronan's Well.	Surgeon's Daughter.
Count Robert of Paris.	Black Dwarf.	Castle Dangerous.
The Betrothed.	Legend of Montrose.	Ivanhoe.
Rob Roy.	Bride of Lammermoor.	Talisman.
Old Mortality.	Guy Mannering.	Monastery.
Abbot.	Red Gauntlet.	Fair Maid of Perth.
	Quentin Durward.	Glossary.

WAYSIDE BRIEFS. By John M. Miller. Baltimore, 1875.

WHAT TO OBSERVE, or the Traveler's Remembrancer. By Col. J. R. Jackson. London, 1845.

WILD SPORTS. By Lieut.-Col. Napier. Western Prairies; American in Paris, by Jules Janin. Ireland, by J. G. Kohl. New Orleans as I Found It; Camp Life of a Volunteer in Mexico.

WOOD RANGERS, The. By Mayne Reid.

WORKINGMAN'S WAY IN THE WORLD. By a Journeyman Printer. New York, 1854.

YELLOWPLUSH CORRESPONDENCE. Thackeray. Philadelphia, 1831.

ZENOBIA. By Dr. Ware.

ZOLA, ÉMILE, Novels by. 16 vols.

A Mad Love.	Ladies' Paradise.	Pot-Bouille.
Claude's Confession.	Magdalen Ferat.	The Abbé's Tempta-
Conquest of Plassans.	Markets of Paris.	tion.
Girl in Scarlet.	Mysteries of the Court	Thérèse Raquin.
Hélène.	of Louis Napoleon.	The Rougon - Mac-
In the Whirlpool.	Mysteries of Mar-	quart Family.
La Belle Lisa.	seilles.	

CLASS VI.

MAGAZINES.

CLASS VI.

AMERICAN QUARTERLY REVIEW. [Except Vol. XI.] 22 vols. 1827–1837.

ANTIQUARY, The. A Magazine devoted to a Study of the Past. 1880–4. 9 vols.

BENTLEY'S MISCELLANY. American edition. 1838.

EAST ANGLIAN, The, or Notes and Queries. 3 vols. London, 1864–1869.

HARPER'S MAGAZINE. June, 1850, to November, 1858. Vols. I. to XVII. 17 vols.

HISTORICAL MAGAZINE, and Notes and Queries, concerning Antiquities of America. August, September, October, 1866.

NEW YORK REVIEW. Vols. I., II., IV., V., VI. 5 vols.

NORTH AMERICAN MAGAZINE. Vols. I. and VI. 2 vols.

NORTH AMERICAN REVIEW. Vols. XIII., XV., XIX. 3 vols.

OVERLAND MONTHLY, The. July, 1868, to June, 1874, inclusive. San Francisco, California. 15 vols.

QUARTERLY REVIEW. March, 1822, December, 1824.
—— June, 1827, January, 1828.

SIMMS' REVIEW. Vol. I.

WESTERN JOURNAL. 1853–4, and 1854. 2 vols.

CLASS VII.

POLITICAL AND LEGAL.

CLASS VII.

ADAMS'S REPUBLIC. A Defence of the Constitutions of Government of the U. S. A. John Adams. 3 vols. London, Stockdale, 1794.

DÉFENSE DU TESTAMENT DE McDONOUGH. Argument by Alex. Grailhe. New Orleans, 1852.
DEFENSA DE MEXICO. Manuel Aspiroz. Mexico, 1878.

EWING, THOMAS, of Ohio, Memoir of. By Ellen Ewing Sherman.

JEFFERSON'S MANUAL OF PARLIAMENTARY PRACTICE. 1812.

LOUISIANA, Notes on the Civil Code of. By Albert Pike. [MSS.] Small 4to.

MANUAL DE LA CONSTITUÇION DE LOS ESTADOS UNIDOS. J. Carlos Mexia. 1874.
MEMORIAL ADDRESSES. Life and Character of—
    Carpenter, Matthew Hale, Wisconsin. January 26, 1882.
    Clay, Henry, and Webster, Daniel.
    Garfield, James G., Ohio. By James G. Blaine. February 27.
    Garfield, Funeral ceremonies in honor of. New Orleans, 1881.
    Hill, Benjamin Harvey, Georgia. January 25, 1883.
    Williams, Alpheus S., Michigan. 1879.

PROGRESS OF NATIONS. Ezra C. Seaman. 1852.

RANDOLPH, JOHN, Speech of, in 1806, on Gregg's Resolution for a Non-importation of British Goods.

STATE DEPARTMENT. Papers relating to Foreign Relations. President's Message. 1872.
—— Same. 1879.
SUPREME COURT OF THE U. S., Arguments before the. By Albert Pike.

THOUGHTS ON CERTAIN POLITICAL QUESTIONS.   By a Looker-on.
[Albert Pike].   Washington, 1859.

TYRANNY UNMASKED.   By John Taylor, of Virginia.   1822.

UNITED STATES, Constitution of the.   Hickey.   Baltimore, 1878.

WARD, MATT. F., Trial of.   1854.

White Acre vs. Black Acre.   By J. G., Esq. [William M. Burwell].
Richmond, Va., 1856.

WHITNEY'S DEFENCE OF THE AMERICAN POLICY.

WYANDOTTE GOVERNMENT.   An Address by J. W. Powell.   Boston,
August, 1880.

CLASS VIII.

PHILOLOGICAL.

CLASS VIII.

ADVIS ET DEVIS DES LENGVES : Svivis de Lamartigenée.   Par François Bonivard, Ancien Prieur de St. Victor.   Reprint, Genève, 1865.

CRATYLUS.   The New.   Donaldson.   London, 1850.
CUNEORUM CLAVIS.   The primitive alphabet and language of the ancient ones of Earth.   J. H. Hemsworth.   London, 1875.

DICTIONARY.   Archaic, from the Egyptian, Assyrian and Etruscan Monuments and Papyri.   By W. R. Cooper.   London, 1882.
——— Johnson and Walker's.   Boston, 1827.
——— Etymological, of the English Language.   Rev. W. Walter Skeat. 4to.   London, 1882.
——— The Imperial, of the English Language.   By John Ogilvie. 4 vols.   London, 1882.
DICTIONNAIRE D'ARGOT.   Paris, 1880.
DICTIONARIUM SCOTO-CELTICUM.   A Dictionary of the Gaelic Language.   By the Highland Society of Scotland.   2 vols.   4to. William Blackwood.   Edinburgh, 1828.

ENGLISH SURNAMES, their Sources and Significations.   Bardsley. London, 1875.

GRAMMAIRE ITALIENNE.   Zotti.   1823.
GRAMMAR, English and Portuguese.   London, 1751.
——— Greek.   Goodwin's.
——— Spanish.   Exercises, etc.

INDIA.   Past and Present.   By Shoshee Chunder Dutt.   London, 1880.
INDIAN LANGUAGES, American, Introduction to the Study of.   J. W. Powell.   1880.

LANGUAGE, Introduction to the Science of.   A. H. Sayce.   2 vols. London, 1880.

13

LANGUAGE, Laws of, Primitive and Universal. Callistus Augustus and Frederic Pincott.

—— Origin and Progress of.   By Jas. Burnet [Lord Monboddo]. 6 vols. 1774–1792.

LINGUISTIC NOTES. By Albert S. Gatschet. Pamphlet. Washington, D. C.

PURITAN NOMENCLATURE, Curiosities of.   Charles W. Bardsley. London, 1880.

WORD BOOK OF THE ROMANY. By George Borrow. London, 1874.

WORDS, FACTS AND PHRASES. By Eliezer Edwards.

CLASS IX.

SCIENTIFIC

CLASS IX.

ABSOLUTE MONEY. A New System of National Finance. Britton A. Hill.

ANTHROPOLOGICAL SOCIETY, Abstract of Transactions of the. J. W. Powell. Pamphlet. 1881.

ASTRONOMY. J. Rambosson. Translated by Pitman. London.

—— Myths and Marvels of. By Richard A. Proctor. 1880.

ASTRONOMICAL EXPEDITION TO THE SOUTHERN HEMISPHERE. Lieut. Gilliss, Navy Department. 4 vols.

BABY WORLDS. An Essay on the Silent Members of our Solar Household. J. von Gumpach. London, 1863.

BIRDS OF THE COLORADO VALLEY. Department of the Interior. Coues.

BIRDS OF THE NORTHWEST. Department of the Interior. Coues.

BRIDGING THE MISSISSIPPI. Between St. Louis and St. Paul. Warren, 1878.

CHEMICAL HISTORY OF A CANDLE. M. Faraday. London.

EASY STAR LESSONS. Richard A. Proctor. London, 1882.

ECLIPSE OF THE SUN, TOTAL, 1878. Report of the U. S. Naval Observatory.

ELECTRICITY AND MAGNETISM. Physical Treatise on. By J. E. H. Gordon. 2 vols. 1880.

ENTOMOLOGICAL COMMISSION, U. S. Second Report. 1878–'79.

—— Third Report. 1880–'82.

—— Bulletin of. Nos. 2, 4, 6, 7.

ETHNOLOGICAL SOCIETY OF LONDON, Journal of, 1869. Vol. I.

ETHNOLOGY, Bureau of. Study of Mortuary Customs of North American Indians. H. C. Yarrow.

—— Annual Report, 1879–'80. J. W. Powell.

—— Annual Report, 1881. J. W. Powell.

EXPANSE OF HEAVEN, The. Richard A. Proctor. London.

EXPLORATIONS AND SURVEYS FOR SHIP CANAL. Tehuantepec Route. Shufeldt. Navy Department.
—— for a Route to the Pacific. Williamson, 1855.
—— and Surveys from the Mississippi to the Pacific Ocean. War Department. 13 vols.
EXPLORATION OF THE COLORADO RIVER OF THE WEST. Powell, 1869–'72.
—— of the Red River. Marcy, 1854.
—— and Surveys for Inter-oceanic Ship Canals. 1875. Panama, Lull. Napipi, Collins.

FISH COMMISSION, The. Report of, 1877–'78.
FORTIFICATIONS OF TO-DAY, The. Board of Engineers, U. S. A. 4to. 1883.

GEOGRAPHICAL SURVEYS, Lieut. Geo. M. Wheeler. War Dep't. viz: Astronomy [Part II.]. Geology [Part III.]. Palæontology [Part IV.]. Zoology [Part V.]. Botany [VI.]. Maps. 5 vols.
—— U. S. Lake Survey, Primary Triangulation of. Comstock, 1882.
GREAT SALT LAKE EXPEDITION. Stansbury, 1852.

HALL'S ENCYCLOPÆDIA OF ARTS AND SCIENCES. Wm. Henry Hall. 2 vols.
HEAVENLY BODIES, The. Their Nature and Habitability. William Miller. London, 1883.
HUMAN RACE, The. By Louis Figuier. Edited by Robert Wilson.
HUMBOLDT LIBRARY, The. Nos. 1 to 50. 3 vols.

INFINITIES, Our Place Among. Richard A. Proctor. London.
INTERNATIONAL SCIENTIFIC SERIES, The. 13 vols. D. Appleton & Co. Viz.:

The Forms of Water. Tyndall.	Descent of Darwinism. Schmidt.
The Atomic Theory. Wurtz.	Ants, Bees and Wasps. Lubbock.
Volcanoes. Judd.	Chemistry of Light and Photography. Vogel.
Life and Growth of Language. Whitney.	The Nature of Light. Lommel.
Spectrum Analysis. Lockyer.	Formation of Vegetable Mould. Darwin.
The Crayfish. Huxley.	Conflict between Religion and Science. Draper.

The Sun. Young.

ISLAND LIFE. By Alfred Russel Wallace. New York, 1881.
ISTHMUS OF TEHUANTEPEC. Barnard. 1852.

JAPAN EXPEDITION. Commodore M. C. Perry. 3 vols. 4to. 1856.

LANDS OF THE ARID REGION. Powell. 3 vols. [3 copies.] 1879.
LES ÉTOILES, ET LES CURIOSITÉS DU CIEL. Par Camille Flammarion. Páris, 1882.
LES SECRETS DE LA MER. Jules Gos. Paris.
LIGHT, POLARIZATION OF. William Spottiswoode, F.R.S. 1874.

MALARIA, What it Means and How Avoided. Joseph F. Edwards, M.D. 1881.
MEDICAL AND SURGICAL HISTORY OF THE WAR OF THE REBELLION. Medical, Parts 1 and 2. Surgical, Parts 1, 2 and 3. 5 vols.
MEDICAL STATISTICS OF THE PROVOST MARSHAL-GENERAL'S BUREAU. 2 vols.
MESSAGE FROM THE PRESIDENT. 34th Congress, First Session. Illustrations.
MEXICAN BOUNDARY SURVEY. Emory. 3 vols.
MEXICAN PAPER, its Manufacture, Varieties, Employment and Uses. By Ph. J. J. Valentini, Ph.D. Pamphlet. 1881.
MICROSCOPE, Common Objects of the. By Rev. J. G. Wood, M.A., F.L.S., etc. London.
MICROSCOPICAL DIAGNOSIS, Treatise on. Von Duben. Translated by Prof. Louis Bauer, M.D., M.R.C.S. 1859.
MISSISSIPPI RIVER, Discovery and Exploration of the. By J. G. Shea. 1853.
· MULLAN'S MILITARY ROAD REPORT. 1863.
MUSEUM, U. S. NATIONAL, Proceedings of the. 4 vols. 1878–1881.
—— Bulletin of, No. 23. Bibliographies of American Naturalists.
—— Bulletin of, No. 26. Guide to the Flora of Washington and Vicinity.
—— Bulletin of, No. 32. Avifauna Columbiana.

NATIONAL [NAVAL] OBSERVATORY. Total Eclipse, July 29, 1878.
NATURÆ. TRACTATUS SECUNDUS DE NATURÆ SIMIA. Robert Fludd. 1618.
NATURAL HISTORY OF PLANTS. By H. Baillon. 2 vols. London, 1872.
NAVIGATION AND ASTRONOMY, Tables of. Don Manuel Sans.
NAVY DEPARTMENT. Publications by the Hydrographic Office, Bureau of Navigation, viz.:

NAVY DEPARTMENT.

General Examination of the Atlantic Ocean.   Capt. R. H. Wyman.

General Examination of the Pacific Ocean.   Commander C. H. Davis.

General Examination of the Mediterranean Sea.   Capt. R. H.· Wyman.

Physical Geography of the Red Sea.

General Examination of the Indian Ocean.

Dominican Republic.   Report of Commission of Inquiry to Santo Domingo.

Gulf of Cadiz, Winds, Currents and Navigation of the.

The Magnetism of Ships and Deviations of the Compass.   2 vols. 1867, 1869.

Reported Dangers in the North Pacific Ocean, List of.

Same. [Supplemental.]

Reported Dangers in the South Pacific Ocean, List of.

English Channel, Sailing Directions for the.   South Coast of England.   Part 1.

Same.   North Coast of France.   Part 2.

Mediterranean Sea, Coast and Islands of the.   Part 1.

Same.   Part 2.

Same.   Part 3.

Coast of South America.   Part 1.

Atlantic Ocean, Navigation of the.

West Coast of Africa, The.   3 vols.

Azores or Western Islands.   Pamphlet.

Madeira : The Savages and the Canary Islands.   Pamphlet.

Spain, Northwest and West Coast of, and Coast of Portugal.

The Cape Verde Islands.   Pamphlet

The Voyage of the Vaudreuil through Patagonian Channels and Magellan Strait.   Pamphlet.

The West Coast of Mexico, including the Gulf of California.

Commodore George Dewey, on the Coasts of Lower California and Mexico.   Pamphlet.

Navigation of the Pacific Ocean, etc.

The Coasts of Chilé, Bolivia and Peru

Coasts and Ports of the Bay of Biscay.

Rio de la Plata.

Caribbean Sea and Gulf of Mexico, Navigation of the.

Kattegat Sound and the Great and Little Belts to the Baltic Sea.

NAVY SCIENTIFIC PAPERS. Nos. 1 to 9 inclusive, viz.:
  No. 1. Astronomy.
    2. Tides and Tidal Phenomena.
    3. Lightning Conductors.
    4. Running Survey of an Island.
    5. The Marine Compass.
    6. Chronometer Rates.
    7. Turning Powers of Ships.
    8. Observations for Dip.
    9. Determination of length of Nautical Mile ; Dangers and Ice in the North Atlantic Ocean ; Our Violent Gales, Way to avoid the Centre of ; Barometer ; Thermometer ; Hygrometer ; Rules for their use ; Von Littrow's Method of finding Time at Sea.

NAVAL SCIENTIFIC PAPERS on the Eastern and Northern Extension of the Gulf Stream.
  Supplements to the above, six in number. Pamphlets.
NEW JERSEY, Geology of. Henry D. Rogers, State Geologist. 1840.
NEW MEXICO. Abert. 1846–1847.
NEW REGIONS. Facts. 1879–1880.

OCCULT WORLD, The. By A. P. Sinnet. Boston, 1882.
OCEAN WORLD, The. From the French of Louis Figuier. By E. Percival Wright.

PATENT OFFICE GAZETTE. 2 vols. April to September, 1883.
PLANTS, Power of Movement in. Darwin, 1881.
PLEASANT WAYS IN SCIENCE. By Richard A. Proctor.
POPULAR SCIENCE MONTHLY, from the beginning, May, 1872, to April, 1884. 24 vols.

RECONNOISSANCE of Routes from San Antonio to El Paso. Marcy and Simpson. War Department. 1850.
—— of the Black Hills of Dakota. Ludlow. 1874.
REPTILES AND BIRDS. By Louis Figuier. Revised by Parker Gilmore.
REVENUE STEAMER CORWIN, Cruise of the, in N. W. Arctic Ocean in 1881. 4to. 2 vols. [2 copies.]
ROUGH WAYS MADE SMOOTH. By Richard A. Proctor. London, 1882.

SCIENCE WORKERS, Wages and Wants of. By Richard A. Proctor. London, 1882.
SELBORNE, The Natural History of. Gilbert White.

SMITHSONIAN INSTITUTION : CONTRIBUTIONS TO KNOWLEDGE. 4to.
    Vols. I. to XXIII.
    The Indians of Cape Flattery. J. G. Swan. Part of Vol
    XVI. Duplicate.
    On the Remains of Later Pre-historic Man. W. H. Dall.
    1878. Part of Vol. XXII. Duplicate.
    Sculptures of Santa Lucia Cosumalwhuapa, in Guatemala. S.
    Habel. Part of Vol. XXII. Duplicate.
    Miscellaneous Collections. 8vo. Vols. I. to XXV.
    Reports of Regents. 18 vols. 1863 to 1870, 1872 to 1875, 1877
    to 1879, 1881.
SOUTH CAROLINA, Report on the Geology of. By M. Tuomey. 4to.
    Columbia, S. C., 1848.

TRAVELS IN THE AIR. By James Glaisher. 1871.
TRICHINÆ. How to Detect them, and how to Avoid them. By John
    Phin. Rochester, 1881.

UPPER ARKANSAS AND THE COMANCHES. Abert. 1845. 1 Vol.
    NEW MEXICO. Abert. 1846 & 1847.
    UPPER CALIFORNIA. Fremont, 1848.

WAR IN EUROPE, in 1855-'56. Report of Capt. George B. McClellan.
—— Report of Major Richard Delafield.
WAR DEPARTMENT. Annual Report of the Chief of Engineers,
    U. S. A., for 1882. In 3 parts, 3 vols.
WIND AND CURRENT CHARTS, Explanations and Sailing Directions
    to accompany. By M. F. Maury. 6th Edition. 1854.
—— The same enlarged. 8th Edition. 1858. Vol. I.
WORDS AND PLACES : or Etymological Illustrations of History, Eth-
    nology, and Geology. Rev. Isaac Taylor, M.A.
WORLD, The Vegetable. By Louis Figuier.

YELLOW FEVER, Epidemic of 1878 in Memphis. Its History.

CLASS X.

CLASSICAL.

CLASS X.

BAKER'S LIVY. 2 vols.

CLASSICAL ATLAS, to illustrate Ancient Geography. By Alexander
G. Findlay. London, 1853.

DEMOSTHENES ON THE CROWN.

ORATIONES, EPISTOLÆ, HYMNIQUE SACRI, POEMATA, etc. M. Antonii
Mvreti. Ingoldstadii, 1610.

PLINII. C. SECVNDI PANEGYRICVS, TRAIANO DICTUS. Tanaquilli
Fabri, 1671.

CLASS XI.

ARTISTIC.

CLASS XI.

ART TREASURES OF ENGLAND, The. Philadelphia. Gebbie and Barrie, 34 parts complete.

BRITISH ART, The New Gallery of. Edition de Luxe. 100 plates. Putnam, New York. Cost, $100.

CERAMIC ART, of Great Britain. Llewellyn Jewitt, F.S.A. 2 vols. London, 1878.

CURIOSITÉS DE L'HISTOIRE DES ARTS. Ph. Jacob. Paris, 1858.

DANCING, The Art of. By Kellom Tomlinson. London, 1735.

DOMESTIC ARCHITECTURE OF THE MIDDLE AGES. 4 vols. London, 1851–1859.

ECCLESIASTICAL ARCHITECTURE OF IRELAND. Rich'd Robert Brash. 4to. Dublin, 1875.

GRAPHIC ARTS, The. By Philip Gilbert Hamerton. 1882.

ORDERS OF CHIVALRY, Description of the. By F. H. von Gelbke. Colored plates. Folio. Cost, $40.

PHOTOGRAPHS, Large ; 400 ; of Scenes in Cairo and Monuments of Egypt. In portfolios. Presented to the Grand Commander by S. A. Zola.

PRINTING, The Art of. By T. C. Hansard. 1851.

14

CLASS XII.

AGRICULTURAL, STATISTICAL, ETC.

CLASS XII.

AGRICULTURE, Department of. Reports, 1862 to 1883. 49 vols.

  Same. 2 vols. Special for 1879–1881.

  Same. Special on yield per acre ; cotton, corn, potatoes, etc.

  Pamphlets. Miscellaneous on Wool, Sheep, etc.

  Statistics of 8th Census.

  Statistics of 9th Census.

ALABAMA, Second Annual Report of the R.R. Commissioners of. June 30, 1882.

ALMANAC. Whitaker's London, for 1883 and 1884.

—— de Gotha. 8 vols. 1865, '69, '77, '79 to '83 inclusive.

—— The Royal. Dietrichson and Hannay. 1861, 1862–1869. London.

—— American, The. 13 vols. 1849 to 1861.

—— Same. By A. R. Spofford. 6 vols. 1878 to 1884 inclusive.

AMERICAN STATISTICAL ANNUAL. 1854.

ARIZONA, Handbook to. R. J. Hinton. 1878.

ARMY REGISTER. 1879 to 1883 inclusive.

BROOKES'S GAZETTEER, or Compendious Geographical Dictionary. 1801.

CABINET ATLAS. Thomas Starling. London, 1832.

CALIFORNIA, The Resources of. By John S. Hittell. 1879.

CAPE COLONY, Handbook of the. By John Noble. London, 1875.

CATALOGUE OF THE LIBRARY OF CONGRESS. 5 vols. 1840, and additions in 1868, 1869, 1870.

—— of the Library of the Patent Office. Flint. 4to.

CENSUS, U. S., Compendium of the Ninth. 1880.

  Same. 10th. Parts 1 and 2. 8vo. 2 vols. 1880.

  Statistics of Population. 4to.

  Same. Manufactures. 4to.

  Same. Transportation. 4to.

  Same. Agriculture. 4to.

  Cotton Production. General Discussion and Special Reports. Parts 1 and 2. 4to. 2 vols.

Coast Survey Reports. 4to. 15 vols. 1852–1856.
Commercial Relations of the U. S. 4to. 9 vols. 1856–1861.
—— 8vo. 5 vols. 1862–1867.
—— 7 vols. 1879–1882.

Education, Reports of Commissioners of. 11 vols. 1870, '71, '72, '73, '74, '75, '76–7, '77–8, '78, '79, '80.

Florida, Civil and Natural History of the Territory of. John Lee Williams. 1837.
Fosbroke's Foreign Topography. 4to. London, 1828.

Gold and Silver Production in the U. S. Burchard. 1880.
Golden Northwest, The. Chicago, 1878.
Guides for Tourists. 7 vols.

Handy Royal Atlas. A. Keith Johnston. Small folio. Blackwood & Sons, Edinburgh and London.

Indian Affairs, Commissioner of. Annual Reports. 20 vols.
Indians, Colonial and State Laws relating to. 1633–1831.
Interior, Department of the. Reports of the Secretary. 1876–1881.
International Monetary Conference, Report of. 1878.

Johnson's Atlas. Folio.

Kansas. First and Third Biennial Reports, State Board of Agriculture. 1877–1878, 1881–1882.

Life Saving Service. Report of Operations in 1879.
Lippincott's Gazetteer of the World. A Pronouncing and Geographical Dictionary. 4to.

Michigan Manual. 2 vols. 1881, 1883.
Michigan and its Resources. Compiled by Henry M. Walker, Commissioner of Emigration.
Mineral Resources of the U. S. J. Ross Browne. 1868.
Minnesota and its Resources. By J. Wesley Bond. 1853.

New Zealand, The Natural Wonders of. London, 1881.
—— Handbook or Guide. London, 1879.

Ohio Statistics. 8vo. 4 vols. 1877, 1878, 1879, 1880.

Public Libraries in the U. S.   Department of Interior.   1876.

Railroads, etc.
Railroad Convention, Southern and Western.   1852.
Railroad Guides.   1878–1880.
Register, Biennial, The ; of the U. S. to the 1st of July, 1881.

Santo Domingo, Report on.   Navy Department.
Statistical Atlas of the U. S.   Based on Results of 9th Census.
Walker, 1874.

Transportation Routes to the Seaboard.   3 vols.   1874 and
1881.

Wyoming, Handbook of.   Strahorn.   1877.

CLASS XIII.

MISCELLANEOUS.

CLASS XIII.

MAP OF WISCONSIN, Sectional. Chapman's Pocket Map
—— Kansas.
—— Colorado. Topographical and Township. Nell's.
—— New Mexico. Thayer's.
MAPS OF THE GEOGRAPHY OF THE ANCIENTS. By Herman Moll.
London, 1721.
—— of the States and Territories containing Public Lands ; 28 in
number, mounted. In portfolio. General Land Office.

NAVY DEPARTMENT. Flags of Maritime Nations.

ODD FELLOWSHIP. Grand Lodge of the U. S. Transactions. 5 vols.
1865–1878.
—— Illustrated in an Address delivered before the Grand Lodge of
Kentucky by Tal. P. Shaffner. 1874.
ORATIONS AND OTHER PAMPHLETS. 6 vols.

PAMPHLETS. Miscellaneous. 2 vols. Political. 2 vols.
PARIS UNIVERSAL EXPOSITION. 5 vols. 1878.
PATENT OFFICE REPORTS. 14 vols. 1847 to 1853. 1855 to 1861.
PINKERTON'S GEOGRAPHY. By John Pinkerton. 2 vols. 1804.
POSTAL GUIDE. 5 vols. 1880–1884.
POSTAL LAWS AND REGULATIONS.
POST OFFICE DEPARTMENT. Reports of Postmaster General. 1881
and 1882.
PROBLEMI DI MATEMATICA. By Domenico Anghera. Naples.
PUBLIC LIBRARIES OF THE UNITED STATES. Part I. Washington.

SPEECHES, EULOGIES, etc. 3 vols.

VIEW OF SLAVERY. By Bishop Hopkins. New York, 1864.

LIBRARY C.

THE GENERAL LIBRARY

OF THE

SUPREME COUNCIL.

MASONIC.

CLASS I.

MONITORS AND TEXT BOOKS.

ENGLISH AND AMERICAN.

CLASS I.

AHIMAN REZON OF IRELAND. Dublin, 1807 : and a selection of Masonic Songs, arranged with choruses, in parts, by Bro.·. S. Holden, with lists of Lodges in Ireland and England, 1804.

AHIMAN REZON. Abridged and digested by order of the Grand Lodge of Pennsylvania. By William Smith. 1783.

AHIMAN REZON OF LAURENCE DERMOTT. First American, from Third London edition. New York, 1805.

AHIMAN REZON OF PENNSYLVANIA. Philadelphia, 1825.

AHIMAN REZON OF SOUTH CAROLINA. By Dr. Frederick Dalcho. Charleston, 1807.

—— Same. By Albert G. Mackey. Charleston, 1852.

AHIMAN REZON. By Daniel Sickels. New York, 1867.

ANCIENT AND ACCEPTED SCOTTISH RITE, The. Illustrated. By J. T. Loth. Edinburgh, Glasgow and London, 1875.

ANCIENT YORK AND LONDON GRAND LODGES. Leon Hyneman.

ANDERSON'S CONSTITUTIONS. London, 1723.

—— By John Entick. 1756.

BOOK OF THE ANCIENT AND ACCEPTED SCOTTISH RITE. By Charles T. McClenachan. 8vo. New York, 1867.

—— Same. 4to. New York, 1868.

CATALOGUE OF LIBRARY OF SUPREME COUNCIL OF ENGLAND.

CODE OF MASONIC LAW. Morris. Louisville, 1856.

CONSTITUCIONES DE LA FRANC-MAÇONERIA DEL GR.·. OR.·. DE ESPAÑA. Madrid, 1871.

CONSTITUIÇAõ DO GRANDE ORIENTE LUSITANO UNIDO : SUPREMO CONSELHO DA MAÇONARIA PORTUGUEZA. Lisboa, 1878.

CONSTITUTION DU GRAND ORIENT LUSITANIEN UNI: SUP.·. CONSEIL DE LA MAÇONNERIE. Lisboa, 1881.

CONSTITUTIONS OF THE FREE-MASONS. London, 1723.

DIGEST OF MASONIC LAW. By George W. Chase. New York, 1859.

15

FRA-MAÇONARIA ANTIGA. Constituiçaões da, de Portugal, 1881.
FREE-MASON'S CALENDAR AND DIRECTORY FOR LEICESTERSHIRE AND
    RUTLAND. 1876.
FREE-MASON'S LIBRARY AND GENERAL AHIMAN REZON. Cole. 1826.
FREE-MASON'S POCKET COMPANION, The. Glasgow, 1771.

GRAND CONSTITUTIONS OF 1762 AND 1786. Edition of New Orleans,
    1859.
—— Same. Edition of New York, 1869. [3 copies.]
—— Same. As borrowed without leave and printed by the so-called
    Supreme Council, 33°, of the United States of America, with
    History of that Council. 1862.
GRANDE ORIENTE D'ITALIA, REGOLAMENTI DELLA MASSONERIA
    SCOZZESE, DE TORINO. 1869.
GUIDE TO THE CHAPTER. Sheville & Gould. New York, 1867.

HANDBOOK OF THE CHAPTER. By Thomas H. Caswell. San Fran-
    cisco, 1878.
HUGHAN, WILLIAM J., Masonic Memorials.
—— Masonic Register, Numerical and Numismatical. London and
    Philadelphia, 1879.
—— Old Charges of British Free Masons. .

ILLUSTRATIONS OF MASONRY. Preston. London, 1821.
—— Same. First American, from Tenth London ed. Alexandria,
    Va., 1804.
—— Same, with notes by Oliver. New York, 1866.
IRISH FREE-MASONS' CALENDAR AND DIRECTORY. Dublin, 1876.

KATECHISMUS-REDEN. Manuscript für Freimaurer. Leipzig.
KENTUCKY, Grand Lodge of. By-laws and Digest Code. Louis-
    ville, 1880.
KEYSTONE OF THE MASONIC ARCH. By Charles Scott. Phila-
    delphia, 1866.

LOUISIANA GRAND LODGE CONSTITUTIONS. 1813 to 1850.

MANITOBA, Grand Lodge, Constitution of. [2 copies.] Winnepeg,
    1876.
MANUAL OF THE LODGE OF PERFECTION. New York, 1871.
MASONIC CONSTITUTIONS AND BY-LAWS.
—— Same. Various.
MASONIC LAW AND PRACTICE. Lockwood. New York, 1867.

MASONIC PARLIAMENTARY LAW.   By Albert G. Mackey.
MASONIC RECORD AND DIRECTORY.   By Leon Hyneman, 1859.
MAURERISCHES TASCHENBUCH.   Berlin, 1802.

NEUES CONSTITUTIONEN-BUCH DER ALTEN EHRWÜRDIGEN BRÜDER-
   SCHAFT DER FREIMAURER, zum Gebrauche der Logen verfasst auf
   Befehl der Gross Loge, von Jacob Anderson, D.D.   (Aus dem
   Englischen übersetzt.)   Andreaische Buchhandlung, Frankfurt
   am Main, 1762.
NEW FREE-MASONS' MONITOR.   By James Hardie, A.M.   New York,
   1818.

PERFECT CEREMONIES OF CRAFT MASONRY, The.   Privately Printed
   for A. Lewis.   London, 1873.
—— Same.   Scottish.   London, 1874.
PHILADELPHIA SUBLIME LODGE OF PERFECTION.   Monitor of 1781 to
   1789, with By-laws of the A. & A. S. Rite.   Philadelphia, 1878.
PROVINCIAL GRAND LODGE OF CORNWALL.   1876.

REGULATIONS OF SCOTTISH MASONRY FOR FRANCE.   Honolulu, 1859.

SCOTTISH AND OTHER MASONIC CALENDARS.
SUPREME COUNCIL OF ENGLAND AND WALES.   Rules and Regulations
   of 1869, 1871, 1874.   3 vols.
SUPREME COUNCIL OF SCOTLAND, Constitutions and Laws of.   Edinburgh, 1873.
SUPREME COUNCIL NORTHERN JURISDICTION OF THE U. S.   Extracts
   from Constitutions, with By-laws of Bodies in Philadelphia, Pa.
   1875.
—— Same.   Extracts from the Constitution of.   Philadelphia, 1875.

TEMPLAR'S CHART.   Jeremy L. Cross.   New Haven, 1821.
TEXT-BOOK OF ADVANCED FREE-MASONRY.   London, 1873.

WORLD'S MASONIC REGISTER.   By Leon Hyneman.   1860.

CLASS II.

TUILEURS AND INSTRUCTION.

FRENCH, SPANISH AND ITALIAN.

CLASS II.

DICTIONNAIRE MAÇONNIQUE. Paris, 1825.

GUIDA DEL FRATELLO LIB∴ MUR∴, E LAVORI DELLA R∴ MADRE L∴
LA SEBEZIA. Grados 1–32. 2 vols. Napoli, 1865.
GUIDE DES MAÇONS ÉCOSSAIS, CAHIERS DES TROIS GRADES SYMB∴ DU
RIT∴ ANC∴ ET ACC∴ Edinburgh. 58*⁕* 3 vols. (parts).

INSTRUCTIONS DES DEGRÉS SYMBOLIQUES DU RIT ANCIEN ET ACCEPTÉ.
Paris, 1851.
INSTRUCTIONS DES H∴ G∴, DANS LES CHAP∴ DU G∴ O∴ DE
FRANCE. 1801.
—— Same. [2 copies.] 1835.

LA LIRE MAÇONNE. La Haye. 1787.
LE PARFAIT MAÇON. Cette année.
L'UNIQUE ET PARFAIT TUILEUR POUR LES TRENTE-TROIS GRADES
DE LA MAÇ∴ ECOSS∴, par Tissot, 33d. 1812.

MANUEL DU FRANC-MAÇON. Par M. Bazot. 2 vols. Paris, 1845.
MANUEL PRATIQUE DU FRANC-MAÇON. Paris, 1854.

NÉCESSAIRE MAÇONNIQUE. Paris, 1854.

THUILEUR DE L'ÉCOSSISME DU RIT ANCIEN. Paris, 1813.
—— Same. Paris, 1821.
THUILLEUR UNIVERSEL OU MANUEL DU FRANC-MAÇON. Par Aude
Allyen (de l'Aulnaye) 1810. (MSS. Folio, 300 pp.)
TUILAGE DES GRADÉS PHILOSOPHIQUES DU RIT ÉCOSSAIS. (MSS.
TUILEUR DU RIT DE MISRAIM. (MSS.) Degrees 1st to 66th.
TUILEUR PORTATIF DES TRENTE-TROIS DEGRÉS DE L'ÉCOSSISME DU
RIT ANCIEN ET ACCEPTÉ. Paris, 1846.

VADE-MECUM MAÇONNIQUE POUR LES TROIS PREMIERS DEGRÉS DU RIT
ÉCOSSAIS ANCIEN ET ACCEPTE. 1825.
VERDADERA MASONERIA DE ADOPCION. Havana, 1822.
VOCABULAIRE DES FRANCS-MAÇONS. Par E. F. Bazot. Paris, 1810.

CLASS III.

MASONIC HISTORY, DISSERTATIONS, ESSAYS, TRACTS, TREATISES, ADDRESSES, Etc.

CLASS III.

ACTA LATOMORUM. Thory. 2 vols. Paris, 1815

ADDISON'S KNIGHTS TEMPLARS. London, 1842.

—— Same. London, 1853.

—— Same. Added to and text changed, by Robert Macoy. New York, 1874.

ADDRESS delivered at the 10th Anniversary of Tancred Commandery No. 48 K.T. Penn. By Samuel Harper.

ADDRESSES AND ORATIONS. Masonic.

AHIMAN REZON, Oliver's Dictionary and History of Initiation, Anderson's Constitutions, Constitution of the Grand Lodge of Scotland.

ALMANACH PITTORESQUE DE LA FRANC-MAÇONNERIE. 1844 to 1848 inclusive. By F. T. B. Clavel. Paris.

ANALOGY OF ANCIENT CRAFT MASONRY TO NATURAL AND REVEALED RELIGION. By Charles Scott. Philadelphia, 1850.

ANCIENT CITY LODGE, No. 452. MASONIC ODES. Albany, N. Y.

ANNUAIRE MAÇONNIQUE DE TOUS LES RITES. Par le F. M. Pinon, 18. Paris, 1865 and 1866.

ANNUAL REGISTER, Grand Lodge of Perfection of South Carolina, containing membership of Grand Consistory and Supreme Council. Charleston, 1802. Original : with divers Registers of Lodges in San Domingo, Charleston, and Portsmouth, Va., from 1796 to 1810.

ANTI-JESUIT TRACTS. By Masons of Brazil. 2 vols. 1875.

ANTIQUITIES, ILLUSTRATIONS, INITIATIONS AND DEFENCE OF FREE-MASONRY. Oliver. 2 copies.

ANTIQUITIES OF FREE-MASONRY. Oliver. 2 copies.

ARCHÆOLOGICAL CURIOSITIES OF THE RITUALS OF FREE-MASONRY. Reprints by Enoch T. Carson, 1867.

ARCHIV DER FREYMAURER-LOGE ZU LIVORNO. Leipzig, 1803.

ATENIZON. Frankfurth und Leipzig, 1803.

> Bollendeter aufchluss des Jesuitismus und Geheimnisses der Freimaurer. 1787.

ATENIZON.   Wiederherstellüng der Jesuiten di Underdructüng des
Freimaurerordens.   1815.
Freimaurer Regeln.   1785.
AUFKLÄRUNG UBER WICHTIGE GEGENSTANDE IN DER FREYMAUREREY.
Aus der Loge Puritas, 1787.

BAUSTEINE ZUM TEMPEL DES MENSCHENTHUMS, von Freidrich Auwald.
Leipzig, 1856.
BIBLIOGRAPHIE DER FREIMAUREREI, von Georg Kloss.   Frankfurt am
Main, 1844.
BLAZING STAR, The.   By William B. Greene.   Boston, 1872.

CANDID DISQUISITION OF THE PRINCIPLES AND PRACTICES OF FREE-
MASONRY.   By Wellins Calcott.   New York, 1855.
CENTENNIAL CELEBRATION OF ST. ANDREW ROYAL ARCH CHAPTER.
Boston, September 29, 1869.
CENTENNIAL MEMORIAL, Lodge of St. Andrew, and Mass. Gr.
Lodge.   Boston.
CHRISTIAN KNIGHTHOOD, Text-book of.   By C. L. Stowell, 33°.
N. Y. 1874.
CONNECTICUT VETERAN MASONIC ASSOCIATION.   First Annual Re-
union.   June 17, 1882.
CONSIDÉRATIONS FILOSOPHIQUES SUR LA FRANC-MAÇONNERIE.   Ham-
burg, 1776.
COURS PRATIQUE DE FRANC-MAÇONNERIE.   Par Chémin Dupontés.
Paris, 1847.
COURS COMPLET DE MAÇONNERIE.   Vassal.   Paris, 1832.
COURS PHILOSOPHIQUE ET INTERPRETATIF DES INITIATIONS, An-
ciennes et Modernes.   Ragon.   Paris, 1841.
—— Same.   Paris, 1853.
COUSTOS, JOHN, The Sufferings of, for Free-Masonry and for His
refusing to turn Roman Catholic, in the Inquisition at Lisbon.
London.   Printed for the Author, 1746.
CRADLE OF REBELLIONS.   History of Secret Societies of France.   By
L. de la Hodde.   1867.
CRYPTIC MASONRY.   A Manual of the Council.   By Albert G. Mackey.
CUMBERLAND LODGE NO. 41, The Royal.   History of, from 1732.   By
Thomas Payne Ashley, P.M., P.Z.
CYCLOPEDIA OF FREE-MASONRY.   By Robert Macoy.   New York,
1867.
CYCLOPEDIA, Royal Masonic ; The.   By Kenneth R. H. McKenzie.
London, 1877.

DALCHO FREDERICK, DR., Orations of. Dublin, 1808.
DARUTY, J. ÉMILE. Recherches sur le Rite Écossais, Ancien
Accepté. Paris, 1877.   *
DÉFENSE DE MISRAIM. Paris, 1822.
Order of the Friendly Brothers of St. Patrick. Dublin,
1856.
DERMOTT'S MASONIC SONGS.
DES ÉTANGS. Œuvres Maçonniques. Paris. 1848.
DIE DREI ÄLTESTEN KUNTSTURKUNDEN DER FREIMAURERBRÜDER-
SCHAFT. 2 vols. Leipzig, 1849.
DIRECTORY OF GR.·. LODGE OF THE THREE GLOBES.
Frontenac Chapter and St. John's Lodge, Canada.
Anti-Masonic Convention of 1830.
DISCOURS, etc., dans la Franc-Maçonnerie.
DISCOURS DU F. DESRIVIÈRES, etc. Paris, 1848.
DISCREPANCIES OF FREE-MASONRY. Dialogues on Obscure and Diffi-
cult Passages. Rev. J. G. Oliver. London.
DOCUMENTS UPON SUBLIME FREE-MASONRY. By Joseph McCosh.
Charleston, 1823. 2 copies. One of these in Grand Lodge Library
of Iowa.

EARLY HISTORY OF FREE-MASONRY IN ENGLAND. By James O.
Halliwell. London, 1844.
ÉCOSSISME. Polémique, 1827 to 1842.
ÉCOSSOIS DE SAINT ANDRÉ D'ÉCOSSE, OU DÉVELOPPEMENT DES ABUS
INTRODUITS DANS LA FRANC-MAÇONNERIE. Paris, 1780.
ENCYCLOPÆDIA OF FREE-MASONRY AND ITS KINDRED SCIENCES.
Albert G. Mackey. Philadelphia, 1874.
ENCYCLOPÉDIE MAÇONNIQUE. Par Chémin Dupontés. 4 vols. Paris,1832.
ENCYCLOPÄDIE DER FREIMAUREREI. Von C. Lenning. 3 vols. Leip-
zig, 1822–1828.
ERKLÄRUNG ÜBER SEINE GEHEIME VERBINDUNG MIT DEM ILLUMINATEN
ORDEN. F. Nicolai. Berlin and Stetten, 1788.
ESSAI HISTORIQUE SUR LA FRANCHE-MAÇONNERIE. Bordeaux, 1830.
ESSAI HISTORIQUE SUR L'INSTITUTION DU RIT ÉCOSSAIS. Paris, 1827.
Discours. Par Robert Du Var. Paris, 1838.
Récapitulation de toute la Maçonnerie.
Masonry Dissected. By Samuel Pritchard. 14th edition, Lon-
don, with copperplate list of Lodges. March 25, 1725.
ESSAIS SUR LA FRANCHE-MAÇONNERIE. Par J. L. Laurens. Paris, 1806.
ESSAIS SUR LA FRANC-MAÇONNERIE. À Latomopolis, chez Xiste An-
dron. 2 vols. 1784.
ÉTUDE SUR LA FRANC-MAÇONNERIE. Boubée. Paris, 1854.

Études Historiques et Philosophiques sur les trois grades de la Maçonnerie Symbolique. Par le F. Redarés. 2 copies. Paris, 1858.

Excerpta Latomica. By the Gr.·. Commander. MSS.

Finch, W. Treatise on the Religious and Moral Beauties of Free-Masonry. Canterbury, 1802.

Fondation du Grand Orient de France. Thory. 1812.

Four Cardinal Virtues, The. Extracts : MSS. By the Gr.·. Commander.

Free-Masons' Melody, The. By Brethren of Prince Edwin's Lodge. Bury, 1818.

Free-Masonry, General History of. By J. Fletcher Brennan. 1875.

Free-Masonry, Its Pretensions Exposed. Dwight Farmer, 1828.

Free-Masonry, Early History and Antiquities of. By Geo. F. Fort. Philadelphia, 1877.

Free-Masonry. Letters to Robert T. Crucefix, LLD. By Rev. George Oliver.

Free-Masonry for the Ladies. London, 1791.

Free-Masons' Vocal Assistant and Register, The, of the Lodges of Masons in South Carolina and Georgia. Charleston, S. C., 1807.

Freye Bemerkungen uber die Politsche Verfassung des Ordens der Freyen Maurer. Christian Rose. Leipzig, 1787.

Freymaurer-Bibliothek. Dessau, 1785.

Freymaurer, Der. January to December, 1738. Leipzig.

Freymaurer Reden und Gedichte. Von A. W. L. v. Rahmel. Breslau und Leipzig, 1780.

Frey-Maurer, Der. Newes Constitutionem-Buch der alten and Chrw. Bruderschaft. Dy James Anderson, D.D. Frankfort am Main, 1762.

Friemurare-Ordens Matrikel. 2 vols. Stockholm, 1873 and 1882.

Geschichte der Aeschaffung des Tempelherren-Ordens. Altona, 1780.

Gespräche Maurerey betreffend : Rebst einem Unhange von Rosen-Kreuzern. Leipzig, 1785.

Grand Lodge of Scotland, Laws and Constitutions of. 4to. Edinburgh, 1848.

Harris' Discourses. Philadelphia, 1818.

Hermes ou Archives Maçonniques. 2 vols. Paris, 1818, 1819.

Histoire de la Condannation des Templiers. Par Mons. Pierre Dupuy. 2 vols. Bruxelles, 1713.

Histoire de la Franc-Maçonnerie. Par Edouard Bobrik. Traduit par Edouard Lens. Lausanne, 1841.

HISTOIRE DES CHEVALIERS HOSPITALIERS DE ST. JEAN DE JERUSALEM. Par M. l'Abbé de Vertot. 7 vols. Paris, 1726.

—— Same. Quarto. 4 vols. Paris, 1726.

HISTORY OF THE ORDER OF ST. JOHN OF JERUSALEM. By John Taaffe. 4 vols in 2. London, 1852.

HISTOIRE DES FRANC-MAÇONS. 2 vols. Paris, 1745.

HISTOIRE DES INITIATIONS DE L'ANCIENNE ÉGYPTE. Paris, 1825.

HISTOIRE DES TEMPLIERS. Par J. A. J. Paris, 1805.

—— Same. Par le R. Père Mansuet Jeune. 4to. Paris, 1789.

HISTOIRE DES TROIS GRANDES LOGES DE FRANC-MAÇONS EN FRANCE. Rébold. Paris, 1864.

HISTOIRE DES TROIS ORDRES. Par l'Abbé Roux. 2 vols. 3 copies. Paris, 1725.

HISTOIRE DU JACOBINISME. Par M. l'Abbé Barruel. 4 vols. Londres, 1797.

HISTOIRE GÉNÉRALE DE LA FRANC-MAÇONNERIE. Par Émanuel Rébold. Paris, 1851.

HISTOIRE, OBLIGATIONS, ETC., DES FRANC-MAÇONS. Francfort-sur-le-Meyn, 1742.

HISTOIRE PHILOSOPHIQUE DE LA FRANC-MAÇONNERIE. Par Kauffman & Cherpin. Lyons, 1850.

HISTOIRE PITTORESQUE DE LA FRANC-MAÇONNERIE. Par Clavel. Paris, 1844.

HISTORICAL LANDMARKS OF FREE-MASONRY. Oliver. 2 vols. 2 copies.

HISTORY OF CHIVALRY OR KNIGHTHOOD, The, and its times. By Charles Mills. 2 vols. London, 1825.

HISTORY OF FREE-MASONRY IN SOUTH CAROLINA. Albert G. Mackey. 1861.

HISTORY OF FREE-MASONRY IN FRANCE. (MSS.) By the Grand Commander. 6 vols.

HISTORY AND PHILOSOPHY OF FREE-MASONRY. Rev. Augustus C. L. Arnold.

HISTORY OF INITIATION. Oliver. 2 copies.

HISTORY OF THE LODGE OF EDINBURGH, MARY'S CHAPEL, No. 1. By Murray Lyon. Edinburgh and London, 1873.

HISTORY OF MASONIC PERSECUTIONS. Oliver.

HISTORY OF MASONRY IN PENNSYLVANIA. Alfred Creigh.

HISTORY OF THE MOTHER-LODGE KILWINNING. By Robert Wylie. Glasgow, 1879.

INFORME, emitido por el Ill∴ H∴ Alberto Pike, sobre el Supremo Consejo de España. Madrid, 1882.

INITIATIONS ANCIENNES ET MODERNES.   Par J. M. Ragon.   Paris,
1841.
INSIGNIA OF THE ROYAL ARCH.   Oliver.   London, 1847.

JACHIN AND BOAZ : or an Authentic Key to the door of Free-Masonry.
London, 1791.

KANE LODGE, Reception of Gr.·. Officers, etc.   New York, April,
1871.

LA FRANCHE MAÇONNERIE RENDUE A SA VÉRITABLE ORIGINE.   Par
Alex. Lenoir.   Paris, 1874.
LA LIRE MAÇONNE, ou Recueil de Chansons des Francs-Maçons.   Par
les frères Vignolles et du Bois.   La Haye.   1787.
LA MAÇONNERIE ÉCOSSOISE COMPARÉE, etc.   Orient de Londres, 1788.
LA MAÇONNERIE.   Par Rhegellini de Schio.   3 vols.   Paris, 1842.
LA MESSE DANS SES RAPPORTS AVEC LES MYSTÈRES ET LES CÉRÉ-
MONIES DE L'ANTIQUITÉ.   By J. M. Ragon.   Paris.
L'ANTI-MAÇON.   1747.
L'ÉCOLE DES FRANCS-MAÇONS À JERUSALEM.   1748.
L'ÉCOLE DES FRANCS-MAÇONS ou les Francs-Maçons sans le savoir ;
Comédie en un Acte.   Par André Honoré.   Paris, 1779, and
Apologie des Maçons.
L'ÉCOLE DES FRANCS-MAÇONS.   Par le F. Vernhés.   Montpellier, 1821.
L'ORDRE DES FRANCS-MAÇONS TRAHI, et Le Secret des Mopses
révélé.   Amsterdam, 1745.
LE PARFAIT MAÇON ou Répertoire complet de la Maçonnerie Symbo-
lique.   Montpellier, 1820.
LE PARFAIT MAÇON.
LE SECRET DES FRANC-MAÇONS.   1744.
LES FRANC-MAÇONS ÉCRASÉS.   Amsterdam, 1747.
LES MAÇONS DE CYTHÈRE : Poëme.   Par Jean Louis Bard.   Paris,
1813.
L'ÉTAT ET L'ÉGLISE.   Par Allard et autres.   Documents French and
Belgian.   Letters to Bagary.
L'ÉTOILE FLAMBOYANTE, ou La Société des Francs-Maçons.   2 vols.
1766.
L'ÉTOILE FLAMBOYANTE À L'ORIENT CHEZ LA SILENCE.
LETTERS OF J. J. J. GOURGAS, Gr.·. Commander Northern Jurisdiction,
and others.   (MSS.)   1798 to 1846.
LE VOILE LEVÉ POUR LES CURIEUX.   Paris, 1791.
LE VRAI FRANC-MAÇON.   Par Frère Enoch.   Liege, 1772.
LODGE OF SORROW.   Ceremonies : Addresses, Celebrations, etc.   Pam-
phlets.

LOGE CENTRALE DES VÉRITABLES FRANC-MAÇONS.
—— Same. Paris, 1802.
L'ORDRE MAÇONNIQUE DE MISRAIM. Par Marc Bedarride. 2 vols.
Paris, 1845.

MAÇONNERIE ADONHIRAMITE. 1876.
MAÇONNERIE OCCULTE. Ragon. Paris, 1853
MASONIC ADDRESSES, 1817 to 1860.
—— Same, 1841 to 1857.
—— Same, various.
MASONIC ADDRESSES AND REPORTS.
MASONIC DISCOURSES AND ADDRESSES. By Joseph R. Chandler.
Philadelphia, 1844.
MASONIC DOCUMENTS, Sup.·. Council Northern Jurisdiction. 1860 to '65.
MASONIC FRAGMENTS AND STATISTICS of the Grand Lodge and Grand
Chapter of England. Nicholas Wm. Hodges. London.
MASONIC FRAGMENTS. By William James Hughan. London, 1850.
MASONIC HARMONIA. By Cutler.
MASONIC HISTORY [Falsification of]. By Robert B. Folger, 1862.
MASONIC JURISPRUDENCE. By Albert G. Mackey. New York, 1859.
MASONIC LIBRARY. Robert Morris. Vols. 1 to 5, 9 and 11 to 16.
12 vols.
MASONIC MANUAL, or Lectures on Free-Masonry. By Rev. Jonathan
Ashe.
MASONIC MELODIES. By Luke Eastman. Boston, 1818.
MASONIC MINSTREL. 2 copies. Dedham, Massachusetts, 1816.
MASONIC PAMPHLETS. 9 vols.
MASONIC PARLIAMENTARY LAW. By Albert G. Mackey.
MASONIC POLEMICS, in Louisiana. [A Masonic Trial in New Orleans,
1858.]
MASONIC PORTRAITS. By James Gannon. London, 1876.
MASONIC REPORTS ; Letters ; Essays ; Tracts.
MASONIC REUNION, Oregon, Washington Territory, Idaho, and British
Columbia.
MASONIC SKETCHES AND REPRINTS. By William James Hughan. 2
copies.
MASONIC SYMBOLISM, Lecture on. 4to. By Albert Pike.
—— Second Lecture on. 4to. By the same.
Only 100 *copies of each printed, and plates destroyed.*
MASONIC TREATISE. W. Finch. Canterbury, 1862.
MASONRY. History and Articles of. Matthew Cooke. London, 1861.
MEMOIRE SUR L'ÉCOSSISME. Par Chémin Dupontés. 1823.
MIRROR FOR THE JOHANNITE MASONS. By Rev. George Oliver, D.D.
MONROE COMMANDERY. By-Laws of, No. 12, K. T. Rochester, 1882
16

MONUMENS HISTORIQUES, relatifs à la Condamnation des Chevaliers du Temple et à l'abolition de l'Ordre. Par M. Raynouard. Paris, 1813.

MORRIS, ROBERT, Masonic Odes and Poems.

MUSIC FOR THE VARIOUS DEGREES IN THE SCOTTISH RITE. By Matthew Cooke, XXX°. Part I. 2 copies.

MYSTERIES OF FREE-MASONRY. By John Fellows. London, 1866.

OBELISK, THE, AND FREE-MASONRY. By John A. Weisse. New York, 1880.

OLD DOCUMENTS. French Masonic (MSS.) Quarto.

OLD LODGES, The Four, Founders of Modern Free-Masonry ; and their Descendants. 4to.

ORDER OF THE TEMPLE AND ST. JOHN. By Richard Woof.
Notes on the Order of the Temple and St. John.
History of the Knights of Malta. By George S. Blackie.
Recherches Historiques sur les Templiers. Par J. P——. Paris, 1838.

ORIGIN AND EARLY HISTORY OF MASONRY. By G. W. Steinbrenner. New York, 1864.

ORTHODOXIE MAÇONNIQUE. Ragon. Paris, 1853.

OUTLINES OF THE RISE AND PROGRESS OF FREE-MASONRY IN LOUISIANA. By James B. Scot.

OUVRAGES DE MONSIEUR LE COMTE DE PAGAN, Trouvés dans ses Écrits après sa mort. 1669.

PAMPHLETS, French and Portuguese, Masonic.

PLANCHES, DISCOURS ET CANTIQUES, Fête de la Paix, Gr.·. Orient of France. Paris, 1801.

PORTLAND LODGE, of Maine, History of. By Josiah H. Drummond. 2 copies.

PRACTICAL MASONIC LECTURES. Samuel Lawrence. Atlanta, Ga., 1874.

PRÉCIS HISTORIQUE DE L'ORDRE DE LA FRANC-MAÇONNERIE. By J. C. Besuchet. 2 vols. Paris, 1829.

PRÉCIS SUR LA FRANC-MAÇONNERIE. Par César Moreau. Paris, 1855.

PRICE, HENRY. First Provincial Grand Master of New England and North America. Address upon, by William Sewall Gardner.

PROBIERSTEIN FÜR ACHTE FREIMAURER. Vols. 1 and 2. 2 vols. Erster Theil, 1786.

PROOFS OF A CONSPIRACY. By John Robison. London, 1797.

—— Same. 2d edition. London, 1797.

—— Same. 3d edition. Philadelphia, 1798

PRUDENCE BOOK OF FREE-MASONRY. Catalogue and Directory of all
Masonic Lodges in the World. 1860.
PYTHAGOREAN TRIANGLE, or the Science of Numbers. Oliver.

REBOLD'S GENERAL HISTORY OF FREE-MASONRY.
RECHERCHES HISTORIQUES SUR LES CROISADES ET LES TEMPLIERS.
Par Le Chevalier Jacob. Paris, 1828.
RECUEIL DE CHANSONS POUR LA MAÇONNERIE DES HOMMES ET DES
FEMMES.
L'Orateur Franc-Maçon. Par Le F. Jarrhetti. Berlin.
REGISTER OF ANTOINE BIDEAUD (finished by J. B. Villadieu). (MSS.)
January 10, 1806.
—— OF ALBERT PIKE as Deputy Inspector-General and Inspector-
General, 1857, '58, and '59. (Quarto, MSS.)
—— OF JEAN BAPTISTE AVEILHE, 1797.
—— OF JEAN BAPTISTE MARIE DELAHOGUE, 1798–9.
—— OF MOSES HOLBROOK, Grand Commander.
REPORT OF COMPLIMENTARY DINNER given by George Kenning to
Distinguished American Free-Masons. 1878.
REVELATIONS OF A SQUARE. Oliver. 2 vols. 2 copies.
REVUE HISTORIQUE, SCIENTIFIQUE ET MORALE DE LA FRANC-
MAÇONNERIE. Paris, 1830.
ROYAL MASONIC INSTITUTION FOR BOYS. London, 1877.

SAINT JOHN'S LODGE IN PITTSBURGH. Address on the History of.
By Samuel Harper. 2 copies. 1883.
SAINT JOHN'S LODGE, Philadelphia, Phototypes from Liber B, 1731–38.
Issued by C. B. Day, M. W. G. M. Folio. 1884.
SCOTTISH RITE IN LOUISIANA. Various Documents.
SCOTTISH RITE IN NEW YORK AND LOUISIANA. Pamphlets.
SECTES MAÇONNIQUES. Par J. P. Levesque. 2 copies. 1821.
SENDSCHREIBEN AN DIE UNBEKANNTEN ODER DIE ACHTEN UND
RECHTEN FREYMAURER. 1781.
SIGNS AND SYMBOLS. Oliver. 2 copies.
SILENTIA LODGE, 198, History of. 1823–1869. By John G. Barker,
N. Y.
SOCIAL HARMONY, including several choice songs on Masonry. By
Thomas Hale, of Darnhall, Cheshire, England. London.
SOCIÉTÉ MAÇONNE. Supplement aux Vrais Jugemens sur la.
Bruxelles, 1754.
SPIRIT OF MASONRY. By William Hutchinson. Notes by Oliver.
STATUTS DE L'ORDRE MAÇONNIQUE EN FRANCE. Paris, 1806.

STATUTS ET RÉGLEMENS GÉNÉRAUX DE L'ORDRE MAÇONNIQUE EN FRANCE. À Paris, 1826.

STATUTI DELLA MASSONERIA ITALIANA : Rito Egiziano Riformato. Napoli, 1879.

STUDY OF FREE-MASONRY, A. Translated from Dupanloup.

SUTHERLAND'S KNIGHTS OF MALTA. Philadelphia, 1846.

SWEDENBORG RITE and the Great Masonic Leaders of the 18th Century. By Samuel Beswick. New York, 1870.

SYMBOLISM OF FREE-MASONRY. Albert G. Mackey.

SYMBOL OF GLORY, The. Oliver. 2 vols. 2 copies.

TALES, Poems and Masonic Papers. Emra Holmes.

THEOCRATIC PHILOSOPHY OF FREE-MASONRY, The. Oliver. 2 vols. 2 copies.

THE TEMPLE CHURCH. Addison. London, 1843.

THIAN TI HWUI—The Hung League. By Gustave Schlegel. Batavia, 1866.

TOMBEAU LE, DE JACQUES MOLAÏ. Paris.

TRADITIONS OF FREE-MASONRY. By A. T. C. Pierson. 1865.

UITWENDIGE GODSDIENST-PLICHTEN. Eerste Deel. 6 vols. 1727.

USE AND ABUSE OF FREE-MASONRY. By Captain George Smith.

VERITÉ, la, de l'Histoire des Frères de la Roze Croix. Par G. Naudè. Paris, 1623.

WASHINGTON AND HIS MASONIC COMPEERS. By Sidney Hayden.

CLASS IV.

BULLETINS AND TRANSACTIONS.

CLASS IV.

Annales Maçonniques des Pays Bas. 8 vols. Bruxelles, 1773 to 1828.
Annales Maçonniques, par Caillot. 8 vols. Paris, 1807 to 1810.

Bolletim do Gr∴ Oriente do Brazil, Manifesto and Discourses. 1864 to 1866.
Bolletim do Gr∴ Oriente Unido do Brazil—
        Anno 2, 1873. 2 copies.
        Anno 3, 1874. 3 copies.
        Anno 4, 1875. 2 copies.
        Anno 5, 1876. 2 copies.
        Anno 5, 1876. 2 copies, Part 1. 2 copies, Part 2.
Bolletim do Gr∴ Oriente e Supremo Conselho Unido do Brazil, Anno 1, 2, 3, 4, and 5, 1875 to 1876. 5 vols.
Bolletim do Gr∴ Oriente do Brazil (Lavradio), 1872 and 1873.
Boletin del Grande Oriente del Peru, 1875–1876.
Boletin Oficial de la Masoneria Simb. de Colon, 2d Epoca Tomo 1. Habana, 1878. 2d Epoca Tomo 2. 1879. 2 vols.
Boletin do Grande Oriente Lusitano Unido, 1869–1882. 7 vols. Lisboa.
Boletin Oficial del Gr∴ Or∴ de España. January, 1877, to November, 1878; January, 1877, to December, 1880; January, 1881, to December, 1881, 3 copies ; 1882, 2 copies.
Boletin Oficial del Gr∴ Or∴ de España [*Sagasta* and *Romero*]. January, 1877, to November, 1878 ; January, 1877, to December, 1880; January, 1881, to December, 1881, 3 copies; January, 1882, to December, 1882, 2 copies ; January, 1883, to December, 1883, 2 copies. 9 vols. Madrid.
Boletin del Supremo Consejo del Peru, from January, 1874, to December, 1876.
Boletin del Supremo Consejo y Grande Oriente del Peru, 1864 to 1867. Incomplete.
Boletinos. Supremo Consejo de Mexico. 1879–'80.
Bulletins. Gr∴ Lodge of the Netherlands. 1870–'73. Gr∴ National Mother Lodge of the Prussian States. Berlin, 1875–'76.
Bulletin du Gr∴ Orient de Belgique *ab initio*, 1874 to 1878.

BULLETIN DU SUPREME CONSEIL DE BELGIQUE.
   Nos. 1 to 15, Annual, 1863-'72, folio.
   —— Nos. 16 to 19, 1875-'76, 3 copies.
   —— Nos. 20 and 21, 1877-'78.
   —— Nos. 22 and 23, 1879, '80.
   —— Nos. 24, 25, 26, 1881-'83, 3 copies.
BULLETIN DU SUPRÈME CONSEIL DE FRANCE, 1857 to 1874.
BULLETINS and other Documents from the Supreme Councils of Lux-
   embourg, Grand Orient of Spain, Nueva Granada, Argentine
   Republic, etc.
BULLETINS, ETC., Foreign, 1876, 1877, 1878.
BULLETINS, Registers and other Masonic Documents, Foreign. Odd
   numbers. 1875-'77.
BULLETIN SUPREME COUNCIL OF THE SOUTHERN JURISDICTION. Vol.
   1, 3 copies ; vols. 2, 3, 4, 5 and 6, 2 copies of each.

CALENDRIERS DU GRAND ORIENT DE FRANCE, 1869, '71, '72, '74 to '79
   and 1883. 5 vols. Paris.
COLON, Supreme Council of. Gr∴ Lodge of Colon and Cuba. Sup∴
   Council of France. Gr∴ Lodge of Perfection. Transactions,
   1881-'82.
COUNCILS OF DELIBERATION N∴ JURISDICTION, viz : Maine, 1871 to
   '78 ; New Hampshire, 1869 ; Massachusetts, 1867 to '82 ; Vermont, 1875 to '82 ; New York, 1876 to '83 ; New Jersey, 1871 to
   '73 and '78 to '80 ; Pennsylvania, 1867 to '82 ; Ohio, 1868 and '77
   to '82 ; Illinois, 1872 to '83 ; Indiana, 1867 ; Michigan, 1881 ;
   Wisconsin, 1863, '81, '83. 5 vols.

EL SILENCIO ; y Boletin Oficial del Grande Oriente de Colon, 1875
   and '76.   .
ÉTAT DU GRAND ORIENT DU FRANCE. 1777-'79. 3 vols.
—— Same. Vol. 1. Parts 1 and 2, and Parts 3 and 4. 1804. 2 vols.

GENERAL GRAND CHAPTER U. S., 1797-1856. 2 copies.
—— Same. 1859-'65-'68-'71-'74-'77.
—— Same. 1880-'83.
GRAND CHAPTER OF KANSAS, 1866 to 1874. 2 copies.
—— of California. Proceedings. 1854-1881. 6 vols.
GRAND COMMANDERY OF CALIFORNIA. Proceedings, 1858-1881. 3 vols.
GRAND COMMANDERY OF IOWA, K. T., 1864 to '73.
—— Same. 1874 to '79.
GRAND CONSISTORIES, Transactions of. 4 vols.
—— Louisiana, 1866 to 1870; Kentucky, 1867 to 1870; Virginia, 1869,
   1870; Iowa, 1868.

GRAND CONSISTORIES. Transactions of. 4 vols.—*Continued.*

—— Louisiana, 1870 to 1873 ; Iowa, 1870, 1871 ; Georgia, 1872 to 1874 ; California, 1872 to 1875 ; Massachusetts, Counc. of Delib., 1871; Canada, Grand Priory, 1871 ; Vermont, Counc. of Deliberation, 1875; Illinois, Counc. of Deliberation, 1871, 1872.

—— Kentucky, 1867 ; Maryland (Statutes and Regulations), 1871 ; Louisiana, 1869, 1870 ; Iowa, 1870, 1871 ; Georgia, 1873, 1874.

—— California, 1870 to 1872, 1879 to 1882 ; Louisiana, 1866–'67, 1871 to 1873, 1882 ; Maryland, 1881 ; Virginia, 1870 to 1876.

—— Pamphlets : California, 1870 to 1878, bound, 3 copies of each ; 1871, 1 copy ; 1883, 4 copies ; 1884, 2 copies.

GRAND COUNCIL ROYAL AND SELECT MASTERS, Mass. Proceedings, 1826–1883. 2 vols.

GRAND ENCAMPMENT UNITED STATES, 1816 to 1883, except 1859. 5 vols.

GRAND LODGE. Reports on Foreign Correspondence to : South Carolina, 1861 ; Iowa, 1881 ; Louisiana, 1880, 1881, 1882 ; Nebraska, 1882 ; Quebec, 1880 ; Manitoba, 1881 ; New South Wales, 1882.

—— District of Columbia : Reports on Foreign Correspondence, 1871–1884. By Wm. R. Singleton, Gr∴ Secr∴

—— of Iowa. Proceedings, 1844–1884. 9 vols.

—— of Louisiana. Proceedings, 1880.

—— of Missouri, from its organization in 1821 to 1840, inclusive.

—— of Nebraska, 1858 to 1868.

—— of New York, 1781 to 1815 ; 1816 to 1827. 2 vols.

—— of New Jersey, 1786 to 1857.

—— of Ohio, 1874.

—— of Pennsylvania, Early History of. Three parts. 1730 to 1804.

—— of South Carolina. Transactions, 1861–1881. 3 vols.

—— of Washington Territory, 1858 to 1875. 3 vols.

—— of West Virginia. Proceedings, 1865 to 1882.

GRAND ORIENTS of the Dominican Republic and Colon. Regulations and Polemic.

GRANDE ORIENTE D'EGITTO. Statuti e Memfi Risorta, 1874 to 1876, incomplete.

—— Same. Statuti, 1874.

GRAND ORIENT DE FRANCE. Bulletin from November, 1841, to March, 1859. 11 vols.

—— Same. Bulletin from May, 1844, to March, 1854. 9 vols. in 4.

—— Same. Bulletin 27ᵉ and 29ᵉ, An : 1871–'74.

—— Same. Bulletin 30ᵉ, An : 1874.

—— Same. Bulletin 32ᵉ, An : 1876–77.

GRAND ORIENT DE FRANCE.   Bulletin, 1871–1877.
—— Same.   Bulletin, 1872 28ᵉ, An :
GRANDE ORIENTE DI NAPOLI : Cenno Storico.
GRAND ORIENTS of New Granada and Peru.   Constitutions, Regula-
tions, etc.

MÀGYAROSZÀG NAGY-ORIENSE VEDELME ALATT ALLO Sz.∴ K.∴ EK.∴
Alkotmanyà.   Alapszabalai eş Torvenykezési szabalyai.   Buda-
pest, 000875.
MEMFI RISORTA, 1875 to 1878.   Vols. 1, 2, and 3, in one vol.
—— Vols. 2 and 3.   Sup.∴ Council and Nat.∴ Gr.∴ Lodge of Tunis,
Bolletini e Decreti, 1882.   Uruguay, Constitution of Sup.∴ Coun-
cil, 1881.

PROCÈS VERBAL de la Session Annuel du Suprême Conseil pour la
Juridiction du Sud, with other Documents.   2 copies.   New
Orleans, 1857.
PROTOCOLS, Gr.∴ Mother Lodge of Berlin, 1875 to '76.
          Gr.∴ Orient of Hungary, 1876.
          Gr.∴ Orient and Supreme Council of France, various,
          1812 to 1861.
          Mexico, Supreme Council.   Report of Gr.∴ Minister of
          State and Constitutions, 1878.

RECUEIL DES ACTES DU SUPRÊME CONSEIL DE FRANCE : 1762 to 1830.
Paris, 1832.
ROYAL ORDER OF SCOTLAND.   Provincial Grand Lodge of the U. S.,
Records and Minutes of, 1878 to 1883.   2 copies ; and Constitu-
tion and Laws of the Grand Lodge.

SUPRÊME CONSEIL pour l'Amérique en France and Suprême Conseil de
France, Actes : 1817 to 1843.   3 vols.
SUPREME COUNCIL of Canada, 1874 to 1878, and Statutes, and Great
Priory of Canada, 1876 to 1879.
—— Same.   1874 to 1876, and Grand Priory of Canada, 1875 to 1876.
—— Same.   Transactions, 1874 to 1883.
—— of England and Wales, Rules and Regulations of, 1869, '71, '74,
'80, and '82.   6 vols.
SUPREME COUNCILS ; of Ireland, 1856.
                    of Scotland, 1874 to 1883.
—— of the 33°.   Official Report of Proceedings relative to the establish-
ment of the same in Greece.   By H. I. H. Prince Rhodocanakis.
Octavo.   Athens, 1872.

Supreme Council Northern Jurisdiction, 1813 to 1862. Reprint.
2 copies.
—— Same. 1863 to 1866.
—— Same. 1867 to 1869.
—— Same. 1870, 1871. 2 copies.
—— Same. 1872, 1873. 2 copies.
—— Same. 1874, 1875. 3 copies.
—— Same. 1876, 1877. 2 copies.
—— Same. 1878, 1879. 3 copies.
—— Same. 1880, 1881. 2 copies.
—— Same. 1882, 1883. 2 copies.
—— Same. 1870, with Supreme Council Southern Jurisdiction, 1870.
—— Southern Jurisdiction, 1857 to 1866. Reprint. 2 copies.
—— Same. 1860 to 1866. Original.
—— Same. 1860 to 1866. Reprint. 2 copies.
—— Same. 1868 and 1870. 2 copies.
—— Same. 1872 to 1878. 2 copies.
—— Same. 1880 and 1882. 2 copies.
—— Same. 1868, with Supreme Council Northern Jurisdiction, 1869.

CLASS V.

RITUALS, PRINTED AND MANUSCRIPT.

CLASS V.

Book of the Words, The. By the Gr∴ Commander. (MSS.)

Cahiers, 23d, 24th, and 25th Degrees, Rite of Perfection. French. (MSS.)
——. 24th and 25th Degrees, Rite of Perfection. French. (MSS.)
—— and Instructions, Various. French. (MSS.)
Ceremonies of Inauguration and Installation. For the five different Bodies of the Scottish Rite. By the Grand Commander. (Original MSS.) 5 vols.

Five Jewels of the Orient. 1872.
Funeral Ceremony, Ceremony of Baptism, Reception of a Louveteau, and Ceremony of Adoption. By the Grand Commander. (Original MSS.)

Grand Inspecteur : Grade d'Élu. (MSS.)

Ineffable Words. By the Gr∴ Commander. (MSS.)
Instructions des Hauts Grades.
    Instructions du Rit Moderne, 1801.
—— Same. Rit Moderne, 1835. 2 copies.
Instructions des Trois Degrés Symboliques Écossais du Rit Ancien et Accepté. Paris, 1851.
Instructions Maçonniques, Various. (MSS.)

Liturgies of De Castro. Caracás, 1877.

Maçonnerie d'Adoption, Degrés d'Apprentie, Compagnonne et Maîtresse. Parts of Mistress, Grand Inspectress and Sister Depository. Hérédon, 5807. 9 vols.
Manual de Masoneria. Cassard. New York, 1860.
Manual of the Ancient and Accepted Scottish Rite. Cunningham.

Recueil Précieux de la Maçonnerie Adonhiramite. Philadelphia, 1786.

RÉGULATEUR DU MAÇON : Degrés Symboliques.   Parts of the Master and Wardens.   3 vols.   Heredom, 1801.

RÉGULATEUR DES CHEVALIERS MAÇONS ou Les Quatre Ordres Supérieurs ; Grades d'Élu, d'Écossais, de Chevaliers d'Orient and de Rose Croix.   Parts of the Most Wise, Grand Inspector, Architect, and Orator.   4 vols.   Parts.   Reg. du Gr∴ Or∴ de France.   Paris.

—— Same.   Parts of Most Wise and Orator.

RÉGULATEUR, LE, DU MAÇON.   3 vols. [parts.]   Hérédon, 5801.

RÉGULATEUR SYMBOLIQUE.   Parts of the Master and Wardens.   Paris

RÉGULATEUR SYMBOLIQUE : APP∴, COMP∴, MAÎTRE.   3 vols. [parts.]

RITUAL, Symbolic Degrees.   Rite of Schröder of Hamburg, and Rite of De Castro, of Cuba.   (MSS.)

RITUAL AND SECRET WORK, Southern Jurisdiction, 4 to 14, in German. (MSS.)

RITUALS, (Original MSS.) C. L. de L. and A. P∴ 18th, 30th, and 31st and 32d Degrees.   (MSS.)   3 vols.

—— 9th, 10th, and 11th Degrees.   De Castro.   (MSS.)

—— 18th Degree, in French and English   By Charles Laffon de Ladebat.   New Orleans, 1856.

—— 18th to 30th Degrees of Rit Ancien et Accepté ; and Kadosh of Cromwell.   (MSS.)

—— 15th to 25th Degrees, MSS. in French, certified by Jⁿ. Bᵗᵉ M. De la Hogue.

—— Ancient and Accepted Scottish Rite Degrees, Northern Jurisdiction.   Parts 1 to 4.   4 vols.   New York.

—— Same, Sup∴ Council Northern Jurisd∴   Boston.   Degrees 18 and 30.   2 vols.

—— Kadosh, 30th Degree.   French.

—— Same.   Parts of Gr∴ Master, Grand Sacrificer, and First and Second Grand Judges.   (MSS.)

—— Same.   Parts of Gr∴ Master, First Warden, First, Second, and Third Gr∴ Judges, First and Second Master of Ceremonies and First Herald.   (MSS.)   9 vols.

—— Rose Croix of Kilwinning, 46th Degree, Rite of Misraim.   (MSS.) French.

—— Rose Croix, 18th Degree.   French.

—— Rite of Perfection, 4th to 16th Degrees.   (MSS.)

—— Rite of Adoption, Degrees 1 to 3, French, revised and printed.

—— Same.   4th to 7th Degrees ; revised.   (MSS.)

—— Rose Croix d'Hérédom de Kilwinning, Rite Ancien, Maçonnerie d'York : Grade Mark Maçon, Grade Royale Arche and Passe Maître, Vénérable de Loge ; as worked in San Domingo in 1795, with Instituts Généraux Maçonniques.   (MSS.)

RITUALS, French, MSS.. Maître Expert, ou Maître Parfait, San Domingo, 1800; Élu des 9, 15, and 27, San Domingo, 1798; Sublime Architecte de Couleur jaune, 12th Degré; Grand Élu, 14th Degré, San Domingo, 1801; Le Vrai Maçon, Grade Philosophique, Huet de La Chelle, 1796.

—— —— MSS.: Rose Croix Cabalistique et hermetique; Roy du Sanctuaire, Huet de La Chelle, 1796; Chev.·. de la Triple Croix, same, 1796; Le Vraie Maçon, same, 1796; Souverain Com. des cœurs enflammés de la Reformation, New Orleans, 1811, Duhulquod.

—— —— MSS.: Lycée du 34me Degré, Grade des amis de la Nature et des Arts, 1816; same, Donaldsonville, Louisiana, by Duhulquod, 1818; same, 1817.

RITUAL, LYCÉE des Amis de la Nature et des Arts. 2me Degré *(Aspirants Gens d'Armes)*. (MSS.)

SECRET WORK, Southern Jurisdiction, 1st to 32d Degrees. (MSS.)

VERDADERA MASONERIA DE ADOPCION. Habana, 1822.

17

CLASS VI.

PUBLICATIONS OF OUR SUPREME COUNCIL.

PUBLICATIONS OF OUR SCIENCE
COURSE

CLASS VI.

ANCIENT AND ACCEPTED SCOTTISH RITE, 31st and 32d Degrees. By
Albert Pike and Charles Laffon de Ladebat. New Orleans, 1858.
ANNUAL REGISTER Gr.·. Lodge of Perfection of South Carolina. Fac-
simile. 2 copies. 1802.

CEREMONIES OF INAUGURATION AND INSTALLATION, Southern Jurisdiction, Bodies from 14th to 32d. 5 vols. 2 copies each.
CERNEAUISM, FOULHOUZEISM, ETC., Exposed. 3 Pamphlets bound in
one vol. 2 copies.
CONSTITUTIONS AND STATUTES Supreme Council Southern Jurisdiction, 1855 to 1878, and Tableaux, 1867 to 1878.

DEDICATION, CEREMONIES OF, for a Hall of the Rite.

FUNERAL CEREMONY AND LODGE OF SORROW, Southern Jurisdiction.
2 copies.
—— of a Knight Kadosh. 2 copies.

GRAND CONSTITUTIONS of 1762 and 1786, Southern Jurisdiction.
Quarto interleaved. New York, 1859.
—— Same, same edition. 8vo. 2 copies.
—— of 1762 and 1786, with Historical Enquiry. Published for the
Southern Jurisdiction. 2 copies, 4to. 2 copies, 8vo. 1872.

LITURGY OF THE LODGE OF PERFECTION, 4th to 14th Degrees. 1st
edition. 3 copies.
LITURGY OF THE ANCIENT AND ACCEPTED SCOTTISH RITE, Southern
Jurisdiction, Degrees 1st to 30th. 2 copies of each. 4 vols.

MASONIC BAPTISM, Reception of a Louveteau and Offices of Adoption,
Southern Jurisdiction. 2 copies.
MASONRY OF ADOPTION, Revised. Degrees of Apprentice, Companion,
and Mistress. 2 copies.

MASONIC SYMBOLISM. First Lecture. By the Gr∴ Commander. 2 copies. Large 4to. Script. Only 100 copies printed.

—— Second Lecture. By the Gr∴ Commander. 2 copies. Large 4to. Script. Only 100 copies printed.

MORALS AND DOGMA OF THE ANCIENT AND ACCEPTED SCOTTISH RITE. 8vo. 2 copies.

RED READING for Relighting the Lights, of the Rose Croix. 2 copies.

REPLY to the Encyclical Letter of Pope Leo XIII. 2 copies.

RITUAL (First Revision, large quarto) of the Southern Jurisdiction. Degrees 4th to 32d. Only 100 copies printed. 2 copies.

RITUALS SOUTHERN JURISDICTION. Degrees 1st to 32d. 6 vols. 2 copies.

—— Degrees 31 and 32 : Same, Revised 1879, with Legenda and Readings. 2 copies of each.

—— Degrees 4 to 14, and 15 to 18, with Secret Work. In German. 2 copies.

RITUALS. Reprints of Old Degrees, viz :

> Mark Mason, Royale Arche (West Indies, 1795) ;
>
> Grand Maître Écossais or Scottish Elder-Master and Knight of St. Andrew ;
>
> English Ritual for Knights Templar ;
>
> Royal Arch Exaltation ;
>
> Master Mark Mason (South Carolina, 1796) ;
>
> Wigan Ritual of the Early Grand Encampment.

SEPHAR H' DEBARIM (The Book of the Words). Southern Jurisdiction. 2 copies.

CLASS VII.

PERIODICALS.

CLASS VII.

L'ABEILLE MAÇONNIQUE, Journal Hebdomadaire. Paris. 113 Nos. 1829 to 1832.

ACACIA, The. By William P. Mellen and Giles M. Hillyer. Natchez, Miss. Vols. 1 and 2. 1855 and 1856.

AMERICAN FREE-MASON'S MAGAZINE. Edited by Albert G. Mackey. New York, 1860.

AMERICAN FREE-MASON. Louisville, Kentucky. 1853 and 1854.

—— Vols. 1 and 2. 1858. By J. F. Brennan. New York. 2 copies. Vols. 3 and 4. 1859.

AMERICAN MASONIC REGISTER, The. By Luther Pratt. Vol. 2. New York, 1826.

AMERICAN QUARTERLY REVIEW OF FREE-MASONRY. Vols. 1 and 2. 1857 to 1859. 2 copies.

CHAINE D'UNION DE PARIS, LA. 1872, 1873, 1874 ; 1875, incomplete ; 1876, incomplete ; 1877, 1878, 1879, and 1880, 2 copies each ; 1881 ; 1882, 2 copies ; 1883 ; in all 17 vols.

DER BUND. Budapest, 1878.

EVERGREEN, The. Dubuque and Davenport, Iowa. Vols. 1 to 5. 1868 to 1872. 3 vols.

FRANC-MAÇON, LE. Paris. Vols. 1 to 8, in 3 vols. 1848 to 1859.

FREE-MASON'S MAGAZINE. London. Vols. 1 to 7. 1793 to 1796.

—— Same. Philadelphia, 1811. Vols. 1 and 2.

FREE-MASON'S MONTHLY MAGAZINE. Charles W. Moore. Boston, Nov. 1841 to Oct. 1872. 31 vols.

—— Same. London, 1855.

FREE-MASON'S MAGAZINE AND MASONIC MIRROR. London, 1852. Part 2, 2 copies. 1856, 2 copies. 1857 and 1858, Part 1, 2 copies. 1858, vol. 4. 9 vols.

FREE-MASON'S QUARTERLY MAGAZINE. New Series. Vol. 1. London, 1853.

FREE-MASON'S QUARTERLY MAGAZINE. London, 1834 to 1859. 27 vols.

FREE-MASON'S QUARTERLY REVIEW. New Series. London. Vols. 1, 1843 ; and 3, 1845.

FREE-MASON'S REPOSITORY. London. Vol. XI. 1798.

FREE-MASON, The. George F. Gouley. St. Louis. Vols. 1 to 9.

—— Same. A Weekly Journal of Free-Masonry, Literature, Science, and Art. London, 1879, 1880, 1881, 1882, 1883. Vols. xii., xiii., xiv., xv., xvi. 5 vols.

—— Same. Sydney, New South Wales. 1878–1883.

GLOBE, LE. Archives des Initiations. Par Louis Théodore Juge. 1839 to 1842. 4 vols.

HAJNAL. Budapest, Hungary. 1877 and 1878.

—— Same. Budapest, Hungary. 1872, 1874, 1875, and 1876. 2 vols.

—— Same. Budapest, Hungary. 1877 and 1878.

KELET. Budapest, Hungary. 1876–'79.

LOGENBLATT. Hamburg. Nos. 1 to 160. 1867 to 1883. 2 vols. 4to.

MASONIC ANNUAL. 1871. 2 copies. Edited by Ll. W. Longstaff, 18°.

MASONIC CHRONICLE. 1875–1883. Vols. 1, 2, 3, 4, and 5.

MASONIC ECLECTIC. Vols. 1 to 3. Simons and Macoy. 1860 to '66. New York.

—— Same. G. H. Ramey. 1876 to '81. 5 vols. Alexandria, Va.

MASONIC JOURNAL. Louisville, Ky. 1876.

MASONIC LIBRARY. Hyneman. Philadelphia. Vol. II.

MASONIC MAGAZINE. Vols. 1 to 6. London, 1873 to 1882. 9 vols.

MASONIC MONTHLY. 1864–1867. Boston. 4 vols.

—— Same. 1878–1881. San Francisco. 3 vols.

MASONIC NEWSPAPER, The. 1878–1880. New York.

MASONIC PRESS. London. Matthew Cooke. Nos. 1 to 4. 1866.

MASONIC RECORD, of Western India. 1880–'81, vol. xvii. ; 1881–'82, vol. xviii.; 1882–'83, vol. xix. 3 vols. Bombay.

MASONIC REVIEW. Cincinnati, Ohio. Cornelius Moore, 1852 to 1883 [incomplete]. 18 vols.

MASONIC UNION. Vol. 1. 1850 and 1851.

—— Same. Vols. 1 to 5. 1850 to 1855. Auburn, New York. 2 copies, one imperfect.

MACKEY'S NATIONAL FREE-MASON. Washington, D. C. 3 vols.

MONDE MAÇONNIQUE. Paris. May, 1878, to April, 1883. 5 vols.

ORIENT, L'. Revue Universelle de la Franc-Maçonnerie. Paris, 1844–1845.

ΠΥΘΑΓΟΡΑΣ (Pythagoras), Masonic Journal. Vols. 1 and 2. Athens, 1882–'83.

REVUE MAÇONNIQUE. Paris. 1835 to 1837. 2 vols.

ROSICRUCIAN AND MASONIC RECORD. London. Vol. 1. New Series. 1876 to 1878.

SENTIMENTAL AND MASONIC MAGAZINE. Vol. 2, 1792 ; vol. 4, 1794.

SOUTHERN AND WESTERN MASONIC MISCELLANY. Mackey. 3 vols. 2 copies. Vol. 4, 6 nos. No more published.

STANDARD, The. Dedicated to Free-Masonry in India. Bombay. April to November, 1876.

UNIVERS MAÇONNIQUE, L'. Paris, 1837.

VERITÉ, LA, Journal Maçonnique. Paris. 1871, '72, '75, '76. 4 vols.

VOICE OF MASONRY. July 15, 1869, to June 1, 1861. Folio.

—— Same. Vols. 13 to 21 inclusive. 1875 to 1883.

VRAIE LUMIERE, LA, Journal des Franc-Maçons. Versailles, France, 1851 to 1852. 3 vols.

www.ingramcontent.com/pod-product-compliance
Lightning Source LLC
Chambersburg PA
CBHW030354270326
41926CB00009B/1098

* 9 7 8 3 3 3 7 3 0 2 0 6 1 *